D1063232

Statue of Liberty–Ellis Island
Centennial Series

*A list of books in the series appears
at the end of this book.*

Labor and Community

LABOR AND COMMUNITY

Mexican Citrus Worker Villages
in a Southern California County,
1900–1950

•

Gilbert G. González

University of Illinois Press
Urbana and Chicago

Publication of this book was made possible in part by a grant
from the Ellis Island–Statue of Liberty Foundation.

This book is printed on acid-free paper.

Library of Congress Cataloging-in-Publication Data

González, Gilbert G., 1941–
    Labor and community : Mexican citrus worker villages in a Southern
California county, 1900–1950 / Gilbert G. González.
        p.   cm.
    Includes bibliographical references and index.
    ISBN 0-252-02097-9. — ISBN 0-252-06388-0 (pbk.)
    1. Citrus fruit industry—California—Orange County—Employees—
History—20th century. 2. Mexican American agricultural laborers—
California—Orange County—History—20th century. I. Title.
HD9259.C53C254   1994
307.7'66—dc20   93-36584
                                                                CIP

For wherever citrus production predominates, a rather distinctive social life has long existed. This citrus belt complex of peoples, institutions, and relationships have no parallel in rural life in America and nothing quite like it exists elsewhere in California. It is neither town nor country, neither rural nor urban. It is a world of its own.

—Carey McWilliams,
Southern California: An Island on the Land

In the development of a large part of the citrus industry in Orange County, California, the Mexican has played the role of a humble but nonetheless necessary Atlas, bearing upon his shoulders in an inconspicuous manner the foundations of this prosperity.

—Jessie Hayden,
La Habra Americanization teacher

For My Mother, Maria del Carmen González Torres,
on Her 90th Birthday

Contents

Illustrations follow page 98

Preface

The idea for studying the history of citrus worker settlements formed while engaged in research on Chicano educational history. I happened on references to "model camps" for Mexican citrus pickers constructed by a La Habra (California) Citrus Association, an affiliate of the Southern California Fruit Growers Exchange (to be known later as "Sunkist"). Another source mentioned Americanization programs sponsored by citrus growers' cooperatives in settlements provided by the growers' organizations. It struck me, as I read the materials, that quite possibly an important chapter of the Chicano experience had not been told and deserved to be written. Upon completing the research on education, I turned my full attention to the citrus worker settlements.

My first steps at locating materials relating to citrus workers, citrus worker villages, and citrus association–sponsored company towns produced surprisingly little. A perusal of research on company towns turned up few references, if any, to company towns for Mexican labor, ironically the nationality most often treated to the company town experience in the southwest. Moreover, I concluded, citrus workers were a "forgotten" people as far as historians were concerned and an untapped vein of Chicano social history, at once of a piece with the history of the citrus industry, remained to be mined. In my search for leads, Professor Lou Weathers of the University of California, Riverside, pointed me in the direction of a series on citrus-picker housing appearing in the *California Citrograph* in the early 20s. I immediately scanned the journal index, found the articles and read them with a deep fascination. I found that the citrus industry established nearly two dozen company-sponsored housing projects. These facts and more emerged in reading volume after volume of the *California Citrograph,* which devoted substantial space to picker housing in the 1918–24 period when Mexican labor became the backbone of the industry.

The core of the information gathered to write this book came from interviews with forty-two individuals associated in one way or another with

the Orange County citrus industry. I must thank Mr. Chester Whitten, re-
tired principal of the La Jolla School, who granted me the first interview
and then graciously suggested the names of other possible interviewees.
Local librarians, often historians in their own right, also gladly gave me
names and phone numbers of citrus era residents. Within a few months a
network had formed and continuously expanded. Most of interviewees
were Mexican Americans, some pioneered the settlements under study,
others grew up there and most experienced the labor of picking and packing. A few interviewees were growers, some foremen, and others teachers. This work benefits in so many ways from their recollections, comments, and suggestions. They told of their life experiences eagerly,
candidly, and openly. I know that they expected the same honesty from
me when the time came to write the story of their communities. I hope
that I have respected their trust through reporting as fully as possible their
stories as given to me.

Naturally, a historian cannot be a mirror reflecting in detail all that he
or she comes across—there is the inevitable and necessary analysis and interpretation of data, plus the effect of additional information that may place
interviewees' information in a different light. A historian is compelled to
assess from the totality of information and not from any one strand or
source. All analyses contains a subjective component, and I make clear
where I am coming from and where I am taking the story.

Apart from the many hours of taped interviews, I also gleaned through
a number of resources, including interviews conducted by others, newspapers, minutes of grower associations' meetings, minutes of boards of education meetings, and professional journals serving the citrus industry, principally the *California Citrograph* (the official journal of the Southern
California Fruit Growers Exchange). Newspapers—among them the *Placentia Courier, La Habra Star, Santa Ana Register, Anaheim Gazette*—were
invaluable and from them I obtained an image (albeit from the viewpoint
of the "outsider") of the settlements, their activities and their relationship
to the dominant community over time.

Government reports and publications from various levels also shed light
on numerous aspects of settlement life. Documents containing information
relating to local health conditions, statewide Americanization programs,
labor, and women were integrated into the unfolding story.

Unpublished theses and dissertations, most written in the 1930s by local teachers, provided various and sundry pieces of data that after careful
consideration were either rejected or incorporated into the study. These resources helped to collate an image of the Mexican settlement held by the
dominant community, but these works also provided a catalogue of settlement activities, organizations, and lifestyle.

Finally, a host of small bits and pieces of data, emanating from many distinct sources such as autobiographies, local histories, reports of religious groups, and information passed along in correspondence or informal discussion helped round-out the study.

Such a work as this would never have been possible without the support of family, friends, and colleagues. My wife, Frances, always listened to my latest ideas, which were sometimes expressed in undecipherable snippets. Though her area of expertise is far removed from the Humanities and Social Sciences, her interest and patience heartened me, and comments on drafts were always incisive. My friends and colleagues in the Program in Comparative Culture at the University of California, Irvine have remained over the years a main support network: I am indebted to professors Raúl Fernández, John Liu, Dickson D. Bruce, Jr., and Dickran Tashjian; Professor Emeritus Robert Hine of the University of California, Riverside, read several chapters and contributed invaluable comments and criticisms of drafts of the manuscript.

Several other persons provided welcome editorial assistance. David Goldstein-Shirley, Charles Krinsky, and Robert Hayden of the Program in Comparative Culture at the University of California, Irvine, read drafts, commented, and suggested changes. Several research assistants contributed their energies to my research effort. I am grateful for the work of Dr. Henry Gutierrez, Amalia Kim, Tisha Wong, and Gwendolyn King. I must also thank Ms. Edna Mejia, who played a critical role in this study, and her technical expertise assisted me in many significant ways. Ms. June Kurata, administrative assistant for the Program in Comparative Culture, University of California, Irvine, helped in no small measure by making me aware of the available university resources.

My deep appreciation extends to the librarians and curators from the Anaheim Public Library; the California State Library, Sacramento; the California State University, Fullerton Oral History Program; the Fountain Valley Public Library; the Fullerton Public Library; the Placentia Public Library; the Santa Ana Bowers Museum; the Santa Ana Public Library California Room; the Sherman Library; and the University of California, Berkeley, Bancroft Library. I also wish to express my thanks to the staff of the Interlibrary Loan Service and Special Collections of the Main Library at the University of California, Irvine. These institutions and the individuals who manage them not only made my task considerably easier but also always directed me, in one way or another, toward new and worthwhile research paths. Finally, two grants from the Academic Senate Committee on Research, University of California, Irvine, provided the necessary financial support to carry out the research.

Acknowledgments

Grateful acknowledgment is made to the following journals for permission to reprint portions of published material. Sections of chapter 1 first appeared in Gilbert G. González and Raul Fernandez, "Chicano History: Transcending Cultural Models," *Pacific Historical Review,* forthcoming in 1994. Portions of chapters 1, 3, 4, 5, and 6 first appeared in Gilbert G. González, "Labor and Community: The Camps of Mexican Citrus Pickers in Southern California," *Western Historical Quarterly* vol. 22, no. 3, (1991): 289–312. And a different version of chapter 6 was first published in Gilbert G. González, "The Mexican Citrus Picker Union, the Mexican Consulate, and the Orange County Strike of 1936" *Labor History* vol. 35, no. 1 (Winter 1994). Permission to reprint granted by the journals.

Introduction

Long before the decline of southern California citrus production in the 1950s and 1960s, the industry basked in the glow of a well-manicured myth that has yet to disappear. That mythology is conditioned today, as in the past, by the brightly colored, skillfully crafted illustrations originally glued onto packing crates. Today, entrepreneurs collect and sell the industry's fading art works on street corners and antique shops. Framed crate labels grace kitchen walls, hallways, and dens as well as business office corridors and waiting rooms. The images are romantic and nostalgic: a full moon lighting a silent grove; golden oranges peering through a thicket of green leaves; snow capped mountains rising behind neat rows of citrus trees; scenes of tall sailing ships, Spanish Mission campaniles, or summery seascapes. Beneath the appealing veneer is the reality: the citrus industry depended on the poorly paid labor of minorities—Chinese, Japanese, Filipinos, Mexicans, and women. In so doing, the industry divided minority from majority, at work, in residence, recreation, religion, education, and politics.

Here, I do not destroy the romantic myth; but rather, I juxtapose it with the social realities that the myth serves to obscure. This is a study of the community of Mexican immigrants and their descendants—women, men, and children—whose labor contributed significantly to the heralded prosperity of the citrus industry of southern California.

Community and Economy

By the 1930s, hundreds of Mexican communities ranging in size from the huge urban Los Angeles *colonia* to tiny hamlets hidden within vast agricultural and mining districts were scattered throughout the Southwest. In 1940 at least two hundred Mexican communities of various sizes sprinkled the central and southern sections of California. "Hardly a town of any size or pretensions," observed Dr. Ernesto Galarza "—Delano, Hanford, Brawley, Sacramento, San Diego, Fresno—failed to acquire between 1900 and

1940 its Mexican colonia on the weathered side of the railroad tracks."[1] The small sized rural *colonias*—the general focus of this study—can be appropriately termed *village.*

The category *village* has not been used previously in the literature on Chicano community history. Yet, for countless southwestern Mexican settlements, village is a fitting description. It is particularly appropriate when surveying the history of southern California Chicano communities between 1910 and 1950, the formative years in twentieth-century Chicano history. Various forms of villagelike settlements formed an integral part of that widely dispersed settlement pattern known as the "*colonia* complex."

This analysis is intended as a historical sketch of one village form, the numerous citrus worker villages that were home to as many as one hundred thousand inhabitants. Given the wide geographic dispersion of the many villages, it is impossible to examine each in detail. The author has therefore chosen as a case study the fourteen citrus worker settlements in Orange County, a major agricultural region in southern California and the state. The fourteen settlements are numerically significant, yet manageable enough for drawing out those qualities that distinguish citrus villages. The focus is comprehensive and emphasizes their formation and culture, their social and economic relations with the dominant society, and their eventual transition to urban blue collar barrios.

The citrus worker village is one of several distinctive types of settlement that have appeared in the course of the historical development of the southwestern Chicano community during the twentieth century. Generally, variations in the settlement pattern follow the contours of the local urban and rural economic enterprises employing Mexican labor. Mexican communities share a complementary history with the region's economy. Thus, communities are anchored in and have evolved from the foundations provided by the cattle and sheep industry, agriculture (vegetables, fruits, and field crops), cotton, mining, railroads, urban manufacturing, and the citrus industry. Each of these general economic branches constitutes a particular community style worthy of comparative study and analysis. Many of these communities, in their role as company towns, exerted varying degrees of intervention into the life of the residents. Most previous historical studies of Chicano communities have ignored this heterogeneity and, consequently, have neglected a significant element in Chicano social history.

Although Chicano historiography has contributed significantly to understanding southwestern social history, there has been little comprehensive analysis of the varied community forms and virtually none encompassing the rural *and* urban continuum of community life. The 1920, 1930, and 1940 censuses demonstrated an equal rural and urban division of Mexican communities.[2] Yet, an unquestioned thesis has upheld an urban pattern for these years, consequently distorting the formative period in twentieth-century

Chicano history.[3] The 1930 census listed half of the Mexican population as rural, thereby verifying the need to expand the scope of our historical study beyond the urban setting. By so doing we can study the varied processes through which communities are constructed, community life is organized, and social relations and divisions of labor evolve. This matter deserves immediate attention inasmuch as there is a growing national trend toward comparative ethnic studies. The unsupported and unchallenged notion that Chicanos have been an urban group either throughout the twentieth century, or at least since 1930, requires serious reevaluation before adequate nationwide comparative ethnic community studies can be realized.[4]

A defined analytical perspective guides this study of the social history of one minority group living in a subregion of the United States. The analysis examines the formation and evolution of Chicano communities, including their culture and organizations, working and living within the parameters of one specific economic context, the citrus industry. Without reference to the significance of the citrus industry, that history is understated and only disparate elements of the social landscape would come to light. This approach contextualizes the social group under study within a clearly demarcated economic environment.

Historical social study often sidesteps the critical influence emanating from the economic sphere in structuring social relations, particularly when assessing minority and non-minority relations. The result is an emphasis on race relations, and racism, as the explanatory model for minority history. Far too frequently the historiography of minority studies underscores the "race factor" as the key to the minority experience. These culture-based explanations tend to minimize the role of economic factors, which are crucial in shaping social and cultural forms. Within Chicano historiography, cultural struggles and racial conflicts have become the principal explanatory model. Although there is no doubt that racism is an important component of Chicano history, it is not the only factor that should be considered. The historical ebb and flow of the Chicano community is only partially explained if analyzed apart from the economic context and its evolution over time. Fortunately, some new scholarship moves away from culture-based models and toward more appropriate emphases on economic power and processes.[5] This study places itself within the body of literature that recognizes the interaction of economics and culture in shaping social experience, in this instance, the Chicano experience.[6]

Studies emphasizing racism as the principal factor in molding the Chicano experience separate, isolate, and reduce Chicano history to cultural relations between Anglos and Mexicans. This study expands that narrow cultural focus by adding the economic context, thereby altering the analysis from one limited to understanding paired ethnic relations to one offering a greater appreciation of a shared history across minority and nonminority lines. Upon such an analysis, the history of Mexican citrus workers becomes a study of one sector of the working population in the American system of production. It is, moreover, a study of one community embedded within the larger American economy and society, and its culture connects in a myriad of ways with the nuances of national, cultural, and political change.

The transformation of the Southwest from a Mexican feudal society in 1850 to a dynamic large-scale Anglo-American capitalist economy by 1900 accompanied the end of slavery in the South and the ensuing industrial revolution in the Northeast. Together these changes made possible the rise of the United States to world economic and political preeminence. European and other immigrants of the late nineteenth century made possible the unparalleled development of industrial capitalism in the Northeast, while Mexican immigrants in the early twentieth century (together with other cultural populations) assured the spectacular achievements of industrialized agriculture, transportation, and mining of the Southwest. Both populations constituted a sector of the American working class; moreover, both socioeconomic regions were integrated within a national economic process. The Southwest provided foodstuffs and other products for the burgeoning urban industrial working class, while delivering raw materials to an expanding machine-driven economy. The industrial regions, on the other hand, sent their processed raw materials plus technologies and power machinery to the Southwest. By the turn of the century, agriculture, stock raising, and mining depended on steam engines, and later on combustion engines, to drive railroads, mining equipment, and tractors. All were critical to an economic process whereby the United States acquired the status of leading industrial and financial power in the world. Certainly, the Mexican, Asian, European, and other immigrants were major actors in that national social and economic transformation. Together with the urbanizing African Americans these populations acted, albeit most often in separate contexts, in the capitalist industrialization of the nation, and in turn were profoundly affected by the concomitant social consequences.

Several studies of various communities observe the link between economy, culture, and social relations. For example, Lizabeth Cohen's examination of working-class Chicago of the 1920s and 1930s; Gary Gerstle's exploration of the French-Canadian working class in Rhode Island; Dennis Nodin Valdes's analysis of Mexican agricultural workers in the Great Lakes region; David Montejano's research into the social relations of Anglos and Mexicans in Texas; and Cletus E. Daniel's history of California farmworkers underscore the critical linkage between the economy and social relations.[7] In all of the above studies, the dynamics of community life unfold inseparably from the vicissitudes of large-scale capitalism.

Economic forces have interacted with each cultural population to weave a national experience. If one steps close enough to the tapestry, the particularity and uniqueness of each strand predominates. It is this particularity that has prompted the development of ethnic-specific studies. However, as one steps back, the diverse figures interact to create a unity of experience. This book is written in the spirit, and conviction, that the United States is comprised of many particular ethnic histories that touch and blend at critical junctures. To ignore either the commonality and/or the particularity, or to emphasize one over the other, does injustice to the cultural heritage of the nation.

Through having experienced labor in the same national economic system, Chicanos share elements of a common history with other minorities and with the English-speaking American working-class population. Not all have experienced it the same way, and not all have endured the status of second-class citizenship. Nevertheless, an analysis of Chicano history integrating economy and culture can illuminate a research path leading to studies that will demonstrate the intertwining of Chicano history with mainstream American social history. Moving the focus from cultural models that highlight Chicano-Anglo conflictive social relations in a regional setting to questions of economic power and development can assist in showing Chicano history to be more than the distinct experience and contribution of a particular regional, ethnic group. Rather, it is demonstrably an integral component of U.S. social history as a whole and is of importance to all U.S. historians.

Citrus Culture, Labor, and Social Relations

Southern California tantalizes pleasure and profit seekers. Some come merely to enjoy the healthy Mediterranean weather, but for those in search of profitable investment, the combination of a subtropical climate and rich soils provides irresistible and lucrative attraction. Given that the right conditions for citrus production are relatively rare throughout the world, and that a market existed that far exceeded the potential for production, it should come as no surprise that southern California became the leading producer of citrus of the United States, and a major producer in the world. Mild seasons, cooling ocean breezes, a variety of excellent soils, and the absence of severe frosts and heavy fogs within a belt of land extending from San Diego County to Ventura County make a nearly perfect natural citrus-growing area. Few regions of the globe are suited to such horticulture and while wheat, grains, and other crops can be grown widely, the citrus region is comparatively limited. One of these choice areas is southern California, where a balanced mix of conditions once provided a fabulously productive and profitable citrus industry. Indeed, the industry was destined to change the diet and nutritional emphasis of the nation.

Citrus production extended through twelve counties of southern, central, and northern California. However, the six counties of southern California, known as the citrus belt, contained 90 percent of California's citrus acreage.[8] By the 1930s citrus was the state's principal agricultural product, and the predominant product of the southern California economy. Indeed, from 1890 to 1960 citrus produced more wealth than had gold in California history[9] and ranked second only to the oil industry in California's economy. In 1936 citrus accrued $97,000,000 in profit compared to the state petroleum industry's $159,500,000.[10] At the zenith of citrus's reign, California produced 60 percent of the nation's crop and 20 percent of the world's supply. As the citrus industry expanded enormously after 1900, the size and number of citrus worker communities increased apace.[11]

Citrus production experienced steady commercial success for nearly a century, from 1870 until the combination of post–World War II urbanization and citrus tree diseases cleared the orchards. The citrus belt reached its peak in the mid-1940s and thereafter declined, either disappearing completely or gradually retreating to outlying areas. Engulfed and surrounded, the citrus worker villages merged into the deepening suburban and urban pattern.

Labor history in the citrus industry parallels labor history in California agriculture. The several stages of the development of citrus generally correspond to distinct trends of minority nationalities performing the bulk of the picking labor. The incipient stage, roughly covering the years 1870–1890, witnessed an extensive employment of Chinese as pickers as well as packers. Growers seldom faced a labor shortage as long as Chinese laborers freely entered the country. Although the Chinese Exclusion Act of 1882 cut off this supply, Japanese immigrants were quickly used to resolve the crisis in the 1890s. By the turn of the century, Japanese, along with remnants of the Chinese gangs, filled the demand for citrus labor.

The cutoff of Japanese immigration in the early 1900s was coincident with sharp increases in the state's agricultural production and a steep rise in Mexican immigration. The extension of acreage and increases in production that occurred after 1900 could never have been achieved without the rapid influx of laborers who had the desirable work habits of the Japanese, without their tendency to organize quasi-unions. Mexicans met the need for labor at precisely the time that larger numbers of workers became necessary, as not only was the market expanding but production was additionally stimulated by a wartime economy. Labor agents, taking advantage of the social disruptions caused by the Mexican Revolution and aided by federal agencies, extensively recruited Mexican labor and transported them

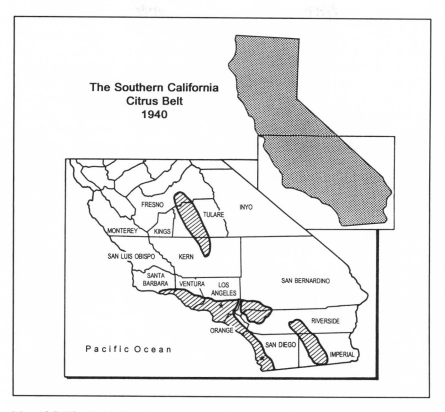

The Southern California
Citrus Belt
1940

FRESNO
TULARE
INYO
MONTEREY
KINGS
SAN LUIS OBISPO
KERN
SANTA
BARBARA
VENTURA
LOS
ANGELES
SAN BERNARDINO
ORANGE
RIVERSIDE
Pacific Ocean
SAN DIEGO
IMPERIAL

Map of California highlighting southern California counties and the citrus belt. Illustration by Karen Christiansen.

throughout the Southwest.[12] Between 1910 and 1930 three quarters of a million Mexicans flooded the labor market and provided a seemingly inexhaustible labor supply.[13] In California, and especially in southern California, their employment followed the pattern established by the Chinese and Japanese.

Most Mexican citrus worker communities formed during the 1910–30 migration, and many later evolved into today's suburban Mexican barrios.[14] Mention of Mexican citrus camps in the literature first appears around 1915, and by 1920 "Mexican camp" had become a common, if misleading, term. In 1915, about 2,300 Mexican orange pickers labored in the groves, by the end of the decade their numbers had increased to 7,004, or 30 percent of the work force.[5] Mexicans numbered some 10,000 pickers in 1926 and by 1940 constituted nearly 100 percent of the picking force, about 22,000.[16] Approximately 11,000 women worked as packers. At the height of the California citrus expansion there were over 50,000 pickers, field hands, packers, and packinghouse employees. Of these, the overwhelming majority were Mexican men and women. Approximately 75,000 to 100,000 Mexicans lived in the many communities, comprised principally of citrus workers and their families, which were dispersed throughout the citrus belt.

In the consciousness of the dominant community, citrus labor quickly came to be associated with the Mexican communities—as if its inhabitants were bound to a single function within the economy. Observers noted that in reality the community had a simple but fundamental connection with the larger society. Mexicans in citrus towns were invariably the pickers and packers; and consequently they were poor, segregated into *colonias* or villages, and socially ostracized, even though they were economically indispensable to the larger society.

Although several historians have referred to camps, that is, residential enclaves of Mexican laborers and their families, no one has sought to study them in depth. So-called camps existed in the southern California citrus belt, in migrant agricultural communities (especially in sugar beet fields), as well as in mining, railroad, construction, and some other industrial communities. In the years 1900–1950, the term camp, commonly applied to any small Mexican community usually on the outskirts of a town, summoned images of a transient, disorganized society that existed on the margins of recognized social norms. However, in many ways these camps reproduced American and Mexican community life and as such were stable, organized, and internally integrated. Mexican customs, traditions, festivals, and celebrations were placed within the American environment and flourished significantly. Citrus worker communities became centers of much more than the routine of picking and packing. They were also systems of social, political, and cultural interaction established on the cultural heritage of a community continually adjusting to the constant stream of cultural infusion from the dominant English-speaking environment. In view of this, *village* is a much more appropriate description than camp for the many picker communities.

Despite the large population of Mexicans in the citrus belt and the extensive social development of the villages, no one has sought to examine these communities in any systematic way. Over forty years ago a distinguished scholar commented that the "social and economic significance" of the "citrus area of southern California . . . has not yet received much study."[17] Since that observation was made, the citrus industry has declined, and as it has, interest in social and economic analysis of the citrus industry has also been lost. Recently, this absence of research has moved two contemporary scholars to write that "despite an extensive literature on agricultural labor in California, there has been little research on the history of citrus workers."[18]

Invariably, mention of citrus labor has been fleeting, general, or contained within a broader focus.[19] Only one historical study of citrus labor, a useful but limited unpublished doctoral dissertation written in 1946, is even available to scholars.[20] This research blind spot persists, and, consequently, social and labor historians have not been particularly interested in examining a principal work force and community that contributed historically to the unparalleled economic prosperity of California.

Three main labor settlement patterns dominated in the California citrus region: (1) full-fledged company towns, owned and run entirely, including businesses and schools, by an enterprise; (2) company-owned tracts within independent communities; (3) and private residential communities, free of company ownership. In the last pattern, housing was commonly family constructed on lots purchased at low prices by the pickers; and house design was patterned after the simple, small wooden structures found in the grower-owned camps. In general, picker housing, whether association owned or picker owned, comprised small wooden frame houses minimally sufficient but, more often than not, substandard as family housing. Just as citrus workers resided in three main environments, patterns of company intervention also differed, ranging from a heavy-handed paternalism via Americanization programs to none at all.

Not surprisingly, scholars have hardly studied the extent to which company towns have affected the Chicano experience. The lone work on company towns in the West scarcely mentions Mexican labor.[21] Mexican *colonias* or barrios—whether in the copper towns of Bisbee, Miami, Globe, Morenci, and Clifton, or in the Goodyear cotton town of Litchfield, Arizona, or in the beet fields of California and Colorado, or in the steel mills of Indiana, or in the citrus-grower association villages of southern California—were part of a larger pattern of company towns in the West, Midwest, and South. Comparisons among the company towns that housed Mexicans reveal similarities and differences. For example, citrus growers, like mining companies, provided community centers for recreational, patriotic, educational, and other activities. On the other hand, a company store dominated all business in mining towns, whereas in most citrus towns Mexican businesses often established themselves beyond the boundaries of the company property. Moreover, mining, lumbering, and railroad company towns generally constituted the entire community. In citrus, the company town was often a housing tract within, or somewhat outside of, the larger noncompany-owned community. Citrus company towns, in the main, were therefore more fully integrated into the social fabric of society. There were exceptions to this pattern—the Leffingwell Ranch in Whittier and the Limoniera Ranch in Ventura County were both similar to the typical mining town. However, in all company towns the social hierarchy and patterns of segregation mirrored the division of labor. Even those places in which

Mexican labor worked alongside other races and nationalities, as in the mining towns of Arizona and the citrus ranches of California, enforced segregation fragmented the town.

Particularity of the Rural Citrus Village

Much of southern California Mexican community history can be studied within the context of the citrus industry, which is neither an urban industry nor one based on migrant labor. Citrus communities were set apart from urban areas by several factors. The most important of these was that citrus communities owed their existence to one form of production, in contrast to the urban employment pattern by which a host of employers and, possibly, many industries employ labor.[22] Second, the social relations of the citrus community reflected the division of labor in one branch of production. Again in contrast to urban employment patterns, the availability of employment for Mexican women was restricted to packing and domestic help; and, until the Second World War, even packing was generally reserved for Anglo women.

Citrus picker communities can also be distinguished from communities of migrant agricultural labor in three main ways: (1) by the absence of family labor as the main unit of productions; (2) by the residential permanency of their inhabitants; (3) by employment in a localized region, and (4) most importantly, by more or less year-round employment. The growing season for the two major orange crops in the citrus belt, Valencias and Navels, did not overlap. Valencias, grown extensively in Orange County, were picked from May to December. Navels were grown in Los Angeles, Riverside, and San Bernardino counties from December to May. Thus, pickers could, and often did, work much of the year simply by journeying from one county to the next (sometimes this meant only a short trip). In the lemon-growing areas—Ventura, Santa Barbara, San Diego, and northern Orange counties—harvests were year round.

This pattern contrasted to that of migratory communities, which were subject to the fluctuations of the demand for family labor over a substantially large rural region necessitating family migration. Although citrus pickers, packers, and their families could become migratory, migration was secondary to their principal line of work. The local economy kept many of them permanently employed during the harvests and resident in their communities—indeed, growers preferred this type of picker community and established housing programs to root Mexican labor in the local area. These factors would affect community organization and strategies to cope with, structure, and control village life.

Similarly, issues related to gender and family evolved within this broad spectrum of community.[23] Employment and educational opportunities available to women and children vary in relation to the organization of labor in particular enterprises. These, in turn, influenced family, culture, and ultimately, community. In citrus areas, women's employment was limited to packing and domestic labor while men provided the family's primary source of income. In cotton and vegetable production, family labor predominated, severely hindering children from attending public school. In manufacturing and industrial centers like Los Angeles, family labor was far less significant; consequently, the employment opportunities for women as individuals, and the educational opportunities for children, were much greater.

Culture and Community

These nonurban, small-sized rural immigrant communities, ranging in population from two hundred to one thousand, shared a lifestyle distinct from that of the dominant English-speaking population. Culturally, occupationally, and geographically the village existed separately from other ethnic groups and the dominant English-speaking community. Cultural traditions of Mexico, although reconstructed, were done so mainly at the most general level. Since the settlers came from various regions, subregions, and villages, the potential to resurrect specific regional or local cultural forms was severely limited. As happened to many other immigrant communities, a cultural synthesis occurred so that the new village partook of a more generalized version of Mexico's culture. Thus, specific localized cultural forms were integrated into a more generalized pattern of a national culture, and in so doing created, albeit unconsciously, an ethnic identity.[24]

The village was not an exact transplant from Mexico, yet much of the culture of the village reflected Mexican rural culture. For example, the village, like its Mexican counterparts, provided its members with protection against poverty, illness, or other misfortune through voluntary reciprocal self-help activities. Even the construction of housing and, in some instances, education was often a village activity. The village experience was to a large extent culturally self-sustaining, especially with regard to patriotic and religious celebrations and rituals, but the villagers also provided substantial portions of their traditional nutritional and folk medicine needs. However, the new cultural, physical, and economic environment presented challenges to immigrants requiring varying degrees of cultural retooling. Adaptations to the new environment, some by choice, others through pressure, were grafted upon the Mexican cultural heritage. In some instances these adaptations inexorably wrought irreversible cultural changes; in other instances change resulted in accommodations rather than radical transformations.

Villagers, in the process of cultural adaptation, perceived their community as a permanent residential site, rather than a temporary stage of a longer migrant process. The citrus village was, for the majority, the final stop of a long family journey from Mexico. The consequence was a maturing community comprised of elders and their children, as the first generation grew old, the second matured within the borders of their community. Two generations imbued with a strong community identity anchored the citrus villages within the dominant Anglo-American context.

Mexican citrus villages were deliberately segregated by the dominant society, and the prejudice and discrimination that was common to the citrus belt promoted the need for self-reliance, creativity, and community organization. In spite of the domination villagers experienced, they managed to create and re-create a dynamic society. What is most significant is that in most instances these communities were formed by recent immigrant workers and their families, many of whom were strangers to each other. Time, however, constructed a community life that was patterned on blueprints drawn from their experience and revised according to the demands of a changing society.

Poverty was the most obvious condition affecting culture in the picker camps. A 1939 Senate committee's report concluded that citrus pickers did "not ordinarily earn enough to supply what is considered a fair American standard of living for a family, [citrus pickers' income averages] from 30 to 35 cents per hour"[25] and amounted roughly to $423 annually. Moreover, pickers and packers were not always fortunate enough to work a nine-hour day, because picking schedules were accommodated to weather, moisture, and demand. Consequently, the season was seldom a full-time working period and crews often would average "only 20 to 30 hours per week."[26] The careful and thoughtful observations of Carey McWilliams captured the gritty mid-1940s character of the Mexican citrus communities or "in the parlance of the region the 'Jim-town.'" "From Santa Barbara to San Diego, one can find these Jim-towns, with their clusters of bizarre shacks, usually located in an out-of-the-way place on the outskirts of an established citrus-belt town . . . always 'on the other side of the tracks' . . . the Jim-towns lack governmental services; the streets are dusty unpaved lanes, the plumbing is primitive, and the water supply is usually obtained from outdoor hydrants."[27] On the other hand, those who lived through that era often recall positive experiences, the strong community bonds and the willingness of the community to share with those in need.

One is impressed with the vibrant sense of community, the organization, complexity, and programming of community life in these pickers' villages. While the outside community generally held a constellation of negative concepts of the Mexican communities, and in spite of the determined social intervention to Americanize them while actively segregating them, these communities remained in many respects islands of Mexican life, maintaining its family traditions, religion, folk beliefs, artisanal crafts, religious and national holidays, celebrations, customs, language, food, and architecture.

These communities were not entirely isolated and independent villages but were linked into semirural regional communities that gave the people a sense of identity and culture beyond the confines of the individual village. Picker villages formed regional ties in the area through employment, intermarriage, union activity, religious and patriotic observances, formal recreation, and political organization. Indeed, when the harvest ended in their area, pickers and packers often traveled to outlying counties and formed secondary ties in those communities in which they temporarily resided. Children, spouses, and relatives, such as aunts and uncles, often made summer treks to the San Joaquin Valley, within the county of residence, and to nearby counties to harvest grapes, fruits, and vegetables. However, the main source of family income remained local citrus picking and, to an extent, packing.

Many women worked either as packers or domestic help, and some operated small businesses; nevertheless, women's primary roles were in the home and family, and included the practice of traditional medicine, conducting religious celebrations, maintaining and conveying folk beliefs, and making handicrafts. Mexican families were quite large and poverty engendered a constant reliance on invention to meet family needs.[28] Women specialized in health care, were knowledgeable about childbirth, as well as the supernatural causes of and cures for illnesses. Villages generally had the services of a *partera* (midwife) and a *curandera* (curer), both of whom practiced traditional medicine that employed teas, roots, flowers, poultices, leaves, prayers, and charms. These skills were passed on to the next generation.

Women were the storytellers, recalling the age-old stories of Mexico, some of which were handed down from pre-Columbian times, and many of which referred to the supernatural.[29] In addition to managing the home, practicing thrift, producing handicrafts, and preserving the oral traditions, women were responsible for the religious celebrations Las Posadas and the *Día de la Virgen de Guadalupe* (December 12), as well as for processions such as for Día de Los Muertos, All Soul's Day, and Sunday church fairs, called *jamaicas*. Women, therefore, created and acted within the oral and visual cultural life of the camps and in no small measure shaped the material and cultural quality of life helping to overcome, to some degree, impoverished conditions.

A comprehensive examination of the social organization and culture of the villages illustrates the creative energies of their residents. Here, unique and culturally dynamic Mexican communities existed on the margins of

Anglo-American society. Bonds stemming from extended family relations, religion, national and regional culture, labor, segregation, history, class, and education forged the Mexican population into a discrete community, self-conscious of its role in the larger society and of the separation between them. In assessing these communities, one begins to recognize the social structure that existed within the village and the significance within it of internal class or political distinctions, including those caused by the inter-vention of the Mexican consulate.

These communities did not forge their experience solely within a region-al context—international issues impacted significantly on the villages. Generally, Chicano historians have noted revolutionary activity among Mexican immigrants, the Partido Liberal Mexicano and the Flores Magon brothers have become celebrated examples of Mexican political ferment aimed toward Mexico from north of the border.[30] What has been less well recognized has been the political activity that extended from within Mex-ico, aimed northward across the border and into the dispersed Mexican communities. The Mexican government appreciated the previous role of the expatriate community in Mexico's internal affairs. Consequently, no sooner did the revolutionary violence subside and an immigrant commu-nity appear in the United States than an active consulate, bringing with it Mexico's domestic policy concerns, established intimate links.

Most historical accounts of consulate activity have tended to ignore, dismiss, or downplay the influence that the consulates exerted into *colo-nia* political and cultural activities.[31] In this analysis, I follow the thread of consular functions in the villages, examining their pervasiveness, and in the instance of union action, their influence. In so doing, I examine the close relationship between *colonia* leaders and consular officials. Through such an inquiry, I provide a more rigorous understanding of the place and role that the consul held in Chicano history.

Logically, much of this study concerns the dominant role of the first generation, the immigrant generation, in shaping the affairs of the village. This group, and its nature as a bipolar group, contoured the cultural and political quality of the village. Many immigrants were political refugees; some had been petty government or lesser army officials at one time. On the other hand, the majority came from a peasantry escaping the violence and death of the revolution. We have, then, two subgroups within this first immigrant generation of citrus workers. Those of the first group were gen-erally of the middling and professional classes; some were educated and enjoyed the advantage of literacy. Those of the second were from the la-boring classes, primarily peasants, had little if any education, and conse-quently were largely illiterate. The first group, conscious of its class sta-tus, positioned its members as the political and cultural leaders of the community. And in the discriminatory and prejudicial atmosphere they found, these leaders turned inward and relied on a fervent nationalism to counterbalance the oppression they faced. It was in this context that the Mexican consulates found a willing partner to jointly exploit a patriotic defense not only of their communities but of Mexico and its government as well. Consulates initially organized community self-help organizations, then committees hosting patriotic celebrations, eventually expanding their influence through attempts to lead labor unions.

Postwar Evolution of the Village

In spite of their apparent insularity, the regional economy in general, and that of the citrus towns in particular, were not immune to international stresses. Enormous economic changes occurred during the war and postwar period and redefined the villages. Only a half-century ago, citrus towns were anchored in southern California on an extensive scale. As happened to many of southern California's agricultural endeavors, the economic boom-and-bust pattern caught up with the citrus industry. The incessant, seemingly inexorable process of change, rooted in the economic sphere, affected all levels of society and was manifested particularly in the area's community lifestyle. Larger and more aggressive economic structures en-croached and eventually engulfed the towns, submerging them into manu-facturing, light industry, and suburbia. As the citrus towns evolved, so did an integral part of the citrus industry, the Mexican villages that sheltered the picking and packing crews. Rather than disappear, many of these com-munities remained, although occupation gradually shifted from the groves to industry, construction, and other nonagricultural lines. But before that economic transition had matured, Mexican contract labor, braceros, filled the labor gap created by wartime draft and industries. Braceros arrived in the citrus region in 1942 and were but one more change in the labor pro-cess that answered the growers' needs. The era of the Mexican family be-ing attached to a picker ended, and the era of the temporarily migrant sin-gle Mexican male as the typical picking laborer began. As the family-based labor force ran its course, so did the original Mexican camps.

With the decline of the citrus industry, association camps were eventu-ally demolished, and their inhabitants moved to nearby housing. Many of the original houses that had been privately constructed or purchased by the pickers in the teens and twenties remained, although remodeling and new construction had altered the communities so that they now only faintly resembled their citrus era image. The urban blue-collar barrio replaced the rural picker village. An urbanization process, that was without migration makes the evolution of these communities novel in the context of urban history. With the emergence of the suburban and urban barrio in the old citrus belt, the qualities that distinguished the segregated picker village gradually declined. The strength of purely Mexican cultural forms evolved into the bicultural nature of today's barrios. Many Mexican American urban barrios, with their particular and complex culture and economic, political, and social structures, now occupy the space in which many former picker villages once stood.

This study of the Mexican citrus picker communities is therefore an analysis of the internal and external forces that have operated to construct, shape, maintain, or modify the community. A certain dynamic within the Mexican community has revolved around a cohesive culture, ethnic, and political consciousness, and a common class experience; and a sociopolitical tension between the Mexican community and the dominant society that has stemmed primarily from the economic life of the area. At the most general level, these are the dynamic processes that have shaped the community's history. It follows, then, that I will examine two processes that have operated both independently and interdependently: (1) the development of the citrus industry and its larger community form; and (2) the consequent development of the Mexican community (or perhaps, subcommunity) and the application of their creative energies and intelligence in the construction and reconstruction of their community. I emphasize the group processes through which an immigrant people, many of whom are strangers to one another and come together only because of a specialized economic function they perform, pioneer the development of a quasi-independent community, well defined in its boundaries and clearly segregated from, and politically dominated (but not entirely controlled) by, the larger society.

Our story begins with an overview of the rise of the citrus industry and proceeds to the process of community formation in a southern California county—the appropriately named Orange County.

• **I** •

History, Labor,
and Social Relations
in the Citrus Industry

The citrus industry was well-rooted in southern California long before Mexicans assumed duties as its pickers and packers. By 1900, the outlines of the future industry, the social relations of citrus towns, and the utilization of minorities as picking labor had been established. Before examining specific villages, it is useful to review the historic origins of citrus culture that preceded the industry's formative years in southern California. By the end of the formative period, roughly between 1910 and 1920, uniform industry-wide practices regarding the nature of picking and packing labor processes, and industry-sponsored housing programs were well established. Such an overview provides background and context to the discussion and analysis to follow of those villages in the heart of the region's Valencia district, Orange County.

Historical Origins of Citrus Culture

Citrus culture was well developed before the late 1700s, when it was brought by the Spaniards to what is now southern California. By then, citrus cultivation had had at least a six-thousand-year history as practiced in Asia, Europe and the Middle East.[1]

The sweet orange, however, did not make its appearance "in Europe until approximately A.D. 1400."[2] Subsequently, seeds were brought to the New World by Columbus and later explorers. Spanish colonial policy, concerned with replicating Spanish institutions in their colonies, expanded citrus production and in so doing confirmed over time the areas suitable to citrus culture. In the early 1500s, Garcilaso de la Vega observed orange harvests in what is today Guatemala. Orange cultivation spread to the West Indies in 1600 and reached Brazil by 1648. The orange was also grown successfully in Spain's northern possessions, in Florida by 1579, and was introduced by way of missionary expeditions into California in 1769.[3]

Thus the Spanish successfully (although perhaps without plan) identified those regions, including southern California, eventually to be recognized as suitable for modern citrus production. However, during the Spanish colonial and Mexican National periods, production was aimed at satisfying only local consumption, given the self-subsistent nature of Spanish-Mexican feudalism. Thus, the only agriculture in Alta California was within the mission, and later in rancho gardens, vineyards, and orchards; and these were limited to satisfying the needs of the priests and neophytes, local garrisons, *hacendado* families, and the missions' artisans and laborers. Nevertheless, the missions and ranchos presaged California's factory-type agricultural production. One scholar has noted that the "fruits and nuts known to have been grown by the padres included almost all those now produced in California, and some that have not succeeded commercially."[4] Apples, raspberries, almonds, plantains, grapes, olives, as well as, of course, oranges, lemons, citrons, and limes grew abundantly.

The first successful citrus cultivation in California occurred at the San Gabriel Mission in about 1804 or 1805, although only four hundred seedlings were planted on 6 acres contained within a 190-acre farm.[5] The secularization of the missions in 1833 and the division of the lands distributed among grantees caused the gardens to fall into decay and ruin. Nevertheless, William Wolfskill obtained surviving trees from the San Gabriel Mission in 1841 and "planted a two acre site at [what is now] Central Avenue at Fifth Street in Los Angeles." Later the orchard was expanded to 70 acres.[6] Wolfskill, followed by several others, embarked upon the first commercial ventures in an area of production that seemed to grow slowly. The transition from Mexican to American territory did not immediately lead to great changes in production. "Even as late as 1870 there were only eight thousand trees in Los Angeles County and fewer than thirty-five thousand trees in the entire state of California."[7] Their enterprises' success was handicapped by the long, slow rail transit causing critical spoilage, thus limiting sales to a small local market. The restricted outlet contributed to maintaining a limited technology adequate for the level of production but ineffective for larger scales of production and distribution. As long as citrus production remained relatively small, technological advances would be indefinitely postponed.

California agriculture has many characteristics that have made it unique in modern agriculture. A history of successive emphases on particular crops, interacting with an environmentally conditioned pattern of crop production, have formed a series of evolving agricultural belts. Grapes, cotton, citrus, walnuts, sugar beets, corn, truck farms, avocados, to name a few, grow in concentrated production zones throughout California. Crops such as walnuts, sugar beets, citrus, and avocados are concentrated in more or less contiguous areas of southern California. California then is a series of agricultural belts, determined by climate, soil, water availability, and in the case of citrus, the absence of dense ocean fogs and freezing temperatures.

In the late nineteenth century much of the future citrus belt was planted with grapevines, grains, cotton, and, for a time, thousands of mulberry trees. In spite of the early emphasis on noncitrus crops, citrus growing made significant but small advances by settlers who were to colonize and develop the vast stretches of the empty plains, valleys, and rolling hills in the semidesert. In the early 1870s Riverside colonists planted nearly seven thousand trees, and through a process of homespun trial-and-error experimentation gradually founded a thriving citrus industry. Within the decade, Riverside emerged as the citrus center of southern California, sponsoring yearly citrus fairs attracting visitors from the region. Meanwhile, Riverside growers organized citrus institutes that brought together learned experts and practitioners in the field, who presented both scientific and nonscientific papers on a wide range of topics related to citriculture. Production expanded to more than two hundred thousand trees in the mid-1880s, compelling growers to organize the first mechanized packinghouse to handle the substantial volume of production. Thus citrus made its initial appearance as a defined, successful, and organized industry in the 1880s. The Riverside settlement demonstrated conclusively the vast potential that citrus held for the region, and so augured future success. Nevertheless, shipping remained limited to the markets of San Francisco, and the small markets of Arizona and New Mexico, as had been the case with the Wolfskill venture two decades before. However, the Riverside growers went several steps further, streamlining methods of growing, packing, and shipping, thus providing a solid technical and informational base for the later growth of the industry.

The completion of the transcontinental railway and the invention of refrigerated railway cars in the mid-1880s through opening the unlimited and unchallenged national market provided the next major impetus to expanding settlement and citrus ranching. Far from its humble beginnings in the self-subsistence mission gardens, by the 1890s citrus was well on its way to becoming the most celebrated nationally consumed California product. It could do so, however, only to the extent that citrus production was extended and marketing made efficient. The national market for California citrus came about soon after the completion of the transcontinental railroad, and further boosted as a result of the construction of large-scale federally funded irrigation projects at the turn of the century.

Town after town was founded throughout the fertile, relatively frost-free, and well-drained semiarid region; and the success of the Riverside colony seemed to be duplicated across what was soon to be the southern California citrus belt. New citrus areas appeared like spring flowers. Professors Lawton and Weathers convey an impression of the social process in motion. "Pasadena, San Gabriel, Whittier, Pomona, Monrovia, Azusa, Corona, Glendora, Upland, Ontario, Etiwanda, San Bernardino, Redlands and Riverside were to become synonymous throughout the world with citrus growing."[8] Many towns initially experimented with several crops before settling into citrus production, but once the transition was completed growth was insured.

From 1890 to about 1940, citrus was the state's principal agricultural product. Between 1890 and 1900, the number of California orange trees was multiplied by five, and the number of lemon trees by eighteen. Citrus carlot shipments between the years 1885 and 1940 demonstrated steady growth. In the 1885–86 season, all of southern California shipped less than 2,000 carloads.[9] In the 1921–22 season, 28,374 rail carloads were shipped, but five years later, 53,574 cars were loaded. The upward spiral continued, so that by the end of the 1941–42 season, 87,768 cars of oranges had been shipped![10] This dynamic productive expansion experienced few downturns in its history. Orange County, destined to become the nation's leading producer of Valencia oranges, shipped but two cars in 1883–84. That figure cannot compare with the statistics for the 1926–27 season, which cite 13,542 carlot shipments. Not even the Depression could pull down the booming economic edifice. "In 1938, a year of low prices, the returns to California citrus growers amounted approximately to $51,000,000, nearly 10 percent of the total farm income for the state."[11] Not only was California the chief producer of the nation's oranges, accounting for roughly 60 percent of the national crop, it was also a major producer on a world scale, responsible for 21 percent of production in 1938–39.[12]

Nearly 90 percent of the oranges shipped from the citrus belt were consumed nationally. As local production expanded, national consumption followed suit. Studies showed that between "1908 and 1912 the average annual per capita consumption amounted to 35 oranges," but fifteen years later the average rose to 51 oranges.[13] The orange became a symbol of health, vitamins, and nutrition, and, as it did, year-round production increased, while improved marketing techniques and distribution effectively placed the commodity within the main population centers across the nation.

By 1928, 183,066 acres of orange orchards produced 36,526,000 boxes of packed fruit.[14] There were, in addition, 42,832 lemon-bearing acres, and 5,800 grapefruit-producing acres, giving a total of 230,698 acres planted with bearing citrus trees. Ten years later the total acreage figure stood at 281,626 acres of bearing orchards. This was a picture of citrus production much different from that provided by the 25,000-tree orchard owned by William Wolfskill at Los Angeles in 1860. Wolfskill's orchard had contained practically all of the citrus trees in the state.

Citrus includes oranges, lemons, grapefruit, limes, citron, and tangerines, among other fruits. However, the citrus belt was known mainly for oranges, and secondarily, for lemons and grapefruit. Oranges were not of one variety, two main types were grown, the Washington Navel and the Valencia. The Navel predominated in the inland areas, such as San Bernardino and Riverside counties and the foothill areas of Los Angeles County. The Valencia grew well in the coastal areas, provided that they were far enough from denser ocean fogs and colder temperatures. Eastern Los Angeles County and the northern half of Orange County, which together constituted the whole of the county's citrus area, were the major Valencia growers.

Whereas lemons were harvested year-round, Navels and Valencias had an approximate six-month picking season that did not overlap. Navels were picked from January until May or June; Valencia harvest began in May and lasted until November or December. Thus, California orange and lemon production was year-round, with staggered harvesting that insured a steady supply and little price fluctuation.

The extensive acreage devoted to citrus and the overwhelmingly abundant crops from 1900 to the 1940s can be attributed to a variety of factors, some of which—such as climate, soil, drainage, water, and capital—are mentioned above. Given that orange trees are one of nature's most prolific producers, good conditions and knowledgeable cultivation easily ensured successful production. Consequently, distribution and marketing, and not production, were the major problems faced by growers during the early history of the industry. Understandably, the first crops were primitively harvested, packed, and marketed. It was one thing to grow and harvest the product, it was an entirely different matter to sell it and realize a profit.

One citrus expert's comment on the method of distribution during the early phase of production illustrates this difficulty. "The prospective buyer visited the orchard, and after looking it over made a Yankee guess at the quantity of fruit on the trees and bid a lump sum for the crop. If a bargain was struck, [the buyer] assumed all responsibility from that time forth, picking, packing, shipping and marketing the fruit."[15]

Each individual grower then bid with one or several buyers, but by so doing the grower "transferred a part of his customary functions to the commercial buyer."[16] Growers no longer picked, packed, or supervised the process. Moreover, they no longer marketed and sold the product, except to local buyers.

In this early period, individual growers sold their crops to a packer or a dealer, who then marketed the product and realized a profit based on the difference between the purchase price and the selling price on the market. Growers quickly grew entirely dependent on middlemen, and shortly "as fruit became more abundant and surpluses began to appear," the earlier method evolved into a consignment or brokerage system. Under the consignment system, the distributors continued to protect themselves at the expense of the growers. This marketing method, remarked Charles C. Teague, owner of the large-scale Limoneira Ranch, "was largely under the control of dealers and speculators who had no interest in the problems of the growers and sought to handle the crop as much as possible to their own advantage."[17] By 1890 only five or six commercial distributors dominated the business and none would guarantee a price, nor even a sale, because they sought to protect their interests quite apart from the problems of growers. Marketing fiascoes, in the form of periodic gluts and wild price fluctuations, exacerbated an already untenable situation.[18] This process did not result in a profitable success paralleling production levels, but, in many cases, in yearly deficits for the grower. Distribution became gross speculation, and anarchy seemed the rule so that "the larger the crop the grower had, the more he was indebted to his packer at the end of the season."[19]

This situation led growers to organize cooperatives to control the distribution of their product. The most significant of the organizations was the Southern California Fruit Growers Exchange, established in 1893. Its objective was to correct poor marketing conditions through an organization governed by a centralized plan, administered by a board of directors elected by the membership. The organization was both local and district-wide and assumed the functions of picking, packing, and distribution, and, most important, allowed its members to rationalize production and distribution. By 1905, after several years of experimentation in order to overcome organizational and technical problems, this early organization was succeeded by the California Fruit Growers Exchange (which in 1952 assumed the name Sunkist). To succeed financially, the growers gave up some control of the private enterprise to a larger organization.

The local grower associations formed the base; above the base was the district association, which connected directly to the central Exchange headquarters. This three-tiered structure dominated "all phases of production."[20] The association then stood above each individual grower, and supplied "all harvesting labor . . . furnishing picking crews, hauling facilities, and all equipment, and undertaking upon request, to take charge of pruning and insect control."[21] The association generally supervised picking schedules, packing, loading, and shipping; rationalized distributing; and provided professional scientific guidance for its members. Perhaps the highest service provided to the individual grower by the Los Angeles central office was its powerful nationwide advertising program. Through newspapers, magazines, billboards, and radio broadcasts, the message that oranges, lemons and grapefruits were delicious and healthy fruits caught on with the American public in a way unmatched by any other agricultural product.

Although the association-grower relationship was the best possible arrangement to satisfy the growers' commercial interest, it was the local association that gave orders to the grower. The grower, it seemed, owned the grove, but the association dominated the grower. Paul S. Taylor, an economist from the University of California at Berkeley, described the function of the grower and the association:

> The citrus industry affords a clear illustration of the manner in which the traditional functions of "farmers" are lost by those still classified as "farm operators" in the census. Of course, the packing of fruit is usually performed in large packing plants cooperatively or privately owned, and not located on the farm. But more than that, even the work in the grove of pruning, fumigating, spraying, picking, and so forth, is commonly performed by gangs of laborers under contract, or employed and directed by the manager of the citrus association.[22]

Add to this the role of the central exchange office in coordinating the district and local exchanges, as well as the massive advertising efforts,[23] and the role of the individual grower is diminished considerably. Nevertheless, no later than "five days from the sale of his oranges in some Eastern market, he receives a check for the proceeds."[24] Consequently, the individual grower was not a farmer in any sense of the word, but functioned as a businessman involved more with a bureaucratic cooperative and less with actual farming itself.

Across the United States no other agricultural enterprise was as tightly organized into cooperatives as was California citrus. In California, 248 packinghouses, each with one to two hundred members, were affiliated with either the Southern California Fruit Exchange or the Mutual Orange Distributors.[25] By the third decade of the century the Exchange shipped 75 percent of California's crop through 226 local co-ops; the remainder was shipped through 22 co-ops operated by the Mutual Orange Distributors and 55 large independent packers.

Further, the Exchange established the Fruit Growers Supply Company in 1907, which was intended to furnish the local associations "at cost, the principal supplies that are necessary for packing and production . . . boxes, nails, wraps, fertilizers, insecticides, fungicides . . ." and a long list of other items consumed in production, packing, and distribution.[26] The Exchange operated its own lumber business and a modern mill that in 1943 "could cut 200 million feet of lumber a year"—enough to meet the year's demand for 43 million boxes.[27] Thus, the California Fruit Growers Exchange and its supply arm, the Fruit Growers Supply Company, were the critical organizational factors shaping the citrus industry and ultimately determining industry-wide policy and practices.

While the cooperative method was considered a democratic system with voting rights allocated equally among the members, in practice it was the larger and more successful growers who dominated the local associations and the central exchange. General policy was established at the level of the central exchange, although members of the association had latitude within that policy. Moreover, the association, governed by an elected board of directors, independently managed its own affairs. However, the board members were not elected on a one-man, one-vote system, but on the basis of shares. The size and quality of the crop determined the value of each grower's contribution to the co-op, which in turn determined the distribution of voting shares. In the final analysis, the larger growers in the association held disproportionate power in relation to the smaller or less successful growers. A 1938 U.S. Senate report confirmed that "not only do the larger growers have a controlling voice in the direction of the local associations but, through them, they control the district and central exchanges."[28]

Although the average citrus farm was from eight to ten acres, figures of the size of farms, production, and returns demonstrate that only a handful of farms and commercial enterprises actually dominated. The concentration of acreage was a hidden aspect of the romanticism associated with the citrus belt. At the end of the Depression, only 3.7 percent, or 714 growers, owned 92,652 acres, or 40.8 percent of the state's orange acreage. From another perspective, the concentration of orange growing can be appreciated further. In 1940, 161 growers, or .8 percent of all growers, owned nearly 15 percent of all orange acreage. On the other hand, nearly 12,000 growers, constituting 62.4 percent of all growers, owned 49,649 acres, less than 22 percent of the state's total orange acreage.[29] The data on lemon growers is similar: 3.8 percent of lemon producers owned nearly 58 percent of lemon grove acreage, 29,626 acres; 74 percent, or 3,555 growers, owned 26.5 percent of the acreage, 13,389 acres.

Generally, the larger growers held the better groves, thus increasing the imbalance in the distribution of political clout within the industry.[30] Citrus ranches represented a large capital investment and, on the average, the per-acre valuation in 1937 was $1,581. However, the average valuation does not take into consideration variation in productivity, and in the quality of climate, soil, trees, and water supply. Selling prices for orchards varied from farm to farm and county to county. Accordingly, in 1945–46 the best orchards sold for as much as $6,000 an acre, but the average price was around $2,500. In Tulare County, the average price was $933, considerably below the state average. The Exchange and the local associations incorporated this disproportionate distribution of acreage and valuation into their structure and decision making.

Given the variation in climate, soil, quality of trees, and productivity that often distinguished one district from another, and even areas within districts, it follows that associations also varied in productivity and wealth. For example, in 1938, of 226 packinghouses, or associations, 11, or 4.8 percent employed 21 percent, or 7,485, of the labor force in the Exchange's packinghouses.[31] On the other hand, 42 percent of, or 92, packinghouses, employed 13 percent of the labor force. Data taken in 1937 on the value of facilities and acreage of 91 packinghouses also demonstrated a concentration of wealth within the structure of associations. The average investment for the 91 facilities was $101,846, but the North Whittier Heights Citrus Association was valued at $178,629, and the Sierra Madre–Lamanda Citrus Association was valued at $250,746.

The California Fruit Growers Exchange, contrary to the public relations image it had constructed for itself, was organized like a pyramid with the locus of decision making in the hands of a minority of its members. "The center of power in the industry," wrote Carey McWilliams, "is not to be found in the elegant residences on Smiley Heights in Redlands, but in the offices of the California Fruit Growers Exchange in Los Angeles, [furthermore the commercial growers] dominate the central exchange and its local and district offices."[32] One may deplore the concentration and imbalance in the cooperative system, but the fact is that citrus growing was not a common farming enterprise. Investments in groves required sufficient capital that the average person lacked. Consequently, the citrus belt was colonized, settled, and extended by people who had "succeeded" elsewhere, quite often in professions other than ranching. The continuation of their success dictated that they transfer their independence to the association becoming subordinate to it.

The Citrus Industry Division of Labor and the Labor of Nationalities

Since the beginning of citriculture some six thousand years ago, no methods other than handpicking and handpacking have been developed to remove the orange from the tree and to pack it for transport to market. Many areas of agriculture have benefited from the invention of harvesting and packing machinery, but citrus has not. Consequently, the high volume of citrus production required an intensive labor process, one that greatly distinguished it from wheat and corn harvesting. In 1920, estimates of the man-to-acreage ratio necessary to handle production in the Dakotas was one man to 135 acres. In the United States as a whole, it was one man to 40.5 acres. But in southern California the labor of one person was "required to properly care for two or three acres of full-bearing lemons, pick the fruit and pack it for shipment."[33] A similar amount of labor was required to the same type of work on three to four acres of oranges. Thus citrus production involved heavy expenditures for labor, insuring a need for both a large supply of workers and their steady availability.

As mentioned earlier, although seasonal production depended on subareas within the belt, the need for labor for the belt as a whole was year-round. Nevertheless, the length of the season and the variable conditions (wind, rain, climate, and buyer's orders) provided for peaks and valleys in the picking and packing schedule during the harvest period. Labor needs were often known only on a day-to-day basis.[34] Lack of uniform production, however, did not mean that a large and steady supply was unnecessary; on the contrary, the length of the harvest, made it mandatory to establish a local, permanent labor supply. Under such conditions labor could still be mobilized according to variations in climate, moisture, wind, frost, or a marketing order, determining the daily or weekly picking schedule during the harvest.

Unlike the storied family farm, picking and packing labor has seldom, if ever, been the work of the growers or their families. That area of production has generally been reserved for other nationalities and, to a lesser extent, poor Anglo-Americans. In that regard, labor history in the citrus industry is parallel to that of labor history in California agriculture. The incipient stage of development that roughly covers the years 1870 to the 1890s witnessed the extensive employment of Chinese as picker gangs as well as packers. The Chinese were preferred because as gang laborers, they could be obtained quickly, in time for the harvest, would work long hours for low wages, and were willing to live under conditions white workers would not tolerate.[35] There were additional incentives, it appears that many Chinese had some familiarity with citrus culture and knew some of the picking and packing procedures later adopted by the industry.

One packinghouse manager recalled that in the 1880s "practically all the labor performed in the preparation of citrus fruits for market was done by Chinamen. I was much impressed, especially by the dexterous manner in which the fruit was wrapped in paper and placed in the boxes by these Chinese packers."[36] Charles C. Teague, who for a quarter of a century was chairman of the California Fruit Growers Exchange Board of Directors and a large commercial grower, considered that the Chinese were "good workers, loyal and dependable and were skilled in fruit and vegetable handling and made excellent domestic servants."[37] Early growers seldom faced a labor shortage problem as long as Chinese were allowed entrance to the country. However, the effect of the Chinese Exclusion Act, problematic for the industry in the 1890s, was shortly resolved with the influx of Japanese. Until the teens, citrus pickers were mainly Japanese although Chinese crews were occasionally hired by the grower associations. Consequently, the availability of labor was not an issue in the early development of the industry equal to the problems of marketing and distribution. Labor seemed to be as abundant as the oranges on the trees.

However, the enchantment of the growers was soon cut short by the reluctance of the Japanese gangs to work within a disorganized labor market. Japanese pickers, as did their countrymen in field and truck crops, organized themselves into associations led by a "boss" who mediated with an employer. The gangs, transformed into associations, did not compete with each other and worked for the wages settled upon by their boss. If the wages offered by the employer were too low, the boss merely kept his men out—with the knowledge that no other association would underbid for the contract. The associations acted in the fashion of a union and proved successful because they were the main supply of labor. The reluctance of the Japanese to work in a disorganized market dismayed the growers, prompting Teague to remark that the Japanese lacked the "loyalty and reliability that characterized the Chinese," but that the Japanese "nevertheless were a very useful source of ranch labor."[38]

The Japanese considered labor an instrument to improve their social status, but the growers associated the Japanese with the type of labor performed. Moreover, growers consistently opposed the organization of labor because it placed a significant area of decision making in the hands of laborers. As such, the labor system became an instrument by the Japanese to achieve goals quite separate from those of the grower. In time, the Japanese first underbid other nationalities, then eliminated them as competitors, and finally monopolized the labor market. In 1911 the Immigration Commission concluded that the Japanese underbid and drove out the Chinese and "have maintained their position because their bids have been lower than those occasionally made by white laborers."[39]

The associations often acted as a trade union by engaging in "quickie" strikes, refusing to scab, keeping enough men out of work to threaten spoilage of the product until wages are raised, and also by organizing boycotts.[40] Through such tactics, the Japanese established themselves successfully in farming via tenantry and leasing. But it was the gangs' monopoly of the labor market that soured growers to such an extent that agitation for exclusion of the Japanese became a major political issue in California politics. From 1905 to 1930, a "succession of state and federal measures were enacted designed to diminish the importance of the Japanese in California agriculture."[41] The effects were dramatic. By 1915 the once-predominant Japanese labor supply dwindled, and in some areas was eliminated.

The fortunes of growers, however, did not suffer unduly as a consequence of the exclusion of the Japanese. A steep rise in Mexican immigration, especially in the 1920s, filled the labor vacuum that had been created also in part by vast increases in the state's agricultural production. It is highly probable that without Mexican labor the spectacular achievements in southwestern agriculture between 1900 and 1940 would have been post-poned indefinitely.[42] Moreover, although Mexican work habits paralleled those of the Japanese, unlike the Japanese, Mexican labor displayed no tendency to form unionlike associations. Growers' concerns shifted from the quality of the work force to the quantity of workers available. An intensive recruiting campaign sponsored by agricultural interests in the Southwest contributed enormously to attracting the large numbers of Mexican migrants who arrived in California—southern California in particular. The employment of these migrants followed an established pattern that divided nationalities according to the division of labor. The California Fruit Growers Exchange was one of the many organizations that lobbied for an open border policy during the late teens. As a consequence, during this time, barriers to Mexican migration were relaxed by immigration officials.[43] The Exchange worked closely, for example, with the state chamber of commerce, especially its agricultural branch, to seek legislation favorable to its interests that were finally realized in a 1917 immigration act allowing for the importation of contract labor and suspending the literacy test.[44]

Agricultural districts throughout the Southwest and especially in southern California soon had a new racial class structure: Mexicans were now the laborers while Anglo-Americans remained the dominant group, either as owners, managers, or service personnel. Cheap agricultural labor soon became synonymous with Mexican immigrants and a vast literature, as well as a popular perception, emerged that maintained that Mexicans were by nature farm workers. Charles C. Teague, for example, remarked that Mexicans "are naturally adapted to agricultural work, particularly in the handling of fruits and vegetables. . . . Many of them have a natural skill in the handling of tools and are resourceful in matters requiring manual ability."[45]

The production of citrus involved several specialized tasks, some of which were unskilled, while others necessitated highly trained personnel. The typical cooperative enterprise included growers and the cooperatives' employees: supervisors, managers, chemists, middle-level office employees (accountants, for example), secretaries, graders, packers, haulers, fumigators, pruners, foremen, and pickers. At some locales, the list might include night watchmen, labor camp supervisors, and packinghouse maintenance workers. Statistics taken in 1938 show that grower association payrolls numbered anywhere from ten to over five hundred—about 60 percent employed one hundred or more workers. The two costliest labor expenses, picking and packing, were performed by relatively cheap labor.[46] Pickers and packers constituted the two principal laboring groups—they were the lowest paid employees and were the employees most subject to indeterminate work periods.

Picking was a particularly arduous labor and not an unskilled task—it required that workers follow exacting instructions and make informed decisions. In 1921, the Central Exchange instructions on the handling of fruit cautioned pickers never to pull fruit from the tree, but to always cut the fruit squarely "across the stem right next to the button."[47] They also instructed that "straight ladders should be placed as nearly perpendicular as possible so as to put less weight on the branches";[48] gloves should be worn so that the fruit may not be cut by fingernail scratches. Further, pickers were not to "fill the picking sack too full" and were not to "allow it to bump against the ladder, box, or any hard objects."[49] When the fruit was transferred from the bag to the field box, care was to be exercised in emptying, "allowing the fruit to roll gently," lest the fruit sustain injury. Further, the bags and boxes had to be free of twigs, leaves, and debris that might injure the fruit. Thus the picker, standing on a twelve-foot ladder, hauling a bulky canvas bag capable of holding fifty pounds of fruit, and working with trees that were often thirty to thirty-five feet high and had rough and thorny branches, was required to work delicately and quickly, to measure an orange, and pick it.

Picking was carried out according to schedules devised by the packinghouse manager, who also determined which groves to pick, the quality of the pick, and the requisite size of acceptable oranges (oranges were measured by a set of rings of varying sizes carried by the pickers). The crew foreman assembled his men at dawn, generally at the pickers community or at the packinghouse, and transported them to the grove. Crews of from ten to twenty men worked under a single foreman instructed to ensure that association picking policies were being carried out. In the teens and 1920s, as a general rule some associations employed an Anglo-American foreman to oversee Mexican crews.[50] As Mexican pickers grew predominant during the 1920s, associations sometimes hired foremen from the picking crews and in some areas, as in Orange County, many foremen were former pickers.

The length of the work day was dictated in part by factors other than the supervisor's wishes. Orchards could not be picked in high winds, or on damp mornings, under foggy conditions, or when it rained. Pickers were not always fortunate enough to work a nine-hour day as picking schedules were contoured to weather and moisture (a wet orange or lemon easily spoiled in the box). At the beginning and end of the season they might have worked only one to two days and only a few hours per day. Consequently, crews often would average "only 20 to 30 hours per week."[51]

In 1939 the average hourly wage of a packer was 43 cents an hour, with work available only thirty-five weeks during the year, and only four days each week.[52] For pickers the situation was much more difficult in that they averaged only from 30 to 35 cents per hour, probably working the same number of weeks, and consequently their average annual wage was below that of packers.[53] Moreover, because of the accepted practice of utilizing the unpaid labor of male children (nicknamed *ratas* [rats]), the wages earned by the average picker were inflated. The harvest came in summer in the Valencia districts, allowing the *ratas* to accompany their fathers (or another close relative) to the groves to work as assistants. John Arce was typical of the *ratas*, when at the age of eight he picked for the first time to help his father. By the age of eleven, he could, in his words, "handle the job fairly well" and by thirteen he considered himself a skilled picker—a vocation he followed each summer until he was eighteen when he joined the service in 1946.[54] In the winter-harvested Navel districts the *ratas* usually worked only on Saturdays since school was in session. *Ratas* usually picked from the lower branches of the tree, received no pay, instead they deposited their filled bag into their father's numbered field box. Generally only sixteen-year-olds were eligible for crewmenship, but examples of fourteen- or fifteen-year-old full-time pickers were not uncommon.[55]

The organization of the picking force had two aspects. On the one hand, the laborers were usually unorganized as a class of workers; on the other, their labor was structured by the nature of an industry dominated by an organization of growers. Consequently, there was "no bargaining, collective or individual."[56] This allowed the packinghouse manager and the association directors to set the prevailing wage rates, frequently after consultation with other associations at the district level. Associations established the wages, hours, schedules, hiring practices; retained a fee for transport to groves and equipment costs from pickers' wages; and determined the criteria for distinguishing between "good" and "bad" pickers. Moreover, if a picker lived in an association dwelling, he was obligated to be available for work at any time during the year. "The workers have no choice," stated one Senate committee's report, "but to accept the terms offered or get no work."[57] The division of labor, whether packinghouse or picking, was virtually free of unionization for most of the history of the southern California citrus industry.

Wages were paid not on the basis of hours worked but according to one of several standards: by the number of boxes picked (a box equaled a full picker's canvas bag weighing fifty pounds); a straight day's salary for a nine-hour day, an hourly wage, or a combination of a box rate with an hourly rate. Seldom were pickers paid solely by the hour; they were sometimes paid solely by the box. The variations combining the box and hour system, were aimed at compelling the pickers to increase their output without lowering the quality of the pick. Many associations paid on a quality-quantity system whereby a picker earned a base wage and a bonus on boxes picked over a certain amount. However, the bonus varied with the quality of the pick—that is, the percentage of "defective" fruit. (A defective fruit was usually one with damaged skin or a protruding stem possibly damaging to other fruit.) If defective picks constituted less than 1 percent of the fruit packed, associations paid 6 cents on all boxes over forty. They paid 5 cents if defective picks were less than 1 percent, 4 cents if less than 3 percent, and 3 cents if less than 4 percent. If more than 4 percent was defective, associations paid no bonus.[58]

The quality-bonus system generally paid an hourly base wage and a bonus based on the quality of the pick such as 2 cents per box if defects were less than 1 percent. The bonus was lowered to ½ cent per box if defects were less than 4 percent. The quantity-bonus paid a base hourly wage, and an automatic bonus of 1 to 1½ cents on all boxes picked. The straight day or hour wage was a simple straightforward wage, which in 1921 (a year of labor shortage) ran from $2.70 to $4.00 per day, depending on local conditions. In this instance, growers thought that tight supervision over the crew would ensure a quality pick. The box basis again was a simple payment based on quantity, say 5 to 10 cents per box. Under this system the incentive to the picker was definitely not quality. The seasonal bonus system paid a base rate of so much per hour and "at the end of the season a bonus is paid to all the men who are still with the crew, providing the quality of their work is satisfactory."[59] The bonus paid, say 3 cents on all boxes over forty if defects were less than 5 percent up to six cents if defects were less than 2 percent. The end-of-the-season bonus kept the laborers from working for other associations or seeking alternative employment during slack picking periods. Pickers accepted the bonus system, but they did so under duress.

In contrast to urban employment, agricultural wages in general, and citrus pickers in particular, were considerably lower. Except for cannery and garment work, urban employers paid hourly rates, and in one 1930 survey sponsored by the State of California of 312 industrial establishments that employed Mexican labor, 85 percent of Mexican workers earned $3.50 per day and above. The average weekly rate ranged between $16.00 to over $30.00. At least one-half of industrial establishments surveyed paid their Mexican labor a minimum of 50 cents per hour, or about 20 cents above the hourly rate paid to citrus pickers who were forced to depend on the piece-rate bonus to increase their pay.[60] The historian Cletus Daniel studied California farmworkers and compared urban and agricultural employment. He wrote that "farm employers, with few exceptions, sought to squeeze the last measure of profit out of their businesses by cutting labor costs to the bone," while urban employers sought to mollify workers with various welfare schemes.[61] Lizabeth Cohen found a similar pattern of company welfare programs in her work on the working class in Chicago.[62] Such were not to be found in the citrus districts.

Citrus associations employed different wage systems as they wished, usually dependent on expected returns on the harvests, availability of labor, or other factors. During difficult periods, associations leaned to the seasonal bonus system because they knew that not all men would last the entire season and unpaid wages would be returned to the association. During periods of labor shortage, a straight hourly rate was more attractive to pickers than were the systems that utilized a bonus. Growers then had flexibility in establishing wage rates, that they did so was mirrored in the wide variations in wage systems found in the belt. Labor costs were generally calculated on the cost per box of picked fruit. Research had demonstrated that when an hourly or daily wage rate was combined with a quality and quantity bonus system that the costs were lowest.

Generally, associations determined picking wages by a combination of quantity and quality, and they established no guaranteed wages under any of the systems. In essence, the wage system was a piece rate system, and differentials in speed of pick as well as quality of the pick determined a picker's wage. There were in any crew both excellent and average pickers and, even if each received an identical base wage the potential existed for a substantially different piece rate. Because pickers were not given sick pay, when one was sick, one's wages were simply lost. In addition, medical costs for injuries suffered on the job were assumed by the worker, rarely by the packinghouse. The danger of a ladder falling remained a permanent work hazard and physical abnormalities from the continuous weight of the bag over the shoulder affected many a picker, especially those with years of toil behind them. An easy identifying mark, a drooping shoulder and a strap tattoo, distinguished the picker from workers in other fields. Moreover, industry-wide policy required pickers to pay for equipment such as clippers, gloves, and, in some instances, for the canvas bags into which the fruit was placed when picked. Associations also generally charged the picker for transporting them to the groves whether they utilized the service or not. Consequently, a portion of the growers costs were recovered through placing them on the shoulders of the workers.

If the picker slacked off, the crew foreman and the field supervisor reminded him to mend his ways. Poor picking was grounds for dismissal and at the Leffingwell Ranch a picker was fired "if the character of the picking falls to more than one percent defective."[63] Inspection was done "every day and averaged out for the week."[64] Former pickers recall that foremen would select oranges randomly from the field boxes and run the stem over their cheek; if they felt a scratch, the orange was rejected. If enough "rejects" were discovered, foremen were authorized to either dismiss the picker or punish him with a "furlough."[65]

Very little fruit was shipped without a packinghouse process whether packed into seventy-pound crates for interstate trade or in loose bulk for intrastate shipment. From the receipt of the fruit in field boxes at the packinghouse loading platform to the stacking of packed boxes in railroad cars, a series of industrial-like precision movements moved the citrus from one step in the process to the next requiring a substantial labor force. Hauled there in open boxes on flatbed trucks, once at the packinghouse the picked fruit was unloaded into large bins and washed, dried, graded, and stamped with a brand (most often "Sunkist"). Color is then enhanced in a gaseous chamber, later polished with wax, and then packed.

In packing prepared fruit for long-distance rail shipment to markets, often to auctions or directly to buyers, the appearance of both the fruit and the container had much to do with the price it fetched.[66] It was imperative that the product marketed and advertised by the Exchange or association be impeccable in quality and presentation. Consequently, great care was exerted in the packing operation to ensure that the commodity was visually attractive (looked tasty) and was uniform in flavor and size. The local grower's cooperative packinghouse was often the scene of marathon work schedules when the oranges rolled in, but no sooner did the supply dwindle then idleness set in. Generally the packing in both the Navel and Valencia districts was done only during the harvest season, but at the peak of the season nine- and ten-hour days, six days a week were not uncommon.

In the California citrus industry approximately 27,000 employees labored in the packinghouse at peak seasons, 65 percent were women, or about 16,500. Of these 10,000 to 12,000 hired on as packers employed in 248 packinghouses and the fifty-five independent grower-packers.[67] Women predominated in the packinghouse labor force, yet were employed in only a few of the available positions as secretaries, forewomen, graders, and packers. Women's labor divided primarily into two exact and demanding tasks: grading and packing. Graders were a distinct category of labor, far fewer in number and paid on an hourly basis and were recruited from the nonminority population. Packers, the majority of packinghouse employees, were piece-rate labor (much like the pickers in the field) and were paid on the basis of the number of boxes packed. Here Mexican women were more likely to find employment as packers. Men were the other packinghouse workers, the loaders, drivers, technicians, maintenance force, foremen, and supervisors, and they also were paid on an hourly basis.

The principle packinghouse activity and the job of the packer centered on the precise placement of oranges or lemons of a certain size and quality into a standard-sized crate in a specified manner. Selected fruit was hand-graded according to quality, and if sizing was not already done by the pickers, machinery separated the various sizes. Packing accorded with both size and quality: A "392" was an orange size because 392 oranges filled a shipping crate. A "288" was the largest orange size, a 392 was the smallest. Early in the citrus era, sizing was done entirely by pickers using a set of wire rings. Later on, machines at the packinghouse sorted according to size and rolled oranges down chutes for packing. When the oranges rolled in each packer made sure, as best she could, that her bin would not overflow. As one picker put it, "When the oranges came in my adrenaline would go up."[68] In packing, then, she was not just in a race against herself to pack quickly; packers like many industrial workers were pitted against machines that determined the speed of the flow of oranges down the chutes and into each packer's bin.

With gloved hands, the workers wrapped each orange with the stem facing downward, the thin tissue folded around the stem with the "Sunkist" label facing up. The wrapping had to be precise and neat, with the tissue covering the entire orange. Good packers moved with an impressive dexterity and swiftness, making them a prized association resource. "Their hands flew so fast . . . you couldn't see their hands," commented one former citrus worker.[69] The oranges then had to be packed in the box in straight lines from side to side and back to front. When the oranges were placed in the crate, the Sunkist label needed to face outward, so that it would be visible through the side slats of the crate and the top slat. A common policy among the managers required an upward bulge at the middle of the crate to give the pack a more appealing appearance.[70] This required the packer to squeeze down the oranges at each end, carefully though so as not to break any orange. If the prescribed criteria were not met, the box could be rejected, in which case the packer would earn nothing for her efforts and would be required to repack the box. The largest fruit required less time; smaller fruit more time. For example, a 392 took, on the average, ten to fifteen minutes, while the mid-size orange took only five to ten minutes. The pay in the early 1940s for the mid-size stood at 8 cents a box, increasing to about 16 cents for the smallest-size fruit.

When fully packed, the seventy-pound box was then lifted by the packer onto a conveyor belt, which then took it to a pressman who operated a machine that nailed a slotted lid onto the box. The packed crate, bulging slightly, with *Sunkist* displayed through each of the open slats, was then readied for railcar loading and shipment to market. Meanwhile, another box was being filled. The same process was repeated hour after hour. Neither packers nor graders were allowed to talk with each other, to sing, or to talk with anyone (such as a visitor) in the plant. Standing was the rule—only on breaks, usually at morning coffee break and noon lunch—were they allowed to sit.

Whether or not packers were physically present their pay depended upon the flow of oranges. If the picking schedules alternated from a slow to a fast pace, packers could have speedups, slowdowns, and complete standstills. Nevertheless their pay depended on the boxes packed, not on the number of hours at the plant. Piecework then was a function of the quickly alternating demand for labor dictated by the nature of the industry. Piece rate, however, guaranteed the grower a cost-efficient labor system, but it did not compensate the total hours the packer was required to be at the ready. Only an hourly wage could do this. Packing labor, like picking labor, was organized in accordance with the grower's interests and decisions, and the piece rate was the most cost-efficient for them.

Moreover, the length of the season did not necessarily decide the number of days worked, since "most plants average only a few days of packing each week throughout the season." Even lemon-packing plants, which packed the entire year averaged "only 180 working days." The average for those plants packing one variety of orange was only 108 days. The typical packinghouse was active "for only a part of the week during the packing season."[71] Thus the average number of weeks California plants operated, thirty-five, did not coincide with the average number of packing days during the season, only 126, or about twenty-five weeks of work.

One federal survey found considerable variation in the length of the packing season from plant to plant. Based on a survey of ninety-four plants, the average season was found to be thirty-five weeks. But 15 percent operated anywhere from fifteen to twenty-six weeks while one-third operated thirty-nine weeks or more. Packers, like their counterparts in the fields, had neither a full-time or a year-round job. The variation in work schedules did not necessarily deter women: For Mexican women it was the only employment other than domestic work available to them, and they accepted it.

Managers generally expected a minimum of fifty packed boxes per nine-hour day, a difficult requirement that led many women to break regulations and pack the bottom rows haphazardly. Naturally packers broke regulations when possible, generally by not wrapping each orange with a full twist called "flagging." The foreman, as well as the mechanic and pressman, were on the look-out for "flaggers," and were "extremely strict." According to one ex-packer, anyone caught flagging was called out by the foreman, taken to the office, and "in a loud booming voice he dressed them down."[72]

The work was demanding and straining resulting in a very tired work force at the end of the day. "I mean," recalled Julia Aguirre, "we were exhausted."[73] Legs and back ached as the day dissolved into the evening hours when the "second shift," cooking, washing, and cleaning house took over.[74] Irma Magaña recalled that after work she, like others, "stayed home, made dinner, did the wash, and made beer for my dad."[75] After years of packing, Angelina Cruz's mother suffered rheumatoid arthritis, a condition that she and several former packers claim was caused by packing. Other work, the chores at home—especially washing—probably contributed as well to a pattern of arthritis among former packers.[76]

Girls, too, worked in an informal apprenticeship system in the packinghouses. At fourteen, Angelina Cruz began packing on a part-time basis alongside her mother, one of five such pairs at the Placentia Orange Growers Association packinghouses. By her eighteenth birthday, Angelina was a skilled veteran, but never reached the *campiona* level of her mother who could pack a hundred boxes per nine-hour day. Angelina vividly recalls the experience. "You were so absorbed in packing that you lost track of time . . . you just kind of lost yourself."[77]

Houses usually employed a set crew of women year after year and filled in with replacements when necessary. The packers came to be well known in the houses in which they worked, and, like the men, they quite often moved from Valencia to Navel areas, and not infrequently into the central California Navel region. Following the season, a migration of packers paralleled the movement of pickers. There was no uniform movement of both groups, some made the seasonal trek annually, others occasionally, or seldom if ever. Yet, migration was not uncommon and thus it became a fairly accepted part of the citrus workers' life.[78] Rarely, however, did the Mexican pickers and packers venture outside of those communities established for them. Citrus workers moved from citrus village to citrus village when migrating, and when so doing hired on with foremen or packinghouse managers who knew them well enough. Managers came to know the available and experienced local and distant personnel hiring them at each season. An informal seniority system functioned, the same work force seemed to reassemble year after year. As in many other occupational lines, packers had a strong respect for their occupation. Those who performed their job well especially those who could pack one hundred boxes, the *cieneras,* or *campionas,* received considerable respect, which translated into a camaraderie enjoyed exclusively by women.[79]

California Fruit Exchange Housing Program

Very early in the history of the citrus belt, labor was relatively easy to secure, and bunks or dormitories were generally provided for the Chinese, and later, Japanese men. Single men were usually easily recruited and housed—some were local, others migrated. One grower noted in 1920 that "only fifteen years ago . . . Japanese were available in abundance and cheaply housed in dormitories" and in "1910 it was an easy task to secure detached Mexican workers."[80]

However the growers confronted a different problem with the full transition to the Mexican labor that was made up mainly of married men with families. With the appearance of the immigrant Mexican family, and with the supply of Japanese dwindling, "the farmer and fruit growers [gave] more and more attention to the family unit as a source of labor."[81] However, growers quickly understood that men with families were available, "almost always if comfortable housing [could] be supplied them."[82] By 1920, the labor policy of many local grower associations included the construction of housing for their picking labor—and this usually meant housing for Mexican families. Charles C. Teague recalled that the "original housing on the ranch for dormitory housing" was for single men. With time, and especially during the war years, the supply of single men dropped, and citrus cooperatives "were obliged to begin constructing family housing, and thus were able to get labor for the fields."[83] Between 1905 and 1920, housing assumed a distinct character as single men, without much social organization, disappeared, and large family units organized into a distinct community setting emerged.[84]

The manager of the large Limoniera Ranch in Santa Paula (California) remarked that "homes for agricultural workers in close proximity to their work is the most promising permanent solution of our agricultural labor problem."[85] At the ranch, 160 cottages for Mexican families were built in groups that ranged from ten to thirty-six over the 1,750 acres of citrus and bean fields, "We had no alternative," continued the manager, "but to house our labor on the ranch."[86]

By 1918, the California Fruit Growers Exchange ran a series of articles in its journal, the *California Citrograph,* informing growers of the various housing programs developed by several associations. The Exchange acted as a clearinghouse for the member associations by providing the objectives—as well as the plans, including architecture, building materials, floor plans, and financing—for their housing programs.[87] Evidence suggests that what began at the local level soon grew into generalized citrus association housing policy.

Depending on the decisions of the association directors, various housing programs were promoted. Some associations, such as the La Habra Citrus Association in Orange County, built and rented housing to their pickers. Others, such as the Sespe Ranch in Ventura County, provided lots, and the "Mexicans [built] their own houses," the size of which depended on the family.[88] The objective of the Sespe Ranch managers was to rivet firmly the laborer to the employer. "In allotting them this piece of land and allowing them to build their own house, it creates a home-like feeling" and it gives "the Mexicans the . . . feeling of permanence." At the Sespe Ranch the building materials were purchased for the picker, the cost later deducted from their wage "until the bill of lumber is paid for."[89] If the worker left before paying the bill, he stood to lose the equity on the house; if he was discharged, his equity was returned. However, the effect of such a policy promoted a labor supply with less free choice given that they stood to lose money if they moved before paying off their debt.

Generally picker housing was modest by most standards, and in many cases it was substandard and inadequate for the needs of the picker families. At the Limoniera Ranch, the 160 cottages were of a plain uniform wood construction, two rooms, 18 by 22 feet, built on a "plot of ground, about 40 feet by 100 feet in area."[90] Each house was supplied with water and, in some cases, shower baths were provided; however, the ranch charged no rent, the only obligation was that one steady laborer be available for work at any time during the year and that two be available during "the heavy picking and packing season."[91] A public school for the children, in which Americanization classes—including hygiene, sanitation, English—were taught, was located on land donated by the ranch.[92]

By late 1918, the *Citrograph* discussed differing views regarding housing, and it borrowed some models from the sugar beet industry. The two-family adobe home model extensively constructed in the Ventura County beet fields was prominently discussed and suggested as a desirable type of picker home for the citrus industry. Each two-room dwelling was 12 by 24 feet, but shared a toilet with an adjoining house. In addition, a small plot was provided for a garden, chickens, or a goat. According to the author of the series on housing, the privilege of having enough ground for a garden on livestock promoted "true thrift and [served] to attach the families to their homes" and that "by providing decent homes and surroundings and treating the Mexicans like human beings the labor problem on citrus ranches . . . [could] largely be solved." The author further suggested that the Mexicans build their own adobe homes, "thus giving [them] employment when not needed for agricultural work."[93] The total cost of such a house was placed at $400.00. Most associations that provided housing generally built dwellings from wood. Such dwellings were rather small and were placed on a 40 by 100 foot lot. The association also charged rent, usually providing a school building, and often a community center.

A typical Mexican village was built by the Upland Citrus Association on ten acres of land, with room enough "for future housing development."[94] The community of twenty houses was "arranged with main streets running north and south" and one street "[ran] through the middle of the camp from east to west." The houses were nearly square, being 18 by 22 feet on a plot "40 by 80 feet in size."[95] Each house was identical—uniform in size and color, with running water, toilet, screened doors and windows, and wood-burning chimneys for heating. The houses were rented for $7.50 per month, which was deducted from the employee's wages.

By 1919, the housing programs were widely discussed in articles and in forums sponsored by the Exchange.[96] And in March 1921, the *California Citrograph* announced that "Many associations are building housing for their employees."[97] The literature mentions twenty-one associations and independent companies providing picker housing. Undoubtedly there were more. Any association that followed the articles in the *California Citrograph* and were wishing to construct housing could request plans "of most of these houses from the Industrial Relations Department, California Fruit Growers Exchange."[98] However, the Limoniera Ranch became the model suggested most often in the pages of the *California Citrograph.*

The reasoning behind the housing policy was simple: Without housing little else attracted married workers to settle permanently in the citrus towns. "The sole object of building a labor camp," stated George Hodgkins, an official of the Industrial Relations Bureau of the California Fruit Growers Exchange, "is to provide a satisfactory supply of labor to do good work at the lowest possible cost."[99] And in a *Citrograph* editorial appearing in September 1918, other "sound" reasons for camp housing were offered. According to the editors, a Mexican laborer would be more likely to remain in the local area and less inclined to seek higher wages if he "has a comfortable little cottage."[100]

Numerous associations not only provided housing for the pickers but also, in many cases, for the administrative and technical personnel. However, as a general policy, associations segregated each of these categories of workers from each other. Further, they housed Japanese, white, Filipino, and Mexican pickers separately, and collectively they segregated all pickers from the town and other employees. The basic pattern of segregation followed the division of labor in the industry, as well as the segmentation of nationality according to the division of labor. Consequently, Anglo-American employees were housed separately from Mexican pickers.

Not only was there a clear physical line dividing nationality, that is, separate living areas, there was also a clear distinction of the quality of housing for each group. The managers and technicians and their families lived in large, comfortable houses, complete with gardens and modern conveniences. Thus, the associations incorporated a class and nationality structure into their housing programs. When associations discussed housing, they did so in reference to the nationalities they hired, the work they performed, and the labor needs of the association. Anglos were not, as a rule, housed with Mexicans; but Anglo-American managers and technicians were not mixed with Anglo-nonmanagerial employees. Consequently, segregation fit both the hierarchical division of labor *and* the nationality segmentation in the organization of labor.

Where there were Japanese, Filipino, and Mexican pickers, a general policy established separate living quarters for them. It was not because the groups were culturally or linguistically distinct, nor was it because the Japanese and Filipinos were primarily single men and the Mexicans were married. The general housing rule established separate living quarters for every nationality constituting the picking labor. Thus whenever Anglo-American, Japanese, Filipino, or Mexican pickers labored in the groves, they worked in separate crews and lived in separate quarters of the housing provided. However, after 1920, Mexicans were the overwhelming majority of pickers. Yet, where more than one nationality was employed, their segregation continued, a practice visible well into the 1930s and 1940s.[101]

At the Leffingwell Ranch, in Whittier, housing for the Japanese and Mexicans were called camps, there were more polite terms for housing for the managers. Unmarried Anglo heads of departments lived in a clubhouse. Married managerial employees lived in what were termed "very attractive cottages surrounded by beautiful flower gardens and ornamental plantings."[102] In addition, these employees were provided with tennis courts and a park. The unmarried managers of the ranch lived in the "new clubhouse," which was described as a "well-kept hotel, except that the surroundings and furnishings are far more attractive and home-like than those of the average hotel."[103] The "old-clubhouse" was used to house unmarried Anglo-American nonmanagerial employees and was similar to the "new clubhouse." The Mexican camp housing 125 unmarried male employees was "located alongside a barranca" (a gulch).[104]

There were then several separate levels in the quality of housing provided for citrus employees. Picker housing was much inferior to the quality of that provided for Anglo-American workers. Mexican houses were often tiny, wooden, adobe, or hollow-brick buildings constructed on the less desirable and often dangerous sections of the association property. Floods continually plagued the camps at Richfield, La Jolla, Anaheim, Fullerton, Stanton, and others in southern California.

The Limoniera Ranch boasted of its housing for employees. The two hundred houses for Mexicans "cost about $300.00 each"; the ranch also had thirty-six houses for its Anglo workers "at a cost of $2,000 each."[105] Generally, Anglo-American workers were treated to a clubhouse, such as the one provided by the Azusa Foothill Citrus Association. The description of the Azusa clubhouse conforms to the pattern of distinguishing characteristics dividing the Mexican from the Anglo sections. "The furniture is in keeping with the architecture, simple, comfortable and pleasing to look at. There is a pool and billiard table for the active and for the literary there are chairs and writing desks; tables and shelves full of magazines and books furnished by the county library. The most attractive feature is the fireplace. . . . Here the men lounge about during their off hours."[106]

Single Mexican and Filipino workers lived either in barracks, or dormitories, but never does the literature mention a "club-house," with billiards, a fireplace, and a library.[107] The Chase Plantation, in Corona (California) provided thirty-six adobe houses, each ten by ten feet; however, "Apart from the houses are a set of barns and other buildings where the Mexicans keep their horses, chickens, and vehicles."[108] Usually, the house included "a little garden patch," perhaps a small community hall was placed in the camp, and an empty field for a baseball diamond. Besides the house, which included running water and an outdoor toilet, not much else was provided the pickers. Of course, for the Mexican picker this was an improvement over rural Mexican conditions. But by American standards, both the wages earned and the housing provided were, at best minimal, and in many cases, below minimum.

Typifying the distinctiveness in housing was Sespe Ranch, which had housing for unmarried white men, married white men, and for Mexican pickers. The single white men lived in a two-story dormitory that comprised twenty rooms, exclusive of a "large living room, dining room for the general class of employees, private dining room for officials. . . . The cost of this building was about $7,000.00." Each sleeping room measured eight by thirteen feet. Hot and cold running water, clean bedding, a library, a billiard table, and a fireplace made for a rather comfortable environment.[109] The quarters for the married Anglo-American personnel were equally attractive. Each house had four or five rooms, and "free water . . . all with plumbing, painting and repairs included." Rent was from $5 to $8 per month and the average cost was from $1000 to $1200.

The Sespe Ranch had a different housing program for its Mexican workers, who lived in what was called the "Mexican village."[110] Pickers were obliged to *build and pay* for their own homes, the land was furnished (there is no record of whether the picker was required to purchase it) along with "free water . . . piped to each lot."[111] Photographs appearing in the *California Citrograph* indicate that the "Mexican village," in comparison to "white" housing, was vastly inferior, reflecting a rough and undesirable location and at best the housing resembled rural shacktowns.[112] The rooms of even those houses built for single Anglo-Americans were larger than the rooms of family housing for Mexicans. For example, the eight-by-thirteen-foot rooms for a single man were larger than the ten-by-ten-foot house furnished for a Mexican family at the Chase plantation, and more than one-quarter the size of a family house provided by the Limoniera Ranch, which measured eighteen by twenty-two feet, and comparable to the La Verne Citrus Association house, a twelve-by-twelve-foot, two-room adobe.[113]

A kind of satellite settlement pattern emerged in the construction of some of the large commercial ranches, with the packinghouse as the center of all activity. Emanating from the "great packinghouse," the core of the Leffingwell Ranch, in Whittier, California, were camps for Mexican and Japanese laborers, a "boarding house for drivers and mechanics," a club house for office personnel and lab technicians, and finally a grocery store.[114] This pattern was more or less followed by the local associations as well.

The widespread construction of housing successfully attracted and retained the requisite number of pickers. Housing construction proceeded at a much slower pace after the mid-twenties, most association-sponsored picker houses were built between 1918 and 1924. A leading figure in the

Exchange's discussions on housing rather confidently stated the reasons that the critical labor shortages of the teens and early twenties no longer concerned growers in 1924. "The establishment of suitable camps, throughout the citrus districts, for the housing of Mexican labor, has to a large extent solved their labor problems as far as picking is concerned."[115]

· 2 ·

The Economy, Migration, and Community Formation in Orange County

Our focus narrows to the local communities dispersed in and about the citrus towns of Orange County—a key citrus region in southern California. The origins of many southern California Mexican American communities are enmeshed with citrus, although the presence of small numbers of Mexican laborers predates citrus. Orange County's social history, like that of southern California in general, is bound with its agricultural development. Particular patterns of social relations formed in the precitrus era, during which Chinese, Japanese, and native Americans were the more significant labor supply. However in the teens and twenties, Mexican immigrant labor assumes dominance as agricultural labor. Immigrants settled into a social organization that long before institutionalized norms and practices that maintained social relations between majority and minority.

Social and Economic Development in the Precitrus Era in Orange County

In the decade following the Anglo-American conquest the semidesert lying between San Clemente to the south and Los Angeles to the north remained virtually empty. Standing silent above an expanse of shrubs and grass broken by trees lying along the creeks and the Santa Ana River banks were the occasional adobe mansions of a *hacendado* (landowner), small laborer hamlets dispersed about a hacienda, or the San Juan Capistrano Mission. Some three hundred persons inhabited haciendas and villages surrounded by sagebrush, cactus, and mustard-covered plains and slopes.[1] Deer, quail, jack rabbits, ducks, foxes, owls, hawks, gophers, rattlesnakes, skunks and coyotes shared the landscape. To the coastal south, abundant artesian springs created-swamp lands (hence the name of present-day Fountain Valley); bears and wildcats inhabited the hilly and mountainous northern areas. Throughout most of the semiarid region, a fertile well-drained alluvial land and year-round mild weather made an ideal agricultural area. And if by some misfortune a settler could not easily grow a seasonal crop, abundant game and ocean fish fed the family.

Between 1855 and 1885 that same area changed dramatically. Mexican landowners either lost their land or held on only to insignificant portions of it. In either case, the independent Mexican culture of the rancho era slowly died, so that by 1900 little of significance remained. Surviving landowning families, no longer economically dynamic, quickly grew dependent on the economic process set in motion after 1850. Some, especially of the younger generation, found employment in the Anglo-American enterprises; a few women of the landowning class intermarried with Anglo-Americans, usually an ambitious Anglo entrepreneur, and thus some family landowning traditions were passed on through marriage.

Once the skills of the *rancho* artisans, the carpenters, smiths, and *vaqueros* were no longer needed, they evolved into wage laborers in the new agricultural enterprises being established throughout the region. Indeed, the early Anglo-American-owned cattle and sheep ranches employed many of the Mexican *vaqueros* and sheep-shearers. Meanwhile, Indian peonage laborers either returned to their traditional native villages, or transferred their labor to the new enterprises.

While some social vestiges of the rancho merged into the new economic order, they were overwhelmed by a handful of Anglo-American entrepreneurs who assumed ownership of the large ranchos that make up present-day Los Angeles and Orange counties. Abel Stearns's two hundred thousand acres included portions of today's Orange County; Juan Forster acquired seventy thousand acres to the south; Bixby, Flint and Company owned one hundred thousand acres in the heart of the county. From huge tracts such as these, Anglo-Americans carved colonization and community settlements. Smaller speculators such as William Spurgeon, William Glassell, and Columbus Tustin acquired town-sized tracts in the late 1860s and early 1870s and lost no time in advertising their commodity extensively in the East and Midwest. Handbills, pamphlets, and newspaper ads told of rich soils, an ideal climate, magnificent scenery, and abundant potential, and included a long list of successful as well as "can't-miss" enterprises. The attraction was more than the adventurous entrepreneur could resist. Prospective buyers, spurred by religious, vegetarian, utopian, temperance, or purely profit motives, came by the trainloads to the southland as potential partners in colonization projects. They were treated to a circus atmosphere dominated by barking auctioneers. One early settler recollected that "hardly a week passed without a special excursion train coming from Los Angeles with tourists to buy lots in a subdivision laid out by professional promoters; a brass band would accompany the train, and, on arrival, the crowd joined by our own residents would march to the new subdivision where good free lunches would be provided; then an experienced high-powered auctioneer would open the affair with a glorious description of the lots."[2]

Most citrus towns did not originate as citrus communities. Rather, settlement, or colonization, preceded the development of the citrus industry. Towns later to be identified with citrus began in a variety of ways: as religious, temperance, farming, or ranching communities. Often these were immigrant communities, as was the case with Anaheim, master-planned and settled by German immigrants in 1857; Westminster and Garden Grove began as temperance colonies; others were religious in origin like El Modena, which was settled by Quakers.

Santa Ana was established in 1869, Orange in 1870, and Placentia in 1889. By 1890 Buena Park, Tustin, Laguna Beach, Fullerton, Richfield (today's Atwood area in the city of Placentia), Garden Grove, and Newport secured a niche in the county's prosperous development. In the place of expansive feudal estates devoted to modest farming gardens and vast cattle range tended by peonage labor and at times slave labor, there now stood thriving entrepreneurial rural villages with well-tended orchards, vineyards, irrigation ditches, and gardens.

Invariably the settlers were professional, successful, and middle-class people of means, owners of capital, but with little experience in semiarid farming or ranching. Moreover, most of the soon-to-be citrus towns were laid out as town sites, master-planned long before the town lots and outlying areas were sold to eastern and mid-western buyers. Developers and colony leaders often prepared the settlement in advance of the buyers. Thus, while the citrus communities owed their economic well-being to oranges, their origins lay in different sources. This was the case especially in Orange County, in which dirt farmers settled, which may account for the more rural flavor in Orange County citrus areas. It has been noted that the Riverside, Pasadena, and Redlands areas were more suburban in character and had larger populations than areas such as San Dimas, Monrovia, La Puente, and Whittier in Los Angeles County and Placentia, La Habra, Brea, Stanton, Buena Park, and Tustin in Orange County.[3] Nevertheless, the distribution of towns, their neat layouts, with town centers and street grids, were defined before settlement.

Settlement in southern California was by no means a simple purchase of an inexpensive piece of an empty town lot. Those who could buy land, and there was much of it to be had in the early years of the century, "needed capital, commercial habits, and business ability."[4] Most settlers came with a mixture of the ideal and the practical, hoping to create a new society but their daily work, and even their ideal society, revolved about a classic profit-seeking capitalist economy. Ranching was a business run on the principles that governed capitalist enterprises. "They were gamblers, these early farmers," wrote a long-time packinghouse manager, "but they were hard workers."[5] Above all, they expected returns on their investments. Indeed, their investments and efforts were well rewarded, especially in the case of citrus—a particularly productive industry in spite of the geographic limitations of climate, water, and soil.

Within the newly formed towns and villages appeared schools, churches, government, newspapers, and civic, professional, and fraternal organizations. Settlers brought with them their eastern and midwestern small-town culture and morality. Beliefs grounded in the primacy of private enterprise, individualism, patriotism, sobriety, Protestantism, racial separation, and identification with an English-speaking heritage guided the steadily developing region. In sum, early settlers were expressors of late nineteenth-century American capitalist culture, and constructed their community upon that foundation.

Transportation and irrigation were two critical factors affecting the pace of economic development. In 1875 the Southern Pacific Railroad connected Anaheim with Los Angeles and San Francisco, and the breaking of the Anaheim Water Company's monopoly on the Santa Ana River allowed for expanded irrigation especially on the east side of the river.[6] Both contributed to the expansion of markets, thus increasing crop acreage and enriching the potential for growth. Early settlers thereupon planted more widely marketable and less perishable products, and, consequently, a pattern of shifting crop emphases emerged. The completion of the transcontinental railroad and the invention of refrigerated cars in the 1880s, and then federal irrigation projects at the turn of the century, further accelerated the pace of development.

Precitrus Agriculture and Labor

Orange County's agricultural history was marked by an initial period of alternating emphases on the growing of various crops, such as grapes. Later in the twentieth century there emerged a settled pattern of crop growing with a steady extension of acreage. Citrus was a relative latecomer to the agricultural history of the area. A number of crops preceded citrus or were contemporaneous with it before problems arose forcing them out of production. Grapes, raisins, peanuts, celery, sugar beets, and some deciduous crops such as peaches and walnuts, were tried and failed, sometimes often succeeding for a time before succumbing to diseases, poor market conditions, or soil exhaustion. Boom and bust cycles describe the history of wine grape, raisin grape, celery, sugar beets, and walnuts, and eventually citrus.

Two products, sugar beets and walnuts, illustrate the cyclical pattern. Sugar beet production grew from twenty-five hundred acres in 1891 to fifty thousand acres in 1913.[7] By 1918 Orange County was the principal sugar beet producer in the state (and the largest producer of any county in the nation), producing about a quarter of the state's total. Together with Los Angles and Ventura counties, it accounted for 55 percent of California's sugar beet crop.[8] The heyday of sugar beets was a boom era for local farmers, who by 1906 "were shipping 400 to 500 tons per day at an average $5.50 per ton, or over $200,000.00 per crop."[9] However, labor shortages, overplanting, and the expansion of more profitable crops played the biggest role in reducing the county's sugar beet acreage to four thousand acres by 1939. Meanwhile, the five sugar refineries operating in the county in 1915 (there were only seventy-six in the entire United States) were cut to only one in operation by 1926.

Walnuts, first planted after the decline of grape growing, followed the demise of sugar beets. In 1892, the *Los Angeles Express,* participating in the boosterism of the day, enthusiastically reported that the "growing of walnuts is assuming immense proportions in Orange County. The crop in this county last season brought to the pockets of the producers $100,000."[10] By 1889 Orange County was producing more walnuts than any other county in the state, reaching its peak in 1923 when the county processed 17,740,209 pounds of nuts from 17,150 acres of trees. At the time Orange County "was the greatest walnut shipper in the world"[11] and crop income for that year was $3,540,841.[12] By 1931 walnut fortunes, too, began to follow the decline of grapes, celery, raisins, and sugar beets, so that by the 1960s the only walnut trees were found along residential streets, or provided shade for backyard barbecues.

Very early in California's agricultural history seasonal production became synonymous with agriculture and, along with this, seasonal labor demands. The "bundle-stiff," the "foot-tramp," the "vagrant" were early characteristics of California agriculture and became a permanent part of the state's social relations. Shortly after this social pattern became fixed, nonwhite foreign nationalities became the main supply of seasonal labor. Thus, Chinese, Japanese, Asian Indians, Filipinos, and Mexicans, along with blacks and poor whites, had been recruited by growers to fill their seasonal labor needs.

Consequently, the class structure in rural areas has generally divided along the lines of nationality. At the top, the growers, native-born white; at the bottom, the foreign-born migrants, or his or her children. The pattern of filling the migrant labor rung with national minorities was strengthened by the conscious efforts of growers and their managers to hire only from the nonwhite community and, if they were not readily available, to import them. Thus, production in the countryside was achieved by a racial and national segmentation; race or nationality tended to correspond with particular rungs on the class structure.[13]

Successive concentrations of particular nationalities further characterized the agricultural labor force. One nationality dominated the labor supply for a period, eventually giving way to another, and the pattern repeating itself. Thus, Chinese were supplanted by Japanese; Japanese by Mexicans; Mexicans by bracero labor; and more recently braceros by newer Mexican migrants.[14] In between these trends, Asian Indians, Filipinos, American blacks, and, in the 1930s, Dust Bowl refugees, have rounded out the supply.[15]

Orange County agriculture fit the general California pattern early in its economic evolution (before separating from Los Angeles county in 1889). Chinese, Mexican, local Indian, and imported Yaqui labor were important as a harvest labor supply. Anaheim, founded in 1857, is an example. The colony quickly developed into a major wine region, producing seventy-five thousand gallons in 1876, but by 1884, eight Anaheim wineries produced "a million and a quarter gallons." Harvest labor became indispensable in this rapid growth spiral. An observer noted that viticulture required "large amounts of seasonal, semiskilled labor" and that recruiting this labor necessitated reaching beyond the community itself. One historian observed that in the colony's early period the chief help were the Indians and Mexicans who came from a distance.[16] By the 1870s Chinese and Mexicans were the main supply, and in the 1880s, as many as four hundred laborers were employed on a seasonal basis by the Anaheim colony, augmenting the town population of some two thousand.[17] The evolution of the colony did not progress without a pattern of the periodic utilization of particular racial or national groups to fill that labor need.

Nearby towns—Tustin, Santa Ana, and others—demonstrated an identical propensity to use cheap foreign labor. Indeed at one time Chinatowns existed on the San Joaquin Ranch (presently site of the city of Irvine), and at Anaheim, Tustin, Santa Ana, and Bolsa. Once the Chinese had built the railroads, they filtered into the cities and were eagerly sought-after as labor. In the 1890s, during the phase when Orange County agriculture was being placed on a solid foundation, the Chinese were a willing and experienced reservoir of hand labor.[18] In Tustin, the 250 to 300 Chinese constituted the majority of the population. The expansive seventy-thousand-acre San Joaquin Ranch brought Chinese crews from Los Angeles to perform ranch work and that at "one time three or four permanent Chinese camps" thrived on the ranch.[19]

In the nearby city of Orange, raisins became the major crop and grew to fairly significant proportions as ten thousand acres were planted with grape vines.[20] One of the first settlers in the town recalled, "in 1886 I was in the field overseeing a gang of Chinamen who were picking. There were one hundred and twenty-five Chinese pickers."[21] Another early settler recalled, "A Chinaman called Jim ran a wash-house in Orange in the late '80s. Whenever settlers wanted help in the grapes or on the [irrigation] ditch, they went to him and got as many Chinese laborers as were wanted."[22] In the distant "marshy wasteland known locally as La Cienega," later known as Smeltzer (the present site of the city of Westminster), the Chinese, and later the Japanese, provided most of the labor on an extensive celery-growing area that covered six thousand acres by 1906. Historian Fern Hill Colman sketched an image of the celery boomtown:

> The village was a company owned town with many of the earmarks of a boom town. A warehouse for storing lumber . . . a building for housing the company offices . . . A small hotel, company blacksmith shop, a huge barn for housing fifty teams of five draft horses, a store, post office and telephone office made Smeltzer a center for celery growers. A dozen houses for American teamsters of the company, a bunkhouse for the seventy Japanese employed in hand work, and numerous shacks for the Chinese completed the town of Smeltzer.[23]

However, the supply of Chinese steadily dwindled in the 1880s, as a result of the Chinese Exclusion Act, and the Japanese assumed the prominent role in the continued economic growth. The Chinese dominated hand labor until the late 1890s, thereafter the Japanese became the "majority of farm laborers, quiet, steady and rapid," or so observed one reporter.[24] By 1920, the Japanese population stood at fifteen hundred, up from three in 1900. This increase in numbers of Japanese agricultural workers roughly paralleled the rise of the citrus industry. (Attempts at establishing grapes, raisin, celery as major crops, as well as other attempts, had already failed due to soil exhaustion or blight.) Consequently, Japanese became the majority in the picking crews, and Japanese bunkhouses become a not uncommon part of the early phase of Orange County citrus towns.[25] La Habra and Placentia, for example, had dormitories for Japanese picking crews.

While Japanese were laboring in the Bolsa celery bogs and in the groves, others of their nationality were farming nearby and threatened the Anglo settlers with economic competition. At the very time that the Japanese were the main supply of picking crews they also became "the berry-growers of Orange County." The *Fullerton Tribune* reported, "A colony of Japs have established themselves a half mile north of town and have gone into the strawberry business. Their patch of about fifty acres is in first-class condition and has bloomed beautifully."[26] By 1915 a Japanese Community Hall thrived in Talbert (today's Fountain Valley) and, in that year, representatives of the Japanese government were invited to the hall as guest speakers.[27] In nearby Huntington Beach the Japanese Agricultural Association was established to promote the common interests of "Japanese celery growers."[28] The *Santa Ana Register* announced, "Of course, there are a large number of [strawberry] patches grown by whites, but nevertheless the little brown man has most of them. In the last year many Americans have deserted the business while the Japs have held onto their patches and planted more."[29] Such success, unfortunately, had its downside.

Orange County farmers, in step with the prevailing sentiments of the state, were against "Japanese immigration, ownership or even leasing" of land. In 1920 the County Farm Bureau polled its members and 150 questionnaires were returned. Of the 150 respondents, 89 were in favor of immigration restriction for Japanese, 98 were against any land leases and 115 were against the sale of land to the Japanese.[30] By then, however, the Japanese were farming a considerable amount of land in the estimation of the county assessor, Jim Sleeper (Sr.), who placed the figure at ten thousand acres.[31] The statewide anti-Japanese campaign was very much a topic of discussion in Orange County as newspapers devoted substantial space to reporting on local agitation against Japanese landownership. The county Board of Supervisors took action, and appointed a committee "to look into the aggressions of the Japanese in the matter of land holdings." That committee produced a resolution "favoring a change in the treaty with Japan so as to exclude undesirable Asiatics."[32] Other organizations took similar stands. The Orange County Farm Bureau passed a resolution declaring the Japanese to be an "unassimilable element" and urged a severe restriction on immigration, landownership, and constitutional rights of Japanese with American citizenship.[33] In the teens and twenties, Orange County was not a friendly place if one was Japanese. The hostility against them, however, did not often spill over into violence, as it did against the Chinese.

By 1910 the Japanese were restricted politically and economically by oppressive legislation and popular opinion that attempted to bar them from agricultural endeavors. However, not only their success in agriculture was of major concern to growers. Their organizational propensities as farmworkers provided a foundation for a kind of collective bargaining that lessened their desirability as hand labor.[34] Growers found the Japanese to be not only the main supply of hand labor but also an organized supply as well. Consequently, in time their value and their numbers dropped and Mexicans quietly stepped in and assumed the center stage of farm labor.

The dominance of Mexican immigrants was preceded by many decades of Mexican farm and ranch labor—going back to the missions, ranchos, and continuing with the Anglo-American settlements. As hand labor, this history deserves mention before proceeding to a discussion of the rise of citrus and Mexican picking labor. Mexican labor was not unappreciated in the nineteenth century. And as, mentioned earlier, Mexicans were employed in the vineyards of Anaheim. There is also evidence of Mexican employment in livestock and in field crops. One early citizen of Santa Ana, Michael Watt, recalled that on his nineteen-acre farm planted with peanuts "sixty Mexicans were employed" for the October harvest. Apparently peanut farming was extremely successful; one farm produced sixteen thousand sacks in a season. Mexicans were employed in the olive production in El Modena, as well.

Mexican labor was used extensively in the beet fields as attested by numerous references in news articles. In the 1913 annual report to the State Board of Charities and Corrections, County Sheriff Ruddock alleged that the increase in crime was due to "the large influx of Mexican peons, attracted by the work in the beet fields."[35] Another article referred to two Mexican "beet contractors" who boarded "beet topping gangs" in Buena Park (the contractors were arrested for selling liquor to the workers "the price of which is taken from their pay").[36] The county Catholic diocese often established missions in Mexican communities, and several were placed next to sugar factories in the county.[37] Finally, in a soil survey of Orange County by the Department of Agriculture, the authors noted that "sugar beets are generally hoed and thinned by Mexican laborers."[38] Estimates of sugar beet industry representatives taken in 1917 of "several thousand Mexicans [leaving] Orange County in the last few weeks going to Utah to work in the beet fields" attest to substantial numbers of Mexican laborers.[39] Nearly simultaneous with the exodus of beet workers are reports of the importation of hundreds of Mexicans to work the Orange County fields.[40]

Mexicans were also the principal labor supply in the walnut groves, although Chinese were quite numerous until 1906, the year in which Santa Ana's Chinatown was burned down by a decree of city officials, causing Chinese laborers to leave the city and area. Thereafter, Mexicans performed nearly all the picking labor in the walnut groves. One local historian stated that "the trees were hand-shaken, the nuts hand-picked and hand-hulled. Every member of the Mexican families—which could run to a dozen—participated."

Two other employment opportunities for Mexicans related to the sheep and cattle industry. Mexicans were the majority of sheepshearers, journeying to the San Joaquin Ranch (Irvine Ranch) each spring.[41] In the southern portion of the county where cattle raising was concentrated, Mexican cowboys (or *vaqueros*) were prominent. And in San Juan Capistrano a regular *vaquero* round-up provided a festive occasion.

However, it was well into the twentieth century, when agriculture in the county expanded enormously, that Mexicans became predominant as hand labor. Their entrance coincided generally with the maturing phase of the citrus industry and the decline of sugar beets, walnuts, and other crops.

Orange County and Valencia Production

While the majority of settler-farmers were busy raising temporarily profitable, and therefore successive, crops, others were planting citrus trees in modest proportions in various locales. Initial plantings were set out in the early 1870s in the Fullerton, Placentia, and Orange areas. The first commercial venture in the county, the Semi-Tropic Fruit Company, chose Placentia as the site for a 110-acre ranch. Organized in 1872 at a cost of $17.50 an acre, the company pioneered Valencia orange production in 1880. Ranchers originally had other ideas than citrus for market products—but nature proved stronger. Thus, during the 1880s and 1890s, when grapes and raisins failed in Anaheim, Tustin, and Orange, oranges stepped in to fill the gap.

At first growers thought that the summer-maturing Valencia "would never amount to much" because it would compete with plentiful summer fruits.[42] History proved otherwise. Limited suitable growing conditions and an ideal supply-demand ratio were irresistible factors compelling ranchers to cultivate Valencias. Citrus subsequently spread across the Santa Ana River to the east and south.

Simultaneous with the founding of the Southern California Fruit Growers Exchange in 1893, two Orange County grower associations, the Placentia Orange Growers Exchange and the Santiago Orange Growers Association (in the city of Orange), were formed. Indeed, Placentia leadership played a significant role in the formation of the central exchange.[43] Other county associations were formed over the years, totaling fifty-five packinghouses in 1945, representing 78,000 acres.

In Orange County citrus spread rapidly during the period from the 1870s to World War II. Shortly after the first Orange County grove was planted at Fullerton, others appeared in nearby areas to the east. But it took twenty-five years for those small initial groves to extend to about 5,000 acres. However, during the following twenty years, the 5,000 acres had expanded to 33,000, and by 1938, 75,000 acres were planted with citrus.[44] Thus, in four decades, citrus production expanded fifteen times! Fullerton provides yet another illustration of spiraling growth: It had 40 acres of planted citrus trees in 1875. Sixty years later, Fullerton's Sunny Hills Ranch alone held over 4,000 citrus-bearing acres.[45] Such a rapid transition could have been accomplished only on the foundations established by the first settlers and pioneers in citrus production. From Anaheim in the west to Irvine in the east, and from La Habra and Brea in the north to Santa Ana in the south, citrus groves covered the soft hills and slopes with a deep green and a sweet and somewhat pungent fragrance.

More people eating more oranges meant more investments in citrus, and the most dramatic increases in the state's production occurred in Orange County, the center of the state's Valencia orange crop. Valencia oranges are juicier than Navels and are picked in the "off-season," that is, during the spring and summer months. However, because of climate and moisture conditions, Valencia production is geographically restricted within the citrus belt. Orange County citrus industry operated at full tilt in the spring and summer, while the dryer and hotter inland counties of Riverside, San Bernardino, and much of Los Angeles were active in the fall and winter. The latter counties competed in the winter market, leaving Orange County most of the summer market. By the blessing of nature, Orange County had the lion's share of the summer crop when the consumer was thirstiest. The dramatic increase in Valencia production is partly explained by the wide open market. Not surprisingly, between 1912–14 and 1925–27, Valencia production increased 249 percent (equaling 7,053,000 boxes). The increase in Navel shipments was considerably less, amounting to 17 percent, or 1,527,000 boxes, during the same period.[46]

Citrus was produced in seven counties of California, but Valencias were grown in only three, and, of the three, Orange County predominated. In 1939, the "smallest of the Orange producing counties" sent close to half of the California Valencia crop to the market. Orange County produced 407,066 tons of Valencias, or 45 percent of the total, while Los Angeles county was the second-largest producer with 186,147 tons, and Ventura County turned in 92,701 tons, for a combined total of 909,677 tons.[47] No other county had such a large share of any varietal production. San Bernardino County, for example, the leading producer of Navels with 188,953 tons, cornered only 30.4 percent of the State total of 622,081 tons.[48] Consequently, the combination of improvements in citriculture, technology, irrigation, transportation, advertising, and increased demand, as well as an open market, made investment in Valencia production a secure rather than a speculative venture in comparison to most agricultural enterprises.

Mexican Migration and Settlement

Fortunately for the citrus grower, acreage expansion occurred simultaneously with the first great Mexican migration to the United States. Nearly 750,000 Mexicans moved north between 1900 and 1930, escaping the violence, destruction, and destitution wrought by the Mexican Revolution of 1910. Indeed, economic development throughout the Southwest proceeded on the availability of Mexican immigrant labor.

Very few of the original Mexican settlers employed in the citrus industry had been born in the United States. Most were relatively young working age immigrants who were raising families. Migrants brought their children, parents, and quite often their grandparents; occasionally teenagers and young adults ventured alone. Whichever the case, migrants were able, willing, and eager to work—indeed, work played an integral part in the life and culture in the villages, haciendas, and ranchos that they had left in the central and northern plateau states of Mexico.

A survey taken in 1930 of the origins of 504 county residents revealed that the central plateau of Mexico was the predominant region of departure. Within the region, the states of Jalisco, Guanajuato, Michoacan, and Zacatecas accounted for approximately one-half of the immigrants; Jalisco alone sent one-quarter of the immigrants, a number that significantly exceeded the percentage for that state found in most areas of the United States.[49]

Composite images of the personal histories of those migrants reveal fears and dangers engendered in innumerable ways by a revolution that threatened survival. Migrants and their children tell individual stories manifesting fascinating parallels. For the most part, they were a laboring people. Many had skills as artisans, carpenters, blacksmiths and shopkeepers; others were small-to-medium landowners; a few were overseers on haciendas, or officials in one or another of the armies fighting in the Revolution. But the majority were of the peasantry and thus illiteracy among the migrants was common; the educated sector, those who could read and write, were those fortunate to have received a grade school instruction. According to one informal study, on average, Campo Corona/Colorado parents of eighth grade children held only a third grade education level.[50] Another study found that 40 percent of Stanton and Independencia adult villagers were illiterate.[51] These findings imply that a substantial number of illiterates and functional illiterates could be found, and they are verified by repeated references distinguishing literates from illiterates among the villagers.[52] Such distinctions accorded a status in the village that was reinforced by the tendency of the packinghouse managers to hire foremen from the literate group. Furthermore, village leaders generally came from the literates and were sought out by the Mexican consulates to act as representatives and community organizers.

Whatever their personal motives, and independent of the various means to reach the border, they all pointed to the Mexican Revolution as the principal force that precipitated the decision to leave. Their migratory route was limited by rail lines to El Paso or the Brownsville-Laredo area. In either case, and for nearly all settlers, the border region merely served as the first stop. Until that point, their lives had been deeply affected by a momentous decision to uproot, followed by continual stresses and strains. In the United States their continuing migration would take on a completely different character. Their survival demanded flexibility and adaptability, yet the enormous changes they faced did not always present insurmountable problems. In Mexico village life was often unpredictable and hazardous—conditions that the extended family and community support networks ameliorated. Migrants invariably brought not only their cultural values but the actual corresponding family network or portions of it and not infrequently, the community network, too.

Very few migrants traveled without some form of social networking extending from their village and/or kinship system. Occasionally, a young man of fifteen or so opted for the adventurous promise of a better life in the United States. Such was the case for Clemente Hernández, who, as a small boy of nine, endured the experience of being rented out as a laborer for a year to a medium-sized landowner by his mother. In return the poverty-stricken family was given a monthly ration of grain.[53] At fifteen he crossed the border at El Paso and arrived in the citrus belt by his twentieth birthday. Most settlers, however, recount a family rather than an individual migration. Not only did a family move together but they often moved to where other family members resided in the United States.[54] In cases of an unattached migrant (a minority among migrants), a village acquaintance or a distant relative at some point in the migration often became a trusted companion. Settlers kept the systematic ways they knew best, and while in the United States such traditions and practices often maintained, albeit precariously, the well-being of the group.

Upon reaching the border, employment was the migrant's first order of the day, an order easily filled. Labor recruiters from southwestern agriculture, railroads, and mining industries vigorously competed for cheap Mexican labor. A balance was struck between migrants desperate to survive and an expanding corporate capitalist economy hungry for cheap labor. Migrants often signed on for railroad maintenance and construction work; the rock quarries near Dallas or the smelters and laundries of El Paso attracted others; perhaps they contracted to pick cotton in Texas or in Arizona. The mines and smelters at the Clifton, Morenci, Globe, or Bisbee districts appealed to some. In a few cases, their work took them to the lumbering camps of Oregon and Washington or to the railroad camps in Kansas. At each stop a variety of work experiences might result: cutting wood for sale to smelters, preparing meals for camp workers, bootlegging, and for a few, gambling. Quite often they lived in company towns or worker camps. Their migratory trek was rarely direct from Mexican village to the citrus camps. Instead it was a multistage process, with the first main stop at El Paso, then on to several points during which they settled and worked temporarily.

Traveling from Texas to Arizona or California was a heavy expenditure involving, of course, many individuals in groups. Rail travel seems to have been seldom used, automobiles and trucks were most commonly employed. Private agreements to transport a family or several families appears in many narratives. Francisco Chico's account illustrates the rigors and perils of travel in 1918. His mother died in El Paso during the 1918 influenza epidemic; his father died in 1921 of unknown causes in an Arizona mining camp. As a twelve-year-old he was thrust into adulthood, with three younger siblings to support, and although he remained under the nominal care of seventy-year-old grandparents and an uncle and aunt, he was obligated to seek work. Francisco contracted to pick cotton in Litchfield Ranch in Arizona. "In 1921," he recollected, "the bottom fell out of the cotton market. Wages dropped to 1 cent a lb. What could one do with a penny a pound? You had to pick 100 lbs. just to earn one dollar. But when it came to pay we were sent to a company store where they handed us groceries instead of cash. Those were the companies then. . . . We lived in a tent at the time so we had no bills or anything like that . . . forty families lived like that in our camp at the ranch."[55]

Hard times compelled the family to continue their migration. Francisco's uncle contracted a truck owner to drive them to southern California. Because of mechanical breakdowns, the trip took six weeks. He recalls that it was all desert, dotted here and there with skeletons, some human. The driver took them as far as Indio, where Francisco worked for several days in odd jobs. Finally, the family moved to Riverside, where at the age of fifteen, he sought work at a citrus ranch and hired on to pick oranges for $1 a day. Three years later the family moved to the La Fabrica village in Anaheim, continuing what would prove to be a long period of employment as a citrus picker.

Julia Aguirre was fifteen years of age when she first packed oranges in 1938. Her life history was similar to that of Francisco. Upon the death of her immigrant father in a Colorado coal mine accident, the family (the mother and four brothers and sisters) moved to the citrus belt. From an insurance policy compensation, her mother purchased a small ranch in Fullerton but because of a prior lien lost the property and the insurance proceeds as well. Left penniless, the family sought whatever employment was available. According to Julia, her mother worked in janitorial jobs and sold prepared food from a cart on weekends. "That is how we survived, to keep us [the family] going." Meanwhile, the several children began working in the local ranches, eventually the entire family migrated annually to pick fruits and cotton in northern California during the summers. Julia describes her experience:

> We did the migratory swing three straight years until 1936 when my mother died. And each time, we traveled the same way. We contracted with a truck owner to take us up north. We'd take our belongings, our wash tub and boards, and our makeshift stove made out of an old steel barrel. My mother made *tortillas* on that old barrel. All of us slept either in tents or in barns. I don't know how my mother managed. We always returned without money—we made only enough to eat. . . . My mother though was very independent, well, she carried a small pistol to protect herself, the family and our belongings when we were migrating.[56]

In 1936, the orphaned family moved to the citrus picker community of Casablanca in Riverside; her brothers entered the picking force and she and her sisters the packinghouse. Eventually the family moved to Placentia, where Julia found employment in a packinghouse, working until she married and became pregnant with her first son in the mid-1940s.

Another account told of a journey from El Paso to Fort Worth, Los Angeles, Portland, Stockton, Riverside, and finally Placentia. At each point a different job: smelter, rock quarry, railroad construction, agricultural labor, lumber camp maintenance work, and finally citrus picking—a job Clemente Hernández held for twenty-five years.

Citrus workers had a variety of labor experiences before arriving in the belt. Picking was seldom the immediate attraction for moving into the area. Usually one was invited by a family member or close friend. Uncles, aunts, and cousins who were sprinkled at various points in the citrus belt served to beckon other family members. Family networking appears to have had primary significance in nearly all migrant accounts of the decision to settle in the citrus towns. In one not-too-unusual case a picker foreman was personally responsible for locating ten relatives in one citrus village.[57] And in another, four separate families under the tutelage of a patriarch settle in contiguous lots at Richfield.[58]

The town lived in, the labor performed, and the personal histories vary in the recollections of different migrants; nevertheless their experiences converge to form an easily recognized pattern. The process of moving westward from the border left in its wake an increase in the economic vitality of the region, a significant spin-off from the migratory movement. However, in the communities in which the migrants eventually settled, their economic importance was permanently established.

Mexican communities in the late nineteenth century Orange County were small residential clusters appearing in Anaheim, Santa Ana, and San

Juan Capistrano. Towns established by Anglo-Americans and European immigrants after the 1850s, based upon agriculture, brought forth these Mexican neighborhoods and laborers' camps. Anaheim in the 1870s had a small Mexican district and Santa Ana's Mexican population amounted to only twelve families in 1900.[59] Between 1900 and 1930 the Mexican population changed qualitatively, reflecting the considerable migration into the county. In 1910 the county census enumerated 1,345 Mexican born increasing to 3,694 in 1920. Based on the method of enumeration then in vogue, we can arrive at a rough population figure for both Mexican- and American-born by doubling the census figures to account for native and foreign born. Thus we get 2,600 for 1910 and about 7,000 for 1920. The next decade witnessed continued growth in both the foreign and native born Mexican population, increasing to 16,536, amounting to 14 percent of the total county population.[60] By 1920, there were at least seven identifiable Mexican communities in the county increasing to twenty by 1930 (In the late 1970s one newspaper reported thirty-one barrios).

Southern California of the thirties was not a monolithic metropolis but was comprised of several counties manifesting differing lifestyles, identities, and economies. Orange County moved to the beat of agriculture and small-scale manufacturing for local trade. The county's population lived in "a network of small distinct towns and villages within a rural region."[61] The largest city, Santa Ana, contained thirty thousand inhabitants surrounded by citrus groves and bean fields. Los Angeles County's population, on the other hand, centered about the city of Los Angeles, which harbored a population of well over one million with suburbs scattered in all directions. The outlying areas formed an imposing agricultural belt, but the heartland, Los Angeles, was becoming a national center for manufacturing, international trade, tourism, and entertainment. Meanwhile, Orange County's economic heart, forty-five miles to the east, pulsated with the citrus and vegetable harvest.

The rural quality of life predominating throughout the county is underscored in contemporary descriptions written in 1937 of the Independencia and Stanton villages:

> . . . the Mexican colony of Independencia . . . is in purely rural surroundings with the exception of the colony itself. The homes of the people, a small church, three or four Mexican stores, and a school make up the colony. The nearest town is five miles distant.
> . . . [Stanton] is located on one side of the tracks in the little village of Stanton. Stanton, itself, is a very small rural type village, with but few business establishments.[62]

Fourteen of the twenty villages were exclusively citrus worker villages, and in several others, primarily in the small sized cities of the county seat, Santa

Ana (30,000), Anaheim (10,000), Orange (10,000), citrus pickers were a sizable segment of the working population.

The process through which a community is formed is fascinating and not simple. There are at least three ways in which Mexican citrus communities form: (1) through private real estate promotions, (2) through company-sponsored housing, and (3) through a move into poor neighborhoods that are usually on the outskirts of a larger town but are bordered by the citrus groves or agricultural fields.

Real estate subdivision was responsible for a good many of today's barrios. A landowner and real estate agent coordinated specifically to establish a Mexican community, usually identified as a "Mexican colony." The headline of the October 5, 1923, edition of the *La Habra Star* read "will Build Town for Spanish Only," referring to *Colonia Juarez* in Talbert (Fountain Valley). The article further reported "residence in the town will be restricted to Mexicans and other Spanish-speaking citizens."

Landowners of one La Habra tract subdivided their property into twenty-eight lots "offered to Mexicans who wanted to become homeowners."[63] All but five lots sold soon after they went up for sale. The lots evolved into Campo Corona. Similar developments for Mexican buyers were built in Richfield, La Jolla, Placentia, Stanton, Fullerton, and Anaheim. Celso de Casas recalls that when as a youngster he arrived in Richfield, the Mexican community of "four or five families" were sharing a barn divided by partitions.[64] The surrounding land was empty, sandy wasteland located along an old course of the Santa Ana River, which had been dammed and diverted for irrigation purposes. The Yorba Linda Citrus Association tapped the picker supply from the distant community of Placentia and needed a more accessible supply. Developers, realizing the market potential, subdivided, built small wooden frame houses on the lots, and sold them, only to Mexican families, for $500 at $10 per month. Some seventy-five two-bedroom-square houses sold quickly in the early 1920s. Like most picker neighborhoods, the community lacked sewers, gas for cooking and heating; had no paved streets, nor even sidewalks. Water lines and electricity did serve the neighborhood, but wood was the primary fuel source. These conditions remained until the late 1940s.

La Jolla lay some five miles distant, along the same former course of the Santa Ana River. This empty and useless sandy expanse proved lucrative for its owner, who in 1921 sold parcels of it to Mexican pickers working for Placentia packinghouses.[65] The first settlers in La Jolla named several of the streets (today one can drive along Tafoya Street) before any of the houses were built. A tent *colonia* was the first stage in La Jolla's history. As a nascent community formed, the character of the village was added to and changed. Within a year the first homes were owner-built and during the 1920s more lots were sold and new homes added. A small store run by Mr. González (there is still a González Market on La Jolla Road), later a Catholic mission, a handball court, and a pool hall had all been established, and by the end of the twenties the La Jolla public school rounded out the community.

The Anaheim Gazette reported in 1925 that "Colonization of Mexicans in one section of [Anaheim]. . . is a project now being considered."[66] The chamber of commerce sponsored the campaign, which featured a highly orchestrated booster dinner, at which speakers extolled the virtues of housing for Mexicans as a means of "promoting a better class of citizens, thereby stabilizing the labor situation."[67] One citizen testified before the two hundred citizens assembled at the Anaheim Elks Club that he sold thirty-two lots in "one tract of land . . . in the sugar factory district . . . all of them to Mexicans [and] were religiously prompt in making payments."[68] The chamber's campaign event brought together educators, packinghouse managers, welfare workers, civic authorities, and citizens. At the conclusion of the meeting a resolution was unanimously adopted, "recommending that the chamber of commerce take early action toward establishing a colony for the Mexican people in Anaheim."[69] Thus the colonia was founded.

Building one's home was much like migration—a family and/or a community affair. Most migrants had a general or rudimentary knowledge of carpentry (in Mexico homes were often made and repaired by the owner) and applied these skills out of necessity. Fred Aguirre reminisced that "in those days you built your own house. My brother built his own house next to where my mother [now] lives. A two story house. The house is still there. In the old days they built their own houses . . . [or] They usually hired somebody that knew a little about carpentry . . . a lot of fellows did nothing but carpentry. They'd go around from job to job. You'd hire him when you'd buy your lumber, and you'd hire him by the day or the hour."[70] The inexpensive homes of small, plain, wooden frame construction, consisted of living room, parents' bedroom, and kitchen. Sometimes materials consisted of scraps, and in many homes the largest size lumber was a two-by-four, usually one-inch planks took the place of siding, and if there was sufficient money, the interior was finished with dry wall. Some lots were sold with inexpensive houses already built on them, but for recent migrants, the cost was nevertheless significant. The Richfield colonia price for a house, $500 at $10.00 per month, was a perilous undertaking for an orange picker. Some moved their homes onto a lot, but these appear to be few. When family size increased, the owner either added a room, or contracted with a neighborhood carpenter to build an addition.

The El Modena colonia, a privately owned subdivision settlement, differed from the general pattern. El Modena housing was always rented, not sold. There were about thirty homes on a forty-two lot subdivision. The tract owner purchased small dwellings (shacks would be a better term) from surrounding ranches, moved them onto a lot, then rented them at $7.00 to $10.00 per month. Each house had one hanging light socket, all had outside privies; some had a gas line for cooking, but most used wood for cooking and heating. A single spigot in the kitchen provided the only water available in the home. The shacks were flimsy, constructed entirely of two-by-fours and one-inch boards standing on concrete blocks. The floors were uncovered planks nailed on to two-by-fours; walls were vertical floors, identical planks nailed on to two-by-fours. Nothing more insulated or protected the home. Over the years the shacks deteriorated badly. In fall the fierce Santa Ana winds blew through the boards, in winter the roofs leaked, and the houses turned into intolerable furnaces in the summer heat.[71] These village conditions remained through the 1940s.

The second method of *colonia* development, grower association–sponsored housing, occurred in La Habra, Fullerton, on the Bastanchury Ranch, and the San Joaquin Ranch. Two types of grower-sponsored housing provide local examples of the wave of housing development that was sponsored by California Fruit Exchange and its affiliates (other nonlocal examples are described in chapter one). These local activities in Orange County are significant for several reasons. First, the La Habra Citrus Association pioneered the concept of Mexican picker housing in 1915, when it contracted for the construction of twelve modest picker dwellings. Second, the La Habra Citrus Association camp, advertised extensively as the "model camp," included a social engineering program advocated by the industry as the correct approach to organizing a Mexican community. Over the years additional housing was built and by the late 1940s sixty-nine houses sheltered a population of about five hundred. La Habra's first colony, Campo Colorado (or "Red Camp" because of its red roofs), was soon joined by the private development Campo Corona. Although divided by a thoroughfare, the two camps existed side by side and interacted as one colony, the total population of the two camps was about one thousand or more. But Campo Colorado was a company town in the true sense of the term. Houses were rented at $7.50 per month only to families with at least one adult male available to work at any given time. Renters were allowed to add rooms and make other improvements provided they pay the costs. One of the first settlers in Campo Colorado raised a family of thirteen in a twenty-by-twenty-foot house, the only size available. The eighth child, a son, remembers, "It had one bedroom, one tiny kitchen and a living room divided by curtains for my parents. The plumbing was outside. With castoff wood he bought from the railroad, my father built another bedroom for us boys. My older brothers got the beds and my younger brothers slept on the floor."[72] A community hall, association-sponsored adult education (i.e., Americanization), and an elementary school were part of the housing program and perceived as such by the Association's board of directors (see chapter seven).

Competition from other enterprises, often from within the citrus industry itself, created labor shortages as acreage to be worked expanded. In July
1920, the need for Mexican labor moved the Placentia Orange Growers
Association to investigate "the problem of housing the Mexican pickers and
[moved] that [a committee be designated] to visit other associations who
have similar problems and find out their solutions."[73] The following month
George Hodgkin of the California Fruit Exchange, who played a major role
in elaborating the Exchange's housing program, attended several monthly
association board meetings "to talk over with the Board the proposition of
housing the pickers."[74] In September and October plans were discussed for
finding a suitable location, and a decision was reached to purchase land in
Fullerton.

The Placentia association's Campo Pomona (so named because pickers
from the Pomona area were settled there) comprised twenty-eight houses
rented at $11.00 per month with four weeks' free rent to those remaining
throughout the year. The Association's 1925 Annual Report reflected on
their settlement:

> The Mexican camp each year proves of great benefit to the Associa-
> tion. At the beginning of the season it assures a supply of men who
> have had the experience with our methods of picking and standards
> required by the Association. It serves to keep the foreman of the crew
> with us throughout the year and makes unnecessary the training of
> new men each season. Aside from this feature, it serves to prevent
> labor troubles since the large percentage of contented employees
> exerts a beneficial influence upon the floating labor which each year
> must be employed to fill out the crews.[75]

The six-thousand-acre Bastanchury Ranch included over four thousand
acres of oranges and lemons. The vast property required a decentralized
form of labor settlement; consequently, six small villages of some thirty
families each were scattered about the ranch. The family-owned Bastanchury Ranch exhibited little interest in providing housing, feeling that by
supplying a plot rent-free their responsibilities and self-interests were met.
Consequently, the first Mexican families to arrive in the early 1920s built
their residences without the benefit of running water, sewers, electricity,
or paved roads. One of the six settlements, called "Tiajuanita" by its residents, was built with "scraps of sheet iron, discarded fence-posts and sign-
boards [and] served by one lone water faucet and a few makeshift privies."[76]

A night-school teacher at the ranch described the houses as "simple little vine-covered cottages" that had gardens that featured geraniums and car-
nations gracing their yards. The garden was watered with a stream diverted from an irrigation ditch. Although picturesque, the houses were, in her
words, "far from elegant and not commodious nor too sanitary. . . . [Some

of them] may have had running water, but very few. [The people] carried their water. . . . [A dusty road] went right through the center of their little village—hamlet would be a better word."[77] In the early 1930s, new ranch ownership altered the previous housing policy, and constructed rental homes with running water and toilets.[78]

The third method of settlement, the move into a poor neighborhood, is illustrated by the case of the Santa Ana *colonias*. Only twelve Mexican families lived in Santa Ana in 1900; but by 1930 nearly four thousand Mexican residents had settled in the Delhi, Logan, and Artesia *colonias*. The settlements had originally housed workers in the sugar factory, beet fields, and railroads. But as agriculture and citrus expanded, railroads completed and sugar production declined, the inhabitants shifted occupations to agriculture and citrus. Although the villages were within city limits, they were situated on the outskirts of town, next to burgeoning citrus groves or vegetable fields. The countryside exerted greater impact on the *colonia* lifestyle than did the city.[79] Virtually all employment emanated from the fields or groves. The little nonagricultural employment that was offered was limited to unskilled labor on road construction or urban rail systems.

Although the same deliberate policy of segregating Mexicans resulted in the *colonia* pattern, citrus workers living in small-sized urban Santa Ana (population thirty thousand in 1930) experienced an environment significantly distinct from those in the rural villages. Delhi and Logan each had approximately 200 households, and some 60 households formed Artesia. These 460 households constituted a substantially higher population than any of the other Mexican communities in a single town or city. In addition, Santa Ana citrus workers shared the occupational stage with vegetable labor (and nut-picking labor during the harvests). Finally the residential areas were established before the influx of Mexican residents. However, in both the small and large versions of citrus worker *colonias* the custom of owner-built homes appeared. In the small urban environment, many of the same kind of community structures and conditions surfaced but on a larger scale, in large measure due to the occupational dependence upon either citrus or agricultural employment. If there is any substantial socioeconomic difference between the Santa Ana *colonias* and those of the purely citrus worker villages (besides size), it is that the former suffered from poorer conditions due primarily to the lower wages paid in vegetable picking and general ranch work. Citrus workers enjoyed better pay, longer working periods, and naturally held higher status in the Santa Ana *colonias*. In the citrus district villages virtually the entire work force labored as pickers or packers, only the foremen garnered a superior status.

In sum, a variety of means secured a home for the recently migrated families, but in the overwhelming majority of cases, it was the planning of Mexican settlements by representatives from the dominant community that

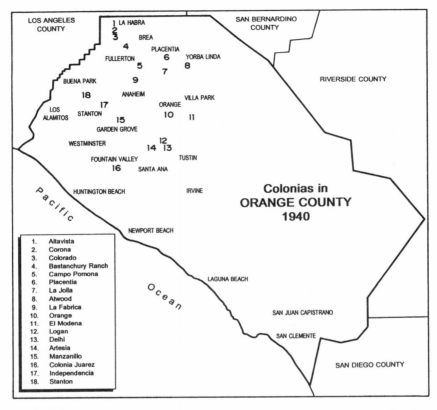

The distribution of Mexican villages in Orange County, 1940. Illustration by Karen Christiansen.

determined their location. Nevertheless, not all schemes to develop Mexican colonies were acceptable to the public and in a few cases sellers were forced to withdraw offers or revise plans. No sooner were plans made public that residents near the proposed Campo Pomona colony site protested the decision and suggested alternate locations. Thereupon the association board voted to investigate other sites agreeable to all parties (excluding the pickers). Apparently no site was completely free from objections, although the association tried to avoid difficulties. The colony was eventually constructed, but nearby residents always harbored a resentment against the community. The head of the Fullerton Unified High School Americanization Department commented years later that the "American neighbors who felt their property had been devalued [*sic*] by its close proximity to the Mexicans treated them with humiliating scorn."[80] Continued requests to change association decisions were ultimately ineffective, in interesting contrast to the manner in which citizens of La Habra forced the reversal of a private landowner to sell to Mexican families. In the former case, the political power of the association proved superior to that of individual residents.

The La Habra developer was besieged by so many complaints from the townspeople that he and his wife "pleaded guilty" and begged forgiveness in a letter to the local newspaper. Under the headline "Will Not Sell Property to Mexicans," they wrote: "[we have] abandoned the plan of selling the tract."[81]

The Yorba Linda Chamber of Commerce gave the matter of a Mexican colony serious consideration before the chamber president, editor of the *Yorba Linda Star,* floated the idea in his newspaper column. Apparently the townspeople read the paper carefully because "an avalanche of disapproval . . . descended upon him." Yorba Linda citizens expressed "little desire for [the] proposal."[82] That the plans became one of the few that were abandoned illustrates the determination of the townspeople to define the parameters of the Mexican community.

Maintaining a Home in the Settlements

Conditions of life in the villages varied from extremely poor to merely poor. Few, if any, reached the lower rungs of middle-class status, and those who did so were invariably merchants. Picking and packing were the principal (and many villagers would say the only) occupations open to Mexican residents.[83] With yearly family incomes ranging from $600 to $800 (when combining the incomes of all adults and working children), it was virtually impossible to rise far above the subsistence level.[84] Yet substantial numbers of families were purchasing homes in the tracts. One 1931 survey found that half of the families in Placentia "and practically all in Atwood and La Jolla were buying their own homes."[85] Similar figures were reported for La Habra's Campo Corona and Alta Vista[86] and the Stanton and Independencia villages.[87]

Making ends meet on meager salaries required inventiveness, creativity, and adaptability on the part of the settlers; examples of which range from the construction of their own homes to the tending of small livestock for food. One observer noted that the Mexican "family income [has] extended beyond limits usually thought possible."[88] Not surprisingly the Mexican community did not require a disproportionate share of welfare assistance before the Depression. In 1930, the county dispensed $10,065 "to the needy," of which only $2,107, or about 20 percent, went to Mexicans; the remainder went to the Anglo-Americans.[89] An editorial in the *Placentia Courier* congratulated the local Mexican communities for low relief appropriation stating, "Mexican residents have their own relief organizations which are functioning."[90] A long-time resident confirms that the villagers cooperated to help out those who fell through the minimal needs level. His statement underscores the editor's comments: "I don't recall cases of families going on welfare . . . if for some misfortune a family's needs were not met, the community would get together and collect from among themselves to help the family."[91] A teacher in a Mexican school offered a similar observation: "The charge that Mexican laborers are an excessive burden upon the community does not appear to be true in the La Habra Valley."[92] Her experiences in La Habra led to her holding an opinion that differed from the then-common stereotype of Mexican profligacy. Mexicans, she commented, "exhibit a degree of thrift unknown to many of the average critics of Mexican thriftlessness."[93] Most families purchased staples, beans, rice, flour, sugar, coffee, and lard in bulk. The more important purchases, especially clothing, textiles, and bulk food items, were made in town, usually in the commercial centers of Santa Ana, Fullerton, or Orange. Large one-hundred-pound sacks of beans or flour, forty-five-pound cans of lard, and five-pound coffee boxes were stored and used daily in food preparation.

Chickens, goats, ducks, and perhaps a pig or two were prevalent in the village yards, supplying a principal source for meat. One study found half of the homes in a Santa Ana village had a milch cow.[94] The same study reported that one in five county village families had a goat to provide its milk supply.[95] Where possible, a wide variety of vegetables, corn, squash, chilies, lettuce, string beans, chayote squash, and cactus were planted in the gardens. Various herbs used for cooking, medicinal teas, and poultices sprouted from lard cans that stood in the yards, segregated from other recycled cans, that displayed perhaps geraniums or mums, and these were separated from a cactus plant or chili plants. The relative geographic isolation of several of the villages, and their inability to meet all their nutritional needs, required purchasing some provisions from grocery trucks that were managed by Mexican merchants who drove through the village once or twice a week. Fresh cheaper cuts of meat (usually tripe for a weekend *menudo* and pigs feet for *pozole*), vegetables, fruit, eggs, bread, pastries, and other small items were used by homemakers to fill in for other goods when these were unavailable or too expensive.[96]

Families, particularly the women, institutionalized a pattern of activities in the home, including the tending of vegetable and herb gardens, recycling materials for additional uses, and canning. Pedal-powered sewing machines were a common and much-used household item employed to sew flour, rice, and bean sackcloth into window coverings, quilts, bed sheets, table covers, shoe-pockets, kitchen towels, handkerchiefs, or other needed items. Angelina Cruz remembers that her mother could "do anything with her sewing machine." Bedspreads, dresses, shirts, pants, socks, table covers as well as knit sweaters, scarves, were common sewing chores for the elder Arce. Mrs. Arce could reproduce a dress simply by examining it closely and then from memory create the garment.[97] In the villages, shirts, pants, and dresses made from store-bought materials, saved considerable expense, and when children outgrew their clothes, they were passed on to a younger sibling or to another family.[98] When clothing wore thin, a patch renewed the item's utility. Men also engaged in sewing, but in these cases within the sphere of men's employment. Some pickers preferred the hand-sewn sacks made by an Independencia resident, Don Onorato, over the factory-made sacks, which were ill-suited to their body dimensions. In various villages, Don Onorato's sacks were popular because they adjusted easily to height, weight, and arm length thereby lessening the burden to the picker. More important, the locally made sacks were considerably less expensive than the sacks sold at the packinghouse.[99]

Canning of foods, especially cactus added to the cost-cutting as did the brewing of beer. During Prohibition and afterward, many homes had a brew-pot to ferment hops, malt, sugar, yeast, and water into a tasty, smooth strong beer. The steady supply of beer was bottled by equipment at home, and was shared with the frequent visits from neighbors, friends, and relatives and for the many birthday, baptism, confirmation, and wedding parties. Brewing was not confined to home use, small-scale bootlegging was practiced in the villages. At La Jolla at least eight individuals sold beer.[100] Home-brewing chores were in addition to the usual home chores, which included meal preparation (and this invariably included handmade tortillas), washing, ironing, sewing, housekeeping, and child care. If the woman worked in the packinghouse, cleaned house for a "high-tone" lady or ran a small store, these were additions to her customary responsibilities.

Numerous business enterprises operated by women served the villages. Common enterprises included selling lunches in the home to workers, or preparing foods sold from a cart or booth at Sunday street fairs (or *jamaicas*). Occasionally women ran boarding houses for traveling pickers and packers. Small family-operated stores selling sundry goods were quite common and an accepted sphere of labor for women. The Placentia *Comercial Mexicana,* founded in the late 1920s by José Aguirre and operated by Doña Martina Aguirre and her daughter from 1934 until its closing in 1943, provided people with smaller staples. Six small Campo Corona/Colorado stores, one of which was a partnership between a woman and three men, maintained villagers with goods. At La Jolla the local pool hall was owned and operated by a woman and at the end of the citrus era, a former packer Erma Magaña, founded Pee Wee's Market, a grocery she ran for nearly twenty years. Villagers had no moral problems with women as merchants, even full-time merchants, as long as they fulfilled their traditional domestic responsibilities (which they often did while tending store).

In the small homes, the kitchen was the heart, where the family clustered, not only for meals, but for social activities. The kitchen, therefore cooking, was almost always the province of the wife or her daughters; it required preparing fresh or unprepared foods. Tortillas, beans, chili sauces, and a variety of dishes—especially those using chicken—were the mainstays of the villagers' diet. Seldom was an evening meal eaten without fresh tortillas. Tortillas could be of corn or flour; older women preferred to grind lime-soaked corn on stone *metates* (grinders) to prepare the dough for the griddle. Traditions changed over the years, flour tortillas, which require less preparation than corn tortillas, became the main homemade variety. Not only were meals served to the immediate family, but when neighbors, relatives, and the younger set's playmates happened by, as they frequently did, they were welcome to enjoy.[101]

For large families, washing laundry was not an easy matter, as it was nearly always done by hand. Children's clothing soiled easily in the dirt streets, and picker's overalls seldom seemed clean. Washtubs, washboards, and the long wooden stirring sticks retained a dampness from their frequent use on back porches. The ash from wood fires for heating water never seemed to cool completely. Occasionally a family purchased a second-hand electric washing machine, which reduced the chore time somewhat for its owner and for those relatives and neighbors eligible to borrow the machine for the minimal cost of electricity.[102] After drying on backyard lines, the finer wash required ironing. The clothes were now ready for the next cycle of wearing, washing, drying, ironing. Laundry was just one of many areas of villagers' labor that was shouldered by the women.

Women were frequently employed in the packinghouses but this required the permission of her parent, or if married, her spouse. If she was a mother, child care was indispensable, and was often provided by an in-law (or *comadre*), a trusted neighbor, or, if he was willing, her husband.[103] Many women packed citrus while also raising families and providing and caring for the home. Erma Magaña thought back to her packinghouse experience and recalled that "all my friends and cousins, we all worked as packers."[104] Some packed on a casual basis, others considered it a full-time occupation. Seldom did women work independently, if they were single, their wages supported her parents' family, and even packers who were married women often set aside a portion for her parents.[105]

However when working, women often earned wages equal to that of males, thereby allowing a measure of economic and social independence. Consequently, packers developed a separate identity from those of their gender who remained at home. But when employed, packers enjoyed a distinctive social life within the packinghouse. Birthdays, wedding engagements or other special events could, and often were, celebrated in the packinghouse with potlucks and parties. Packers shared information regarding employment through informal grapevines, notifying each other regarding those packing-houses scheduled to increase their packing crews. Interestingly, women as fictive-kin or as blood relatives tended to gather together when seeking employment, when employed, and when traveling to local and distant packing-houses. Good packers, especially those who attained the rank of *campiona* (or "champion," because she could pack a hundred boxes a day), earned a special status from her peers. Thus, a unique camaraderie and interaction distinguished packers from other women in the village.

Despite all the efforts to overcome poverty, conditions in the home were understandably meager. A composite description of 35 randomly selected Orange County homes surveyed in a 1940 welfare study captured the quality of homes: "With few exceptions" the homes had no heat "other than that provided by the kitchen stove."[106] Many lived in homes heated by woodburning stoves, consequently woodcutting in the distant hills and hauling wood home were chores commonly practiced by men; some resorted to selling cut wood to help support the family.[107]

The survey further noted that "relatively few homes have inside toilets or baths; although most have running water" and electricity.[108] Refrigeration (if any) was provided by block ice, and cooking was either by gas or wood. The rather large size of households, on the average six persons translated into two persons per bed—required all available space for sleeping.[109] Each community had several exceptionally large families occupying the modest homes. One family of thirteen in La Habra's Campo Colorado occupied each room, including the closet for sleeping; a Richfield family numbering fifteen lived in a four-room house. While the community conditions were poor, they either made-do with very little, or family and community carried over the individual or family in times of extreme need. Shorter-term but no less critical needs often were met at the small local Mexican-owned grocery stores each village utilized, and which offered credit payable the following payday.[110]

Generally most families enjoyed sufficient diets but the cyclic unemployment and low wages often depleted precarious food supplies such that many families periodically sank below minimal nutrition standards. In addition, the poor conditions in the villages, dirt streets, lack of flush toilets, inadequate plumbing and heating prevented basic sanitation practices. Disease and illness found a double entry. Consequently, a number of health problems disproportionately affected the Mexican communities. One illness, tuberculosis, proved deadly, affecting Mexicans three to five times more than the dominant community according to reports.

In 1930, forty-four Mexicans died of TB in the county between January and September, nearly tripling the Anglo death rate. The cases of TB at La Habra's Wilson School in 1935 indicated the widespread problem. Four children were quarantined and thirty more "given a preventative regime."[111]

Deaths claimed a larger number of village infants than those of the town, illustrated in statistics from 1934 when of the county's one hundred infant deaths, sixty were Mexican. Other diseases also took their toll. Trachoma, a contagious eye infection, spread through the Campo Colorado/Corona in 1927 affecting twenty-five children. Meanwhile, only one child in the Anglo district was so infected. When serious illness struck, villagers depended upon the county hospital; lesser health problems were confronted with folk medicines.

The processes of birth and death were the affairs of the home, family, and neighbors. Birthing was commonly performed at home, with the assistance of a mid-wife, or a trusted medical doctor. In some villages, a lone medical doctor or two attended the needs of the people. These physicians usually charged low fees, always made home visits, and seemed to care about the people's welfare. John Arce recalls that a Dr. Foster was the Stanton, Independencia and nearby villages' favorite for helping them through an illness or childbirth.[112]

Funerals were likewise a home affair. Wakes were nearly always held at home, where rosary and other prayers were recited individually and in unison, led either by the mission priest, or a revered villager, usually a woman. Wakes generally began in the evening and lasted throughout the night and into the morning. Food, refreshments, coffee, and liquor were always available for those who came to pay their respects. Attendance at funerals was a good measure of the person's respect and status and thus a particularly revered person would have a considerably elaborate wake. The size of the flower bouquets, the length of the prayers, the silence and reverence for the deceased accorded to the individual's status.[113] In one funeral, that of a county-union leader, the Delhi pool hall, which also served as union headquarters, was transformed into the funeral salon. Since villagers from throughout the county came to pay their respects, the funeral cortege stretched for several city blocks. At his final resting place, the assembled formed a large crowd to hear labor leaders from southern California pay their respects.[114] A memorial *corrido* written by the popular singer and unionist Emilio Martínez captured the sentiments of the villagers:

> I will sing these verses
> with much pain and regret,
> It is nothing less than the story
> of a brother and a union fighter.
>
> You were a loyal comrade
> to all the workers
> You extended your hand to them
> in the fashion of a fighter.[115]

Voy a cantar estos versos
Con mucha pena y dolor
Es nada menos la historia
de un hermano luchador.

Fuistes compañero leal
de todo el trabajador
tu le extendites [*sic*] tu mano
Como todo un luchador.

Corridos dedicated to the memory of a particularly popular individual were heard from time to time, as was the practice of wakes in the local pool hall. The latter occurred infrequently and more often for multiple wakes, as when in 1938 three very well known Independencia athletes were killed in a car accident. Practical considerations decided the matter and the local pool hall served as the funeral salon in order to accommodate the large assembly.[116]

Radios were not as common as the sewing machine even by the mid-1930s. La Habra's villagers owned only five radios in 1934, although forty phonographs provided traditional music. But in the 1940s radios increased in importance as home entertainment in the villages. In the 1920s and 1930s Spanish-language radio programs in the urban centers were on the increase, beaming their broadcasts into the citrus villages and thus provided a source of cultural maintenance. However, as English became better understood by the first generation and spoken by the second, radio programs in that language became popular too. At first, radios in a village attracted curious and awed neighbors, much as television would thirty years later. A particularly special broadcast would bring a living room full of guests. The Aguirre family in Placentia, for example, had one of few radios in the village in the late 1920s, and on evenings when a major program or event, such as a championship boxing match, or a major address by the Mexican consul was aired, the house filled with family and friends. As the years went by, the radio became a favorite form of family entertainment—though challenged by the movies.

In the 1930s only the Santa Ana movie houses presented Spanish-language films, but most villagers lived ten to fifteen miles away. Consequently, viewing silent and later sound English-speaking films in local "downtown" movie houses was much more common, especially among younger migrants and the second generation.[117] Youngsters of the remote villages would ride their bikes—often two to a bike—to the nearest movie house. John Arce recalls biking the seven miles from Independencia to Anaheim in groups of five or six to attend weekend movies.[118] Movies attained a high rank among the community's recreation, even though the films of the period portrayed a culture and lifestyle at variance with those of the village. Not infrequently, the portrayals were stereotypical and racist. Regardless of the themes, movies offered an opportunity to enter into an entertainment fantasy world even if only to escape momentarily. However, there was no escaping the reality of "separate-but-equal" as Mexicans were obligated to sit apart from the dominant community clientele, in sections labeled *Mexicans only.*

Motor transport was a practical necessity and ownership was not uncommon, although cheaper, well-used models were usually purchased, thus recycling unwanted automobiles and trucks.[119] Like many large consumer items, cars and trucks were paid for in cash if purchased from a private party, but credit was often extended by car dealerships. Pickers and packers with a means for transportation traveled to Los Angeles, San Bernardino, and Riverside counties during the Navel season. Families too migrated for summer vegetable and fruit work in the Central Valley. Automobiles and trucks were used primarily to extend the geographic range of employment possibilities serving the family in need of work and the growers' perennial need for cheap temporary labor. When repairs were needed, either the owner or a backyard mechanic from the village could be trusted to solve engine or body problems.

Villagers remained generally isolated from the urban centers in and outside of the county. Public transportation connecting the villages with Santa Ana, the county seat, was nonexistent. La Jolla residents recall walking to Independencia a distance of seven miles to visit friends, and some Placentians never ventured as far as La Habra.[120] Traveling to Los Angeles, forty-five miles to the west, required, apart from concerted effort, an automobile—which not a few families lacked (and if one was owned, the cost for gasoline tempered the range of travel)—or a ride to the terminal of the interurban rail route at La Habra, or Santa Ana. Indeed, Los Angeles remained largely outside the daily routines of the villagers. The rural remoteness stopped well short of constructing a numbing social paralysis as villages engaged in a continuous round of activities set to the cycles of harvests, schooling, religious and patriotic events, recreation, and family life.[121]

No sooner had the villages constructed a routine than the Depression brought more adversity to an already difficult life in the villages. Some families suffered a relentless and often losing search for survival causing fathers to break down and cry, unashamed before friends and relatives. Mrs. Jennie Romoff, Americanization supervisor for the Anaheim High School District, which included six villages, reported "deplorable" conditions: "Some of the Mexican families are in dire straits, with fathers, mothers, and children poverty poor and always hungry. . . . Mothers drawing small hand-wagons, with two or three children toddling along with them, go up and down the alleys, searching the garbage cans of the grocery stores for any kind of cast-off food. . . . What is garbage to a well-to-do family is food to these hungry Mexicans."[122] Things were "pretty tough, pretty tough," recalled Fred Aguirre.

> Because I remember that at least half of the people didn't work because they couldn't find work. Then they paid you hardly nothing. People were always going down to [my parent's] store to beg my dad. That I remember a lot—to beg my mother. They begged them for food. They would say "As soon as we get a job or we get a job promise we're going to pay you." . . . A lot of them paid but a lot of them didn't . . . [but] we ate out of the store, at least we had the store.[123]

Several sources indicate that about 40 percent of Mexican families were forced into some form of public assistance.[124] Available credit in village stores was stretched to the limit. At the end of the Depression, Placentia's *Comercial Mexicana* held sixty bills ranging from a few dollars to $60. Only half were ever paid.[125]

The Depression was seldom attributed to the failings of capitalism rather, opprobrium was heaped on Hoover. Just as Hoover was the culprit, Roosevelt cut a heroic figure among villagers captured in the Corrido de Relief, written in 1935 by Emilio Martínez of Anaheim:

> When Hoover left office
> we were convinced:
> What did he do for the
> people of the United States?
>
> Roosevelt appeared
> like a resplendent sun
> assumed his administration
> and met his senators
>
> One month as president
> He dreamed a profound dream:
> We all have the right
> to live in this world.[126]

> Cuando se separó Hoover
> quedamos muy convencidos
> ¿ Qué se hiso por la gente
> que tiene Estados Unidos?
>
> Apareció Roosevelt
> Como el sol con resplandores
> tomó su administración
> y contó sus senadores.

Al mes de ser Presidente
El soñó un sueño profundo:
todos tenemos derecho
de vivir en este mundo.

The general attitude toward the New Deal was summed up by this villager's statement: "We all knew, we felt, those of us who were around then, that the crisis was Hoover's, a bad president who didn't know how to administer money. Hunger disappeared from one day to the next when Roosevelt took over. There was enough for those who asked for it, such that for all the people, all workers, hunger was stopped in 1933. Strikes too were resolved more easily by the government call for arbitration to judge which side had the better case."[127]

Other forms of help came from within the community, such as self-help lodges that raised modest funds for destitute families; outside of the community, the Mexican became a scapegoat. In 1931 and 1932, local and county governments caught up in the drive across the United States to deport Mexicans sought to cut budgets through repatriating Mexicans.[128] Induced through threats of relief cutoff sweetened with an offer of free transportation, about two thousand left Orange County. The majority left in nine train loads, but others left by private car. Families debated whether to return, and instances of sharp conflicts surfaced between those wishing to stay and those willing to repatriate.[129] The citrus industry was not particularly hard hit by the Depression, but for those who declined repatriation competition from the unemployed cut into work levels, sending already low wages into a decline.

The villages' struggle against poverty was dealt a further blow when tragedy struck in March 1938. Several days of relentless rain inundated vast stretches of the county, the worst flooding in the region's history, washed away large sections of Richfield and La Jolla, and portions of Stanton and Anaheim's La Fabrica colonies, sending twenty adults and children to their death. In the storm's aftermath, the tumbled mass of houses that had been torn from their wood or cement supports stood at odd angles in the muddy streets and nearby irrigation ditches. The pattern of self-reliance and resilience once again pulled the communities together. Shopkeepers donated food; families and neighbors shared homes, food and clothing; labor unions donated money, supplies and their labor; while the Red Cross provided goods, services and funds. Meanwhile, Atwood and La Jolla were once again temporarily established as tent towns. Eventually through community support and federal aid, the devastated villages were rebuilt with better facilities, including indoor toilets and gas for cooking and heating.[130]

Mexican residents were the poorest social group in the citrus belt. Yet by pooling their resources, utilizing materials others considered useless, sewing clothes and other items from recycled materials, building their own homes, producing their food, and caring for themselves in a communal fashion, they managed but never defeated the formidable limitations of subsistence wages, substandard living conditions and natural and economic disasters.

The Mexican community knew well that employment in factories (except for the agriculturally based sugar factory's lowest paid positions), restaurants (including dishwashers), department stores, and shops was closed to all but the dominant community.[131] A lid on the possibility for economic change and social progress tethered the Mexican community to function as cheap labor. Legal restrictive covenants segregating residential zones mirrored the division of labor. In public parks, swimming pools, theaters, restaurants, bars and dance halls, and clubs and societies, Mexican immigrants and their families were either systematically excluded or segregated. At Anaheim's public park, for example, a corner section with a sign "for Mexican use only" was cordoned off by a chain-link fence. On weekends a police officer patrolled the grounds, warning any potential transgressor to stay within the assigned area. Cross-cultural dating was nearly out of the question and intermarriage rare.[132] In sum, the Mexican community was isolated socioeconomically, and subject to the political decision making of the dominant community. Ironically, the citrus industry enjoyed many of its most prosperous years while this social practice was in force.

Most immigrants were strangers to each other, coming from several states in Mexico; yet they founded a dynamic and creative community with a distinctive lifestyle, organization, traditions, and customs. The heritage of the people provided a firm and trusted foundation for their community life in the United States. The Mexicanized Spanish language, Mexican patriotic and religious observances, and folk art flourished. New cultural patterns in the forms of labor unions, baseball, music, language, American food, customs, patriotic practices, and political action were either selectively integrated or engineered by outsiders into the Mexican atmosphere.

Citrus worker villages had the qualities of an extended family. The routines of daily life, marriage, baptism, death, birth, shelter, nutrition, health care, family ties, and friendship were neighborhood concerns. One educator who was active in the La Jolla village observed that in "La Jolla a very friendly spirit prevails, because the inhabitants know each other well; many are related. Therefore, there are many good times at home."[133] Residents of the villages verify the observation, contending that the village was home, neighborhood, playground, and social center and that, as one villager commented, "It seemed everyone was a relative."[134]

In time an immigrant's extended family network merged with other families. Marriage, baptisms, and close and trusting friendships served to broaden family ties cemented in *compadrazgo,* or coparenthood. Thus a La Jolla resident's comment that "everyone was a relative," easily could have applied to the villages throughout the region.[135] Local villages extended to others in the region through the same kinship and *compadrazgo* system forming a type of regional network. This local and regional network obtained in other areas of village life, notably in recreation, entertainment, patriotic and religious observances, and unionization. Since villagers knew one another, a locked door was a rarity, no invitations were needed to a particular family's celebrations, all were welcome.[136] Life was relatively straightforward, yet it was marked by poverty, seasonal unemployment, higher incidence of illness, substandard housing, and social segregation from the Anglo-American community.

In spite of their humble conditions the villager's lives were ennobled by their efforts, to a degree successful, to create an independent way of life. Chafing under the burdens of segregation and feeling the stinging punishments of legal oppression, the residents raised themselves above the onerous customs of the time and constructed their vision of a good society. However, this vision remained confined to their communities and often included political interests not entirely of the community's making, but were most notably guided by the Mexican consulate.

· 3 ·

Village Culture, Lifestyle, and Organization

Adapting to poverty seemed a permanent activity in the lives of the citrus worker families. While poverty appeared inescapable to *colonia* residents, hemmed in as they were from seeking employment beyond picking or packing, the community nevertheless was far less limited in its potential to develop its own internal organizations and activities. Much of the sense of community was rooted in its politicocultural heritage and activities. The heritage centered and anchored the community in an at best suspicious, at worst, unfriendly and oppressive society.

The major organized cultural activities in the villages originated in a strong nationalist consciousness, a devotion to Catholicism, and a variety of extremely popular recreational and entertainment activities. Distinct traditions connected patriotic celebrations, Christmas festivities, sports, and entertainment. Music, dance, drama, pyrotechnics, artisanal crafts, and bazaars all could enter into any of the general community activities to form a complex cultural weave.[1]

More often than not, community functions came from within the historical spirit of the villagers, although not all Mexican cultural activities depended solely on village direction. Cultural and political relations with the Anglo-American community and the Mexican consulates surfaced. Often public schools and Americanization centers (discussed in chapters 7 and 8) involved themselves into an otherwise independent community activity. Meanwhile the Mexican consulate sought leadership in the political and social affairs of the villages. A differing intervention came from Protestants who formed small churches or missions in many villages. A religious minority, Spanish-speaking Protestants conformed to Americanized religious practices and beliefs, and actively proselytized among the Catholic Mexican majority.

An examination of the celebration of Mexican Independence, selected religious celebrations and activities, and various recreational and entertainment activities demonstrates a dynamic, vigorous, and creative community lifestyle. Those who lived through the village era have retained a strong sense of community and identity in their consciousness, even though the physical community no longer exists.

Patriotic Celebrations

The centerpiece of the village's political life, the Dieciséis de Septiembre, returned like the seasons faithfully each year to an anticipating people. Each village hosting the celebration did so under the direction of a local voluntary patriotic committee, some of which were spontaneously organized, many of which were organized through the direct initiatives of the Los Angeles–based Mexican consul. The committees had several titles in the various communities including Comité de Festejos Patrios, Comisión Honorifica Mexicana, Sociedad Mexicana Benífica y Recreativa, Comité de Beneficiencia Mexicana, and La Junta Patriótica. By the mid 1930s, thirty-nine patriotic committees were formed by the consulate throughout southern California. Such political organizations loosely connected the various villages and urban centers with each other, but also infused a political activity in the communities with a Mexican domestic and foreign policy design.

The communities of Anaheim, Campo Colorado, Placentia, El Modena, Delhi, Independencia, and Campo Pomona traditionally hosted Dieciséis de Septiembre celebrations. Of these sites, Placentia, Anaheim, and La Habra appear the most elaborate and popular, attracting visitors from the region. A composite image of Placentia's Dieciséis de Septiembre celebrations provides a clear impression of a typical *16* in the cultural experience of the immigrant settler community in the region.

The Placentia patriotic committee, first formed in the mid-1920s under consulate tutelage, consisted of men from three nearby communities: those in Placentia proper, La Jolla, and Richfield. A founding group of forty-eight men (the number varied over the years) formed the first general assembly, meeting annually to elect members to the patriotic committee who were charged with planning, organizing and staging the Independence Day celebration.[2] An unwritten criterion for leadership was literacy, and committee members frequently were foremen and small-sized shopkeepers with some education. For example, Alejo Diáz, shoe repairman;[3] José Aguirre, barber and small store owner; and José Vargas, foreman were each elected to the Placentia committee for several terms. Nevertheless, most of the committee members were "just regular workers who worked for the ranches, or they . . . picked oranges."[4]

Once organized and having decided on a division of labor, the committee went about raising funds. Celebrations required building materials, dance bands, decorations, floats, and raffle prizes and new dresses for the queen and princesses. The most commonly used fund-raising technique was community dances and *jamaicas,* or weekend fairs. Young women interested in becoming festival queen sold penny dance tickets; each ticket sold meant one vote for the aspiring contestant. The several dances and raffles held during the summer months before the Dieciséis generally produced the funds to cover expenses.

Dances were held in a community hall if one was available, or in a local billiards establishment easily converted into a dance hall. While the fund-raising subcommittee busied itself, other subcommittees prepared for the construction of booths for food sale and games, and of the ramada-like pavilion and platform stage. The last served as the parade terminus and the festival's central location for the queen's coronation, speeches by invited guests, recitations and singing by children, musical entertainment, and dancing in the evening. Months before the Dieciséis, with the design for the open pavilion completed, the collection of donated and borrowed building materials began. As in the construction of houses, anything usable was incorporated, and as the Dieciséis moved closer, the activity of the committee intensified. The son of a Placentia committee activist recalled:

> They put a lot of hours and time up there . . . at least three days before the Dieciséis, my dad hardly slept. He kept saying 'we got to get it done. We don't have that much time.' They had people working in and out. After work, we had a lot of organizing. I remember a lot of people used to go there. We used to see 8 to 12 people at night leveling the ground, putting up two by fours . . . [for the] ramada, every ten feet vertically. They would go back 100 feet . . . [and] 60 to 80 feet wide.[5]

Meanwhile, palm fronds were cut and collected to provide the cover over the ramada.

Subcommittees responsible for the parade, floats, marching groups, guest speakers, and dance band procured the proper permits from the city or county government, and if the community stood on association property, from the association. The various parade participants invariably included a local group of musicians, social and self-help lodges, and always a float on which the queen and princesses rode. A decorated truck, festooned with flags, paper flowers (made by women of the community), and bunting in the colors of the Mexican flag made for a float. Marching children dressed in their best clothes, each with a sash across her or his chest that was the color of the Mexican flag.

The pavilion was the center of the community's life during the two-day celebration. The festivities began at the pavilion on the evening of the fifteenth with the arrival of the queen and her court. Children and welcoming speakers assumed their proper places along with the committee officers on the platform facing rows of seats always filled by an eagerly anticipating and buzzing audience. Ceremonies opened with the playing of the U.S. and Mexican national anthems by a local band or orchestra hired for the occasion, a brief welcome from the master of ceremonies, and a short address by the stellar guest speaker.

The Dieciséis was the more important day, with the organizers assuming their responsibilities in the early morning and working all through the day until the midnight closing. Streets were decorated and cordoned for the midmorning parade, finishing at the pavilion, where speeches, recitations, music and singing were presented before the assembled audience. Children practiced marching in military fashion weeks before the parade. One participant remembered that nearly all the children of the community took part. Children too recited patriotic skits and verses, sang patriotic songs, or delivered short talks on Mexican independence. Children drilled for months in preparation for the recitations and singing. "There was a lady," recalled Fred Aguirre, who marched for several years as a youth, "by the name of Doña Martina González, who for approximately three months before the Dieciséis, was like a teacher. She used to teach us how to recite, how to dance, how to speak, how to perform, so that we would be well prepared."[6]

Evenings turned into a noisy mingling of adults and children. Incandescent bulbs, strung from pole to pole across the grounds, lit food and game booths colorfully decorated with bunting and flags. Finally, highlighting the annual fete, the most important social event of the year, was the long-awaited street dance.

Placentia was a major center of Orange County's celebrations for good reason. The heart of the county's citrus districts, the Placentia-Fullerton region, covered thirteen thousand citrus acres. Each fete was eagerly awaited by the northern county Mexican communities and people came from villages for many miles. "I don't want to exaggerate," stated a Placentia resident, "but I know we had several thousand people here. . . . We had a lot of people from throughout the county—Santa Ana, Orange, and Westminster—that used to come here. They'd come to Placentia to celebrate the 16th of September. That's when all the communities were small here."[7] Each year the crowds increased; in 1928 an estimated one thousand people enjoyed the festivities, by 1930, twenty-five hundred people reportedly attended,[8] and attendance swelled to five thousand in 1935.[9] Several weeks before the event, local merchants gave out raffle tickets according to the amount of the purchase. At the Dieciséis, the ticket stubs were placed in a large drum and when well mixed, the queen reached in and pulled out the lucky numbers. Winners received sizable bags of groceries—a contest that was not only exciting and popular but a most welcome form of community welfare.[10] On occasion a special feature added to the excitement of the festivities. In 1935 a marathon race opened the celebrations, while in 1939 an aviator cruised "over Placentia during the parade."[11]

The *Placentia Courier* generally printed brief articles on the annual events, as did most citrus town newspapers. The 1930 coverage offered glimpses of that celebration "attended by people from many of the surrounding communities," featuring the Colton Pacific Fruit Exchange Mexican Marching Band. Festivities opened on the evening of the fifteenth with the arrival of the queen and her court by train from Anaheim, proceeded to the pavilion where children delivered "a series of recitations arranged by Miss Francisca Estrada." On Tuesday noon "the parade was held along Santa Fe Avenue, with the playing of the American and Mexican national anthems, and firing of salutes to the flags, being a feature [*sic*]. Several floats had been built, and school children and representatives of the various fraternal lodges, marched in line. A street dance drew approximately twenty-five hundred people in the evening."[12] The 1933 Dieciséis impressed one reporter enough to write that the affair aroused "much interest and [was] pronounced the best attended of the seven annual festivals held in Placentia, the celebration of Mexican Independence Day by Mexican residents of Northern Orange County was concluded Saturday night. The streets were crowded for the parade in the morning, a patriotic program was given in the afternoon and the dance ended the festivities."[13]

The problem of maintaining order and decorum with such large crowds obviously concerned villagers. In La Habra the patriotic committee policed the affair by assigning members to keep an eye out for real and potential transgressors of public decorum to admonish them to stay in line. If a celebrator became drunk, too rowdy, or abrasive toward others, they were politely but firmly told to leave.[14] Residents, however, recall very few problems during the celebrations and that for the most part the crowds were quite well behaved.[15] A Placentia villager commented, "Everyone had fun, there were never problems with drunks, well yes some got drunk, but there were no fights. The people were careful . . . everything was peaceful until time to go home."[16] Newspaper articles of the period verify the recollections.[17]

Every celebration immersed itself in nationalism, avoiding any critical discussion or analysis of Mexican politics, indicating the political culture of the community. Eduardo Negrete, a local merchant who delivered the keynote speech in Placentia in 1931, emphasized the significance of the independence of Mexico and the need to protect the nation's sovereignty. Years later Negrete declared that "the labor question" was deliberately excluded from the festivities. In his words, "some wished to speak of political issues, of worker issues. No! [the Dieciséis] was a patriotic celebration, we did not deal with anything other than the patriotic issue . . . of the heroes, but nothing of workers or of such . . . nothing religious; entirely and exclusively patriotic, honoring the heroes, honoring the fatherland, and only that."[18] Naturally, communities' celebrations often had the consul, vice consul, or consular representative as a featured guest speaker. The continual presence of the consulate-inspired activities in the community and the reverence displayed for the consul points to the significance of the consulate in the political consciousness of the villages.

The consulate did not shrink from promoting an image of itself as the defender of the rights of the Mexican people, a defense that has been more symbolic than real.[19] Some of the activities of the patriotic committees were aimed at helping needy compatriots, assisting others in legal matters and, in general, acting as a conduit for consulate affairs such as taking a yearly census of Mexican citizens in the communities.[20] Nevertheless, the consulates were fundamentally politically conservative bodies, opposing all forms of political radicalism and leftist organization and, instead, emphasized cultural nationalism and a political solidarity with the Mexican government (discussed in chapter 7). This characteristic is especially evident in the organization of labor unions, an activity with which the consulate was involved in the late 1920s and 1930s. The consul sought leadership in both the organization of patriotic committees and in the formation of labor unions. Consuls generally acted as advisers of the patriotic committees. Their input was a decisive factor in the planning and staging of the patriot events, stamping then with an "official seal." The main consequence of consular intervention was an emphasis on cultural preservation, thus reinforcing a sense of "Mexicaness," a cultural identity and political solidarity with Mexico and the Mexican government.

In many patriotic committees free elections were generally used to select officers, but the president frequently was chosen by a consular representative. Consequently, only a minority of committees functioned independently.[21] In Orange County, the activities of the consul were particularly visible, operating through a semiofficial representative resident in Santa Ana, Lucas Lucio. Through the ubiquitous work of Lucio, a one-time merchant, who later worked as an interpreter for Santa Ana lawyers doing business with the Mexican community, the Los Angeles office remained in continual contact with Orange County villages. Similarly placed representatives in other areas (e.g., San Bernardino and Riverside), also played key roles in extending the influence and policies of the consul.

By the mid-1930s the thirty-nine *comisiones* formed a network of consular presence in widely dispersed areas, primarily in southern California.[22] Such a network quite possibly served to offer some consular protection into the vast *colonia* system. On the other hand, the consular office openly declared that the *comisión* role included, in addition to patriotic festivals, "civic conferences reminding Mexicans of their duty to their country."[23] The Spanish-language newspaper *La Opinion* summarized the responsibilities of the *comisión* in an interview with Los Angeles Consul Pesquiera: The comisiones "will do what is necessary to preserve the national spirit among the thousands of Mexicans immigrating to this nation."[24] "National Spirit" meant political loyalty to the government of Mexico among the Mexican residents in the United States.

The different village committees in the county held their separate celebrations for twenty years. Finally, at the urging of the Consulate, they formed one countywide Comité Central de Festejos Patrios in 1940.[25] The first Comité Central evolved from a general meeting of twenty-eight organizations active in the Mexican communities.[26] Among the participants were labor unions, the numerous lodges and benefit societies, and of course, the existing *comisiones*. Well experienced in relations with the consulate, the larger organization united the communities' celebrations into one single patriotic event, continuing the general program of the smaller individual *comisiones*. Pascual Rivas, the first county *comité* president, described the continuing high-level participation of the consul: "Well, we of the Comité de Festejos Patrios of Orange County, before proceeding [with the activities] had to first meet with the consulate, telling us his opinion . . . naturally the consulate was in accord with our projects and when the patriotic festival took place often the consul-general attended, or if he couldn't, the vice-consul attended. This was routine."[27]

Anaheim hosted the first countywide Dieciséis; sites then rotated among several villages annually. In the twilight years of the citrus era, the last Placentia celebration, held in 1947, brought "huge crowds . . . thought to be the largest number of people ever assembled [in Placentia] at one time."[28] The main features of the Dieciséis remained fairly constant: A parade with floats, marching lodge and children groups, followed by music, patriotic addresses, crowning of the queen, and climaxed with two dances, one at the traditional ramada-like pavilion, the other a street dance.

The county *comision* held its annual fete for several years, interrupted briefly during the war and resuming in 1947. The organization remained active until it was dissolved in the early fifties. Thereafter the Dieciséis celebrations were the affairs of Anglo-American and Mexican individuals, who often represented business organizations in the suburban center, Santa Ana, and were funded by the contributions of corporations (mainly breweries).

By the 1940s irreversible changes had so modified the Mexican communities that the Dieciséis celebrations were no longer the affair of the small, scattered villages. Indeed, the evolution from picker villages to incipient suburban blue-collar communities wrought further cultural alterations. Nothing better represents that modification than the changes in the occupations of the county *comité* presidents. Pascual Rivas, president from

1940 to 1944, arrived in the county in the early 1930s, and throughout the decade worked in vegetable picking. Acquiring a farm lease from his Japanese employer who, in 1941, was about to be interned, he saved enough to establish himself in the Mexican food business in the late 1940s. The case of Emilio Martínez is less dramatic but equally illustrative. President from 1947 to 1954, Martínez picked oranges through the early 1940s until he was hired as a salaried repairman at Knott's Berry Farm amusement park. Emilio Martínez's and Pascual Rivas's occupational change exemplifies the fundamental reformations undercutting the cooperative cultural activities characteristic of the 1920s, 1930s, and 1940s. World War II [discussed in chapter 8] was simply too great a force for economic and social change; industrialization and manufacturing atomized the communities and their residents in an emerging suburban society. The separation of the consulate from community affairs, especially their active political leadership, in the decade of the 1940s is also a signal that the evolving village was not an extension of Mexico but an integral component of society in the United States.

Religious Celebrations and Functions

The deeply religious convictions of the Catholic majority in the community were manifested in artisanal crafts, song, music, drama, traditional dishes, and elaborate ceremony and ritual. Of all its religious functions, Christmas was the center of the community's yearly religious cycle. As in the case of the Dieciséis, Christmas drew individuals, families, and community into a tighter network. Christmas occupied a good number of persons from each community, not only for the ceremonial and dramatic performances, but also in their preparation. Children, for example, were major players on La Noche Buena (Christmas Eve) and in the Posadas. Both celebrations required not only costumes, singing, recitations, and acting, but also extensive practice directed by prominent women from the community. However, whereas the Dieciséis was secular, much larger in scale, and regional in scope, Christmas was overwhelmingly religious, drawing the various distinct communities separately into themselves.

Several Christmas activities, each expressing particular aspects of the holiday, and all celebrating the birth of the Christian Savior, warmed the winter season. Three deserve discussion: Nacimiento, the traditional, frequently large-scale creche; the second, Las Posadas, a communitywide reenactment of Mary and Joseph's nine-day journey in search of lodging; the third, Pastorelas, a morality play depicting the struggle between good and evil, Jesus and the Devil. La Habra's two main *colonias,* Campo Colorado and Campo Corona (separated primarily by a main thoroughfare) gained widespread acclaim for their Nacimientos. Time has worn the collective memory recalling these significant portrayals, but any long-time resident of an old village will longingly recount the rich experience that was Christmas.

The community Christmases at Campo Colorado/Corona through the 1920s and 1930s featured the most elaborate and detailed Nacimientos in the county. The Nacimiento, however, was not unveiled until at midnight on Christmas Eve, the last night of the Posada. For nine evenings (representing the nine-day journey of Mary and Joseph to Bethlehem) the villagers formed a Posada, a candlelight procession through the village streets stopping at appointed houses, chanting a request for lodging for the evening. The occupants (a group within the procession) then responded that there is no room at the inn. The procession then proceeded to the next "inn." On Christmas Eve, the Posada made its last stop at the community Nacimiento, and, at Campo Colorado, the community hall in the association camp provided the last scene in the final act of the Posada.

The procession entered the hall, symbolizing the entrance of Mary and Joseph into the stable. The ceremony continued with the reading of the Christmas story, followed by Mexican Christmas songs by a chorus of young girls "dressed in white and tinsel."[29] Then the *piñata* (a decorated earthen ware pot), suspended by a rope, was lowered and each child, blindfolded and holding a wooden stick, took turns at cracking it to disgorge the large cache of candy inside. Then the throng, numbering from two to three hundred, waited for the unveiling of the Nacimiento. A highly skilled artisan, Francisco España, prepared the creche, shaping wax and wood into statues of "elephants, donkeys, sheep, dogs, and men" and, of course, Jesus, Mary, and Joseph. At midnight the curtains were pulled back while a chorus of girls representing angels "sang a song of adoration."[30] In the words of a *La Habra Star* reporter, the Nacimiento "was truly beautiful, showed a degree of artistry very surprising in an untutored genius."[31]

At the close of the celebration, *atole* (a chocolate and cinnamon flavored corn gruel), candied fruit and nuts, sweet breads, and *buñuelos* (fried tortillas flavored with cinnamon and sugar) were served. The Nacimiento remained on display in the Americanization center, used as the community hall, until the season's end in early January.

Perhaps the most fascinating and entertaining of the Christmas practices, the Pastorelas was a centuries-old drama often informally presented in the open air in the neighborhood. This biblically inspired morality play, structured along the lines of an epic poem, proved extremely popular with the village folk. The play and its variations developed in the twelfth century as dramatic recitations performed at high masses in celebration of Christmas and Easter. In Spain these ecclesiastical dramas known as *autos del Nacimiento* became widely popular and eventually secularized with variations such as comedy introduced. In the Spanish new world colonies the *autos del Nacimiento* became a major tool for proselytizing among the Indians, evolving into a major element of the religious culture of Mexico.

The Placentia, La Habra, Santa Ana, and Anaheim villages, among others, regularly presented the Pastorelas, a remarkable achievement given the extraordinary memorization required of the twenty-five actors in preparation for presentation. At Placentia, practice began several months before Christmas under the direction of Jesús Ortega, who seasonally migrated for the Valencia crop from the Corona (in Riverside County) picker community. Working on a voluntary basis, Ortega resided with a close friend during the months of practice, which took place in a garage. Participants still recall Ortega, who knew the entire play by memory, sitting silently, head downward with cigarette in hand, listening intently, looking upward only when correcting players' errors.[32]

The play utilized elaborate costumes, masks, robes, and decorated staffs. Some groups had masks sent from Mexico, while others had masks made locally, most probably in Campo Colorado/Corona, where the skill of Francisco España was employed on a wide number of artistic projects.[33] So popular was the play in La Habra that even the families of the actors attended the rehearsals, "seemingly never tiring of the repetition of the old, old story."[34] The La Habra presentations in the 1930s attracted "a large number of visitors" from the "entire district of northern Orange County" as the group added a procession and singing, "led by men [in brilliant costumes] carrying staffs with beautiful colors and adorned with bells."

Placentia's Pastorelas, like those of other communities, were performed by local residents, primarily for the local community. The presentation could be given in any number of places, but the open air was almost always the stage. In La Habra, the players went from "home to home where the Nacimiento altars [had] been arranged"; in La Jolla the Pastorela was given in the main street at a designated hour by the nearby Placentia group. A La Jollan fondly recalled the play. "The Pastorelas players were really good here. Each year they presented the play and people came from everywhere to see them. The Pastorelas was presented for several days and then they'd go and give it at El Modena and from there go to various different places."[35] Traditional foods and singing capped all the performances. The Placentia players achieved distinction in the many villages, as did others, and received invitations to perform in the county as well as in Los Angeles County. A Placentia participant recalls that over the years the group performed in the picker villages of Buena Park, Norwalk, Upland in Los Angeles County, and Corona in Riverside County.[36]

The Pastorelas, unlike the Dieciséis celebration, did not survive; the last presentations were given in the late 1930s. Like much of the original settlers' culture, the Pastorelas, an activity that required much time, effort, and expense, succumbed to the changes brought by the vicissitudes, first, of the Depression, then by the 1936 pickers strike, by the 1938 flood, and finally by the war. The coming of age of the second generation in the 1940s did not include the oral and visual tradition known as the Pastorela.

Perhaps the most elaborate religious procession occurred on December 12, Día de la Virgen de Guadalupe, the patroness of Mexico, commemorating the appearance of the Virgin Mary before the Indian boy Juan Diego on a Mexico City hilltop in 1598. The 1923 celebration in Campo Colorado/Corona resembled the affairs held in the many villages in the region. The villages were decorated on the evening of the eleventh, in the colors of Mexico, a "picture of the Virgin Mary on every house, with three paper lanterns alight below it" created a picturesque subdued brilliance. Early in the morning of the twelfth, the festivities began with the singing of the traditional *Las Mañanitas,* followed by the recitation of the Rosary at the community hall. At 6 P.M. the service resumed with the praying of the rosary and procession through the camp.[37]

The 1931 procession included several hundred children dressed in Indian costume, one group represented the Indian converts to Catholicism, each child held a gift and a "load" of bamboo on their shoulders. Next, an appearance by the Virgin Mary is enacted, and she expressed her wishes for Indian conversion "with great solemnity" to a boy playing one of the Indians, Juan Diego, "the most forlorn and ragged member of the group." A second group of children followed behind the gift-bearing children. They represented those Indians not converted, the "infidels." Dressed in "grotesque costumes . . . some of the children wore masks . . . representing various animal's [sic] heads."[38]

La Jolla's Día de la Virgen de Guadalupe was traditionally closed by a fireworks display.[39] "It was a beautiful celebration," remembered Lionel Magaña. "I only remember that there was a man here by the nickname of *cohetero* ("fireworker"). He prepared the powder, constructed wooden castles, each with many rooms and several floors. A celebration so beautiful that people came from all over to see the display. On December 12 the area was roped off, the large castles were lit, bright colors raced up one side, changed colors and then raced back down, across, with many designs— all a work of art."[40]

Lesser activities, although they were still integral to the community, were the *jamaica,* or outdoor fairs. These fairs, usually held by the local church or mission to raise funds for a specific purpose, were popular Sunday diversions. Food booths, refreshments, games, prizes, music, and possibly a dance or a raffle provided community recreation. The funds collected were applied to a wide number of purposes: the needy, a Christmas scene for the church, repairs for the church, a church group, and so on. Always the work of volunteers, usually women played a prominent role in the preparation of the *jamaicas,* although men also were commonly involved.[41] *Jamaicas* were most often summer activities, when daylight extended into the cool of the evening. A Saturday or Sunday afternoon or evening *jamaica* offered families, and especially young men and women, an inexpensive diversion that filled a recreational void inherent in the rural towns.

Catholics in the county were divided along demographic lines; Anglo-Catholics were concentrated in the larger towns, primarily in and around central Anaheim, while Mexican Catholics were rural, or dispersed along the urban fringes.

The Catholic church responded to the influx of Mexicans by establishing national missions rather than churches under a resident priest serving all Catholics regardless of nationality. This policy contrasts with that of several Catholic archdioceses in the United States that opted for interethnic churches as a means to promote a more Americanized Catholicism. The decision to build Mexican missions emanated from several factors: Mexican Catholic churches had been serving the faithful ever since the Spanish-Mexican era; and second, the efforts of Protestants proselytizing among Mexicans was to be met measure for measure with a Catholic line of defense: the mission.

In each village mission, a local resident assumed responsibility for maintaining the site. That person supervised and cleaned the building, unlocked the doors for services, and locked up at the termination of the service. Sunday Mass, the main form of worship for the Catholic community, was in many villages the only service offered at the local mission church and at the Stanton, Independencia, Manzanillo, and La Fabrica *colonias,* mass was held but twice a month. The diocese ensured the presence of the priest for the Mass but not for lesser celebrations such as the processional on the Feast of All Soul's Day, November 2. If no priest was available for a specific religious activity, a resident stepped forward, recognized for his or her spiritual standing, to lead the ceremony. At Campo Corona/Colorado a number of venerable elderly women known for their devotion generally assumed the priestly duties, reciting the ritual prayers in Spanish and Latin.

Catholic families displayed religious shrines in a prominent corner of their home. The shrine comprised a small decorated altarlike platform on which stood a picture of the *Virgen de Guadalupe,* of Jesus Christ, or perhaps a favorite saint. The shrine was surrounded by decorations. Perhaps a photo of a deceased relative, and lit candles gave a spiritual aura to the home. Prayers usually were recited individually and silently, but were recited together outloud by the family on a special occasion such as the death of a relative or in supplication for a special cause. These prayers and shrines underscore the depth of the Catholic heritage in the daily life of the villagers.

Supernatural beliefs other than those that were strictly Catholic were common, generally emphasizing a belief in the power of good and evil in the world, a dialectic that the church's teachings accommodated.[42] A good many Catholics also believed that bad luck, evil, or illness could emanate from curses, bad omens, evil eyes, and the like. Remedies (or *curas*) ranged from prayers, chants, charms, teas, or special rituals. In many villages a *curandera* (or woman folk-curer) understood the ways to defeat the supernaturally inspired problem, whether illness or bad luck. *Curanderas* were not always necessary as many villagers knew some remedy for curing an illness or curse. Traditional medicines (scientific research now investigates and confirms the effectiveness of some of these) included teas mixed from a variety of substances, aromatic oils, and the like combined with rituals designed to thwart the power of evil.

One mother's cure for her child's fever illustrates reliance on *curanderismo.* Fearing that the prescribed modern medicine would not return her child to health, the resident of Campo Colorado resorted to a folk cure. "I put some castor bean leaves and other herbs into a tea and mixed it with tortilla dough. I placed this mixture into a sack and hung it around the neck of the child. Grandmother stayed here all night saying her charms and finally the child went to sleep."[43]

While some healing rituals were available to everyone and frequently practiced, those chants, cures, and special rituals that were considered the most powerful were known only to a few, usually the older women of the village. If the illness was particularly acute, the trusted woman was called to perform a rite known only to her.[44]

The power of these beliefs in the culture of the village was significant. Even as the first generation grew older and passed away and the younger generation sometimes scoffed at the older generation's reliance on *curanderas,* the younger generation nevertheless continued to believe that particular teas, rituals, or metals (such as copper) could effect partial relief, if not cures. Thus, for instance, tea brewed from the citronella grass remains in use today by the adult children of the first settlers to remedy a broad range of illnesses—from stomach to kidney, liver and lung problems.[45]

In spite of the power of Catholicism, which was the major religion followed by host villagers, Protestantism issued a determined challenge. Protestants established small missions and churches and became a common, albeit minority, part of the religious culture and experience in the villages. Baptist, Methodist and Episcopalian converts were not unusual in the villages, worshiping in separate churches and participating in the unique activities of the Protestant sects. Most characteristic of Protestant church activity is that they perceived the Catholicism of the Mexican as often being practiced in name rather than in devotion, merely superstition dominated by the power of priests, and therefore Catholic villagers were regarded open fields for conversion to a more authentic Christianity.[46]

In 1922, eleven Mexican Protestant churches counted 216 members, 77 enrolled in conversion study, and nine Sunday schools taught 281 children.[47] Over the years the presence of Protestants increased yet never was it a major counterforce to the profound Catholicism that shaped village life.

One of the earliest Mexican Protestant activities occurred at Campo Colorado/Corona. In the early 1920s, the Missionary Society of the Friend's Church conducted religious education and training and provided social assistance with little success, although their efforts received sympathy and respect from the Catholic villagers. Of more significance in the religious affairs of the community, was the Baptist Mission, under the leadership of a Mexican minister, effectively organized an active church. Programs included an orchestra, a Ladies Aid Society conducting community welfare work, a Sunday school for children, and a children's chorus. Eventually villagers were baptized in numbers sufficient to fill the small church (or mission) to capacity during group baptismals, which were held yearly.[48]

Somewhat less active Protestant groups in the community were the Foursquare, affiliated with the Angelus Temple in Los Angeles, Pentacostals, and a small sect of "Jesus Only" believers, had no formal local church but offered free transportation to their churches in Los Angeles. These groups "along with itinerant cults" spent much of their energy preaching on street corners, attracting attentive crowds and engaging them in questioning and discussion. Occasionally an independent church held well-publicized prayer meetings in the community hall or another nearby hall.

Yet for all the success Protestants had in gaining entry into the villages and establishing active churches, Catholicism remained the dominant religion. For example, the small Baptist church in Placentia, founded in 1929, baptized only ninety-one new members from 1931 to 1939, although it sponsored children's clubs, vacation bible schools, a boy scout troop and "well attended" Thursday evening and Sunday morning services.[49]

When pickers, packers, small businesspeople, and their families did convert to Protestantism (conversion was generally a family conversion), the change in religious affiliation ultimately meant little socioeconomically—neither to themselves nor to the community. Whether Catholic or Protestant beliefs were followed, the community as a unit retained its function in the political economy of the region. Yet each group went its own religious way, and viewed the other with suspicion. The Protestants regarded the Catholics as too contented with their lot and lacking in concern for the social needs of the community. On the other hand, Catholics derisively labeled all Protestants "hallelujahs." The community divided during the Christmas season in their particular forms of worship, in social activities, and in marriage. In spite of all this, the village remained unified as a picker's camp.[50]

Recreation and Entertainment

Dances of several varieties afforded an opportunity for a special form of socializing. Saturday night dances and Sunday *tardeadas* (so-named because they took place in the early evenings, or *tarde*) were the most popular and frequently sponsored. But often they took place in celebration of a wedding or birthday. Frequently a small group of local musicians or family members provided the music. These were family affairs, but in the small community setting neighbors and friends were considered welcome guests. Another type of dance was sponsored by a local businessperson, most often a pool-hall owner who converted the space from billiard hall to dance hall for the event, charging a modest price for admission. On these occasions well-known dance bands, either from the region or from as far away as Los Angeles, advertised through mimeographed flyers, attracted dancers from the surrounding communities.

Types of dances mentioned earlier include the *jamaica* fund-raising affair, which frequently included a dance, and the Dieciséis, annual community event, which was crowned with a community dance held either on a street or in a community hall. The Sunday afternoon dances, *tardeadas,* which often were hosted by an enterprising entrepreneur at a set location, proved extremely popular. Food stalls, refreshment stands, and a small orchestra made up of local musicians made Placentia-Fullerton's Rancho de los Panchos and Anaheim's Rancho Daniel popular family recreation spots.

Sunday wedding, birthday, and baptism festivities were commonly family affairs. Saturday night dances were attended by married couples and singles. Young girls rarely, if ever, ventured alone to a dance, but attended with parents or a trusted chaperone, who guarded the young girls from the unescorted young men. Of all social activities, dances were the favorite of the younger set because they offered a chance to mingle in a more intimate setting while staying within the norms of accepted behavior. Organizations comprising younger folk (for example, the La Habra baseball team Los Juviniles) sponsored *jamaicas* topped with a dance, raised funds for equipment and uniforms. Dance bands made up of local musicians eager to earn extra spending money offered low cost dance music, and not infrequently free music. Campo Corona/Colorado formed a youth band, La Chancha, which made appearances in village celebrations. Organized by a local musician and charging parents a small monthly fee for instruction in his home, the students became sufficiently skilled to form a community orchestra, and a popular one, too![51]

The Joe Raya Orchestra in the Placentia area had a similar history. Joe Raya, son of a picker, benefited from several years of private instruction, left Placentia at eighteen to seek professional employment in Los Angeles, landing a job with the Simon's Brickyard Company band. Returning to Placentia in 1926, his line of work changing dramatically as he hired on to pick oranges. Although his main employment for many years would be citrus (he later became a foreman), he never lost his love for music. By the late 1920s, the Joe Raya Orchestra played to jam-packed Dieciséis celebrations, *jamaicas* and private hall dances in Placentia, La Jolla, Atwood, Campo Corona/Colorado, Fullerton, Corona, Murphy Ranch in Whittier, and other citrus towns.[52] One of the members of the seven-piece group recalled that although he and several other band members never formally trained, Joe Raya took the time to instruct them on the various instruments in the band, organizing the band from scratch, so to speak.[53]

Singing, generally accampanied by guitars, sometimes with a harmonica, provided another very popular form of entertainment. The guitar and harmonica were commonly played, and few families were without a guitarist and a singer or two. The traditional Sunday family picnic and/or a party always served as an occasion for the guitar to be passed around the group singing favorite tunes. Usually *corridos* (a ballad form generally mirroring the life of working people) completed the social gatherings. A corrido tune could also serve as dance music, most effectively while played by the Anaheim musical trio Los Hermanos Martinez.

Formed by Emilio Martínez, an Anaheim picker union representative and composer, Los Hermanos Martínez were well known in the north county villages. Martínez composed many dozens of *corridos,* which premiered at baptisms, weddings, dances, fund-raisers, Sunday *tardeadas,* and wakes (sung as eulogies). Los Hermanos Martínez's fame spread to Los Angeles, where they accompanied on several occasions the most popular singer of the era, Pedro J. González, on his musical radio show-aired over radio station KFI. The trio remained an Orange County favorite, singing the villagers' favorite romantic, nostalgic, and humorous tunes. His compositions covered a range of themes, including unrequited love, religious paeans, political changes, and tragedies affecting the local population. The *Corrido de los Inundaciones,* written shortly after the 1938 flood, memorialized the horror. This traditional corrido captured the intense anxiety and fear generated by the rising Santa Ana River:

> The people ran
> completely shaken
> Without knowing that many
> of them would lose their lives.
>
> A night full of pain
> No one will forget

Some lost their children
And others their home.

Toda La gente corría
Todita despavorida
Sin saber que muchos de ellos
Habían de perder la vida.

Fue una noche muy penosa
Nunca lo podré olvidar
Unos perdieron sus hijos
y otros perdieron su hogar.

Martínez wrote many love songs especially of a lost lover illustrated by *Si Veras Que Triste* (If You Only Knew the Sadness [I Feel]):

Oh if you knew how sad life can be
When a man loses his love.
He will abandon the land of his birth
never more to return.

Look dark one, how sadly I live
Always thinking of your love.
I should never have known you
I haven't the strength to forget you.

Ay si veras que triste es la vida
Cuando el hombre pierde su querer.
Abaondona la tierra donde nase
se va para nunca volver.

Mira negra que triste he vivido
todo el tiempo he pensado en tu amor.
Balía [*sic*] mas no haberte conocido
y olvidarte no tengo valor.

Martínez was more than a picker and composer, he participated in the villagers' patriotic celebrations, and was elected president of the county-wide patriotic committee, serving from 1947 to 1954. An active unionist, Martínez organized the Anaheim citrus picker union local, was jailed during the 1936 strike, and was active in the AF of L affiliated citrus picker local during the poststrike period.

If the family was not off working on a ranch, picking strawberries or chiles, then following Sunday church services, the family devoted the day to recreation, and baseball offered a most popular pastime. Many, if not most, of the villages, proudly followed their local club. During the 1920s, Campo Corona/Colorado, Richfield (Atwood), Anaheim, Placentia, La Jolla, Independencia, and El Modena, to name a few, sported well-organized and highly skilled teams.

Campo Colorado/Corona formed a youth team called Los Juviniles in the early 1920s that remained active throughout the 1930s. According to a 1920s *La Habra Star* article, baseball was the "leading sport at Mexican Camp." The team was self-supporting, purchasing uniforms and equipment from funds raised through Jamaicas. Until the team used the *jamaica* in 1930, it had been solely a religious fund-raising event, and some resistance was encountered. Yet the team members persisted, citing the need for "uniforms and bats and balls" and arguing that they had "to give all of our money to help our fathers support the families."[54] Los Juviniles' *jamaica* successfully raised sufficient moneys to launch a team resplendent in new uniforms and equipment. The team eventually became one of the major Mexican amateur baseball powers in the north county area, at one time boasting 16 back-to-back victories over "Mexican teams from other places in this section."[55] Los Juviniles, like the other village teams, primarily played other Mexican teams in an informal league. Although recognition for the best team was generally forthcoming, no one was crowned champion.

A team manager arranged the games seeking to extend the range of opponents. Generally, the non-Mexican opponents were other minority teams. A Pasadena "colored team" challenged Richfield Nine in April 1923, losing that confrontation with a score nine to six.[56] In that same year the Richfield team defeated a Los Angeles Japanese team, six to nine. The same Pasadena team made its La Habra debut in July, 1931, losing to Los Juviniles, twelve to five.

The Richfield Nine, like Los Juviniles, raised their own funds, as this 1923 news excerpt describes: "A big dance for the benefit of the Richfield-Yorba ball team will be given tomorrow night in the new Richfield dance hall. The Vasquez orchestra will furnish music."[57] New and attractive uniforms were a must for the teams as this 1933 article in the *Plain Dealer* makes clear. "[The Richfield Nine] appeared in their new grey and white uniforms. Manager Ray Ortiz carries a smile of satisfaction when he can arrange such a lineup as yesterday. Peralta, a new arrival, occupied the mound."[58]

One of the powerhouses of the citrus circuit, the Placentia Merchants, was well established by the early 1920s. Over nine hundred cheering fans witnessed a 1933 match pitting the Merchants against Richfield, with Placentia winning, eight to four.[59] By the 1940s, the Merchants continued playing organized baseball and had secured funding from the Placentia Chamber of Commerce. The Placentia Merchants continued to challenge amateur teams from the region during the 1950s—their career spanning more than three decades, testimony to the place baseball enjoyed in the village.

Baseball was a serious concern for the community, a core activity combining entertainment and recreation. The seriousness with which the sport was regarded is illustrated by the practice of stealing good players from one team by another. Some packinghouse-sponsored teams sought particular Mexican players for their teams. The more highly skilled players naturally enjoyed a special popularity in the community, and not a few were scouted by the major leagues. One of the better known graduates of the Mexican citrus teams, Jess Flores of Los Juviniles, enjoyed pitching success for the old Washington Senators in the 1940s.

Flores immigrated as a young child with his family from Guadalajara but grew up in La Habra. Among his achievements he became the first citizen of Mexico to play in the major leagues earning him a permanent place in the Mexican League Hall of Fame.[60]

Boxing was a popular activity for men, but never to the same degree as baseball. Nonetheless boxers from the villages gathered strong local following. Tony Moreno and Urbano Hernández, early boxing successes in Placentia under the management of Ralph Pantuso, fought in small arenas in Santa Ana, Anaheim, and Southgate (Los Angeles County). Moreno started his boxing career in La Jolla, training in garages and backyards, honing his skills to eventually box in Anaheim. By 1929 he had won forty-nine fights in a row, earning matches at the Hollywood Legion Stadium and the Los Angeles Olympic Auditorium. Fans from the Placentia area cheered both Moreno and Hernandez at every match.[61]

Boxing was very much a business endeavor and small halls or abandoned factories provided an arena for a match. At Delhi, an old glass factory became a center of boxing for the central to north county area. Juan Torres promoted regular boxing matches during the 1930s, charging 10 cents admission to cheering throngs. Few boxers were as skilled and as eager as Moreno or Hernandez, and Torres was led to motivate other local youths to box for money, paying two dollars to anyone wanting to perform. Many an unemployed vegetable laborer or citrus picker from the county, grasping the opportunity for a seemingly easy, but actually painful, buck, sought a Torres match.[62]

Handball also had its following and in the village either a commercial handball court, or a large conveniently placed wall, was the scene of weekend matches pitting opponents from local and distant communities. The La Jolla handball court on Gonzalez Street, built and operated by Mr. Ortiz, attracted players from as far away as Los Angeles and Pomona because as a La Jolla resident Lionel Magaña recalls, "at that time handball was very popular." Players and fans went to games scheduled as early as seven on a weekend morning, and betting involved substantial amounts of money. At his La Jolla home Mr. German Venegas made and sold custom-made handballs. The handballs were leather covered much like a baseball and were hard like golf balls. Venegas skillfully made balls either with a hard or soft bounce, depending on which player had ordered.[63]

Each village had its local, or not-too-distant, pool hall. It provided entertainment for the men, a gathering place for a beer or two after work, and a game of pool. Pool halls sold soft drinks, cigarettes, and snacks and in some cases only sold soft drinks.[64] Pool halls also served other recreation needs—card playing for small stakes was a popular pastime partaken in the "pool" (as it was popularly referred to by the residents). Alcoholic consumption, whether at home or in the "pool," occurred most often on weekends, because in the words of a former picker, the men did not have the luxury of missing work or working with hangovers.[65] The pool hall was the final touch as far as the community's entertainment and recreation were concerned. Occasionally a relatively rowdier crowd gathered there, and not infrequently a Saturday night fight broke the evening silence. But the pool hall was as much an element of the community as was the baseball team. Perhaps more so, in that the pool hall was sometimes converted to a dance hall or movie house on Saturday night, or to wedding reception hall on Sunday afternoon and, as mentioned above, even into a funeral parlor.[66] Some pool halls included a single-chair barber shop and a shoe shine parlor—the latter task often assumed by local youngsters working for small change. In chapter 7, we shall see that pool halls, handball courts, and other small business establishments also became the meeting places for unionists during the 1936 strike.

Organized village activity differed in significant ways from that of the urban barrios. Mario García found that in El Paso only a minority of Mexican immigrants participated in "secondary institutions such as mutual societies, Mexican patriotic groups, or Church organizations."[67] In the villages, on the other hand, patriotic and religious celebrations, recreation, Americanization, birth and death constructed community and were communitywide rather than the domain of anonymous sectors. Familiar personages, perhaps a relative, comadre, or foreman led village activities and were therefore more accessible. Community life in the villages included strong doses of family life as well as participation in organized activity.

Over time, social networks beyond the small locales supplied a basis for an extended community consciousness. A partial explanation for the community consciousness extending beyond their village was the general practice of working for more than one packinghouse. Pickers and packers regularly sought work wherever employment possibilities appeared that brought them into contact with distant villagers. This extended the opportunity for villagers from several locales to strike up friendships.

The extended community identity was supported by a pattern of village interaction best described as a loose and informal confederation of hubs and satellites.

During celebrations, the villages of El Modena interacted with Orange; Richfield, La Jolla, and Campo Pomona joined with the Placentia village; Campo Colorado served as the hub for Campo Corona and Campo Altavista; Anaheim's La Palma connected with La Fabrica, and Stanton with Independencia. The general pattern for a particular village to become the acknowledged center of cultural and political activities of an area is apparent. Hubs, however, did not garner all cultural or other activities; satellites sponsored sports, entertainment, religious events, *jamaicas* and more. But what distinguished the center from the periphery appears to have been the patriotic festivals and the staging of the Pastorelas. Both events required a centralization of effort that often necessitated participation from outside the local orbit. Other than the size of the event, hubs generally, but not always, were more convenient for staging patriotic festivities. Placentia and Orange, for example, were commercial centers whereas Stanton or El Modena were isolated rural Mexican communities. Streets in the hub had lighting and were paved and the greater availability of resources such as building materials and electricity separated a hub from a satellite.

The emergence and persistence of the hub-satellite pattern did not create animosity or ill-feeling between villages, probably because the inhabitants considered their community to be wider than the particular village they inhabited. This wider outlook would, in the years to follow, serve as a foundation for unionization and the strike of 1936, and the civil rights organizations of the 1940s.

The remarkable achievements of the villagers testifies to the profound creativity of the largely unlettered settlers, pioneers in the social and economic history of twentieth-century California. Picker community culture and organization—as patriotic and religious celebrations, pastimes, and recreation blended and interacted—inevitably clarified a separate identity for the villagers. In some respects, the community articulated a lifestyle that was entirely separate from that of Anglo-Americans, based on distinct and historically conditioned sets of choices and decisions and often enough choices that led to bicultural permutations. At other points, the communities expressed a political and religious consciousness neither entirely of their own making nor entirely related to their cultural heritage.

In sum, the community experienced a cultural push and pull. Not all of the push emanated from outside, nor all the pull from inside. The pull from inside to retain a national identity reflected more than self-defense by the community in the face of a push from Anglo-American cultural intervention; self-defense was considerably shaped by a Mexican government motivated by domestic and foreign policy concerns that were external to the community's needs and welfare. The chapters that follow examine the cultural push, the determined efforts to transform the culture of the villages' adults and children, through public schooling and Americanization.

Pickers in an Upland, California, citrus ranch, 1929. Courtesy of *California Citrograph*.

Packing oranges in a Placentia packinghouse, 1945. Courtesy of Julia Aguirre.

Grower-sponsored housing for pickers, Ventura County, 1920s. Courtesy of *California Citrograph.*

A typical citrus worker's cabin. Courtesy of *California Citrograph.*

A southern California citrus picker company town, 1920s. Courtesy of *California Citrograph*.

Grower-sponsored housing for a ranch manager, 1918. Courtesy of *California Citrograph*.

The Placentia, California, Junta Patríotica, Mexican Independence Day, 1924. Courtesy of Fred Aguirre.

Mexican Independence Day celebration, Placentia, California, 1924. Courtesy of Fred Aguirre.

The Orange County Comité de Festejos Patrios, with the Independence Day queen and her court in the background, 1941. Courtesy of Emilio Martínez.

Actors in costumes, and adornments, for the Christmas drama Los Pastores, Campo Colorado, La Habra, California, 1934. (From Jessie Hayden, "The La Habra Experiment in Mexican Social Education." M.A. thesis, Claremont College, 1934.)

The Placentia Merchants baseball team, 1937, coached by Tommy Muñoz (front row left). Note cheerleaders in traditional Mexican dress. Courtesy of Fred Aguirre.

Eighth-grade class photo, La Jolla School, La Jolla Village, mid-1930s. Courtesy of Leonel Magaña.

The Placentia Americanization center served the four *colonias* in and near Placentia. Photo taken in 1972. Courtesy of Virginia Carpenter.

Americanization class in a citrus village Americanization center (probably Placentia), 1920s. Courtesy of Fullerton College Library.

IF YOU MUST PASS IN FRONT OF SOMEONE SAY "PARDON ME"

Americanization lesson plan for a class in politeness, 1920s. Courtesy of Fullerton College Library.

Graduation ceremony, La Habra Americanization center, 1921. Courtesy of *California Citrograph*.

Placentia veterans, nucleus of the Placentia chapter of the League of United Latin American Citizens, 1946. Courtesy of Fred Aguirre.

Placentia LULAC president Fred Aguirre awarding a scholarship to an aspiring college student, 1949. Courtesy of Fred Aguirre.

Political cartoon, from the *Latin American*, 1949. Courtesy of Hector Tarango.

· 4 ·

Schooling Village Children

By the time the villages had formed, the socialization process of the United States had long since shifted away from traditional sources—the community, church, family, and apprenticeship training—to a bureaucratic state institution, the public schools providing mass compulsory education. In an emerging industrial society composed of culturally diverse and unequal social and economic actors, public schools were charged with inculcating a common normative value system aimed at creating the conditions for harmonious social relations. To achieve these ends, educators, armed with latest sociological theories, fashioned a schooling process stressing, first, a cultural homogeneity for achieving a politically unified and stable population; and, second, an education incorporating occupational skill training but which would be imparted differentially and hierarchically according to measured learning potentials of students.[1]

The cultural aspect of education in village schools manifested itself through an emphasis upon English instruction. Skill training, on the other hand, emphasized a nonacademic vocational, or industrial, education. Both combined to form the core of the curriculum to be imparted in schools constructed exclusively for Mexican children. Segregated schooling assumed a pedagogical norm that was to endure into the fifties and parallels in remarkable ways the segregation of African Americans across the United States. Indeed industrial, or vocational, education was generally applied to both minority communities and for many of the same reasons, that is, an alleged inability to learn equal to that of the majority population.

Late in the 1919 academic year the La Habra school trustees announced plans for the construction of a school "for the Spanish [sic] children in the south part of town." Initially the school intended to enroll only "small Mexican children," building expansion was expected to occur "as the demand grows."[2] At the beginning of the 1920 school year, the *La Habra Star* proudly announced the opening of the West Side School, where "all the Mexican children can be brought in the one building."[3] The school featured

an assembly room and shower baths and intended to provide a "community center for the Mexicans of the town."[4]

In town after town, the formation of a Mexican community brought with
it the development of separate public schooling facilities similar to La
Habra's. School boards throughout the county, in step with the wave of
Mexican school construction across the southwest, established what they
considered a necessary technique for the effective education of Mexican
children. It was thought that linguistic, cultural, and in the opinion of many,
genetic deficiencies in comparison to Anglo children, mandated separate
schooling systems. By the mid-1920s, the segregated schooling process in
the county expanded, matured and solidified, was manifested in fifteen
exclusively Mexican schools, together enrolling nearly four thousand pupils. All the Mexican schools except one were located in citrus growing
areas of the county.[5]

Theorizing Socioeconomic Distinctions

When elaborating theoretical justifications for separate schools, educators
mirrored popular opinion as well as the economic divisions in society. Their
thinking, a mixture of class consciousness and national consciousness,
engendered a simplistic theory of both potential and supposedly already
realized inferiority. Educators argued that Mexicans displayed few schol-
arly skills, lacked ambition for education, and, in the opinion of one La
Habra Mexican school principal, preferred leisure to work (among their
other deficiencies).[6] Another authority, active in the La Jolla School, wrote
that "Mexicans do not see that the conventional schooling is valuable and
they attend as little as possible."[7] Other negative qualities were thrown in
for good measure, including lack of thrift, propensity to alcoholic consumption, gambling, promiscuity, and acquiescence to "things as they are." On
the other hand, nearly all educators agreed that Mexicans were poetic in
nature, philosophical, artistic, and more adept at handwork than at academic
work. In searching for a plausible explanation for the ascribed positive and
negative characteristics of Mexicans, some educators claimed that genet-
ics was the reason, but during the 1930s the majority held culture as the
contributing factor. In either case, bilingualism was considered an overriding handicap, and whether the child was shorted by nature or by culture,
the potential for learning could only be unleashed by acquiring English and
eliminating the use of Spanish. Moreover, bilingualism was commonly
perceived as a political problem for society as well. Junius Meriam, professor of education at the University of California, Los Angeles, and an
authority on language learning and the Mexican child, contended that bilingualism "usually cloaks, if it does not openly express, a conflict of rac-

es."[8] Consequently, language transition emerged as the first order of education, and for this reason the first two years of segregated instruction were devoted to learning English. Theoretically, once English proficiency had been achieved the ultimate objective, inducing children "to develop tastes, standards, and habits of living readily approved in American life," was imminent.[9]

A variety of methods were employed to arouse in Mexican children an interest in speaking English. Most schools utilized various forms of punishment—spanking, ridicule, and standing in the corner were not uncommon—to stamp out Spanish. "They didn't want us to speak Spanish," recalled a former La Jolla School student, "Teachers warned us, 'I don't want to catch you speaking Spanish.'" Unfortunately, he added, "we couldn't help it. That's all we knew at home. They'd tell us "we're going to send you back to Mexico" because they wanted to scare us that way. . . . That's about all we used to hear. . . . I forced myself to learn English."[10]

Some schools applied a positive approach. The Placentia Baker Street School gave a party each Friday "to every boy and girl who didn't talk Spanish on the school ground" during the previous ten weeks.[11] The Richfield School held an annual "Speak English Campaign." "Americanization" a weekly column, written by Mexican pupils, in the *Placentia Courier,* described the "Campaign": "English should be spoken not only on the school grounds but when in the presence of those who don't understand Spanish. We need to use the English language for business transactions. We live in an English-speaking community and are American citizens. We are trying to be able to learn the English language almost as well as English-speaking boys and girls."[12]

Posters drawn by sixth and seventh graders and placed about the school reminded students to speak (as well as to think) in English. The nearby La Jolla School at all times stressed the "fundamentals with a great deal of emphasis on English and the American way of doing things."[13]

Education for Physical Labor

Beyond learning English, educators perceived a narrow range of educational possibilities for Mexican children. They were not given to abstract theoretical work, or "book learning," but, on the other hand, were highly capable of artistic, artisanal, or other forms of manual work. In emphasizing higher-than-average handwork ability, schooling added another dimension to the curriculum for Mexican children. In so doing, Mexican schools not only emphasized language transition but industrial and vocational subjects as well, training children for menial, physically demanding, and low-paying work. Few educators strayed from the prevalent approach to teaching

Mexican children, yet some differentiation within the ranks surfaced. Sympathetic educators emphasized the Mexican pupils' real or ascribed positive characteristics—usually considered to be an artistic flair, but sometimes the potential, of the supposedly rare Mexican child, to perform as well as the average Anglo-American child. Nevertheless, the majority of educators continued to maintain that the Mexican child held little potential for school achievement beyond vocational subjects. They generally looked upon Mexican culture as a burden eliminating the need for schooling opportunity equal to that of the Anglo child.

The emphasis on industrial education did not escape the public eye, and townspeople overwhelmingly supported it. The *Placentia Courier* editor's weekly column contained bits of news from around the town, and on occasion a piece on the Mexican community appeared in it. The May 23, 1930, column praised and highlighted the thinking of teachers in Mexican schools, and the emphasis of their curriculum, both of which accented "the inherent talent of Mexican children for art work, anything done with the hands."[14] The near-universal conviction that Mexicans had only the outstanding ability to manipulate inanimate objects into works of art led administrators to emphasize basic English, and rudimentary reading, writing, and mathematics, combined with large doses of shop or industrial arts for boys, and home economics for girls.

The La Jolla Mexican school curriculum in many respects exemplified those of the county's schools in general. Although the school operated for several years as a University of California, Los Angeles, experiment in "activity education," its curriculum remained on course with those of other districts. The federally funded experiment, which was initiated by Dr. Junius Meriam in 1930 and directed by him, until it was terminated in 1937, underscored the notion that learning proceeded from practical activity rather than being acquired through drill. Thus mathematics was learned through an activity requiring counting, leading to knowledge of numbers. According to Meriam, the old routines, based on "formality, drill, routine, suppression, [were to be] discarded for freedom, expression and self-activity. . . . The new school organizes itself around the child's intentions and desires to learn."[15] Although the townspeople welcomed the experiment, Mexican villagers were unaware of the nature of the experiment, yet generally receptive to the school as the other villagers in the region were to theirs.

Shortly after the launching of the experiment, Placentia school superintendent Glenn Riddlebarger "outlined plans for the enlarged La Jolla School [and] a course of study particularly designed and suited to Mexican pupils. Every effort would be made to include as much manual training, domestic science, and art work as possible along with music and the required subjects."[16] Within the year teachers throughout southern California became familiar with the La Jolla experiment and many considered it a model school. Theoretically, the Mexican child learned the basics through applied manual shop classes, so that three hours of each day, some 60 percent of instruction time, were devoted to such activities as weaving, basketry, drawing, woodcarving, sewing, cooking, and the like.[17] John Cornelius, a teacher at La Jolla for several years, summarized the La Jolla experiment in a 1941 thesis. The Mexican child, he wrote, was considered ill-adapted to academic learning "of the type common to the American public school."[18]

Termination of the experiment in 1937 brought little change in curricula, although the grades were extended to include the junior high school years. The Board's intent for the new junior high school, constructed exclusively for the children of the Placentia, Atwood, and La Jolla villages, was "to give the boys and girls an opportunity that they have not had heretofore," a "practical training." Course work emphasized shop, agriculture, arts and crafts, vocal and instrumental music, and home economics. The shop courses, aimed at boys, included furniture making, "construction of small buildings, painting, plumbing, electric wiring, sheet metal, automobile repair, and other practical work."[19] Agricultural education covered "planting and caring for a garden or other crops . . . [raising] pigs, chickens, pigeons, rabbits and cattle."[20] Every boy was required to have a project involving "either building and repair of farm structures, poultry, citrus or ordinary motor car repairs [sic]."

Homemaking for girls stressed "dress making, cooking, serving of meals, and other training that can be utilized by students when they enter life." Girls could if they wish choose training "to prepare them for work as maids," or other types of training that accorded to the demands of employers.[21] So general was the instruction that no special training was needed to prepare the teacher of Mexican girls. An Independencia village teacher argued, "any lady teacher who has been reared in a well-ordered family with house work to be done can teach the girls much about the improvement of the Mexican homes."[22] An editorial in the *Placentia Courier* assured readers that the girls "enjoy this type of instruction . . . useful to them after they leave school."[23] The underlying educational theory, continued the editor, is that Mexican children seldom "use formal education to attend college." This being the case it was much more practical to "help them obtain and hold jobs."[24]

Quantity and Quality Distinguishing Anglo-American from Mexican Schools

Distinctions between Mexican and Anglo schools included differences in their physical quality. Mexican schools were considerably inferior, some resembled barns and one was comparable to a chicken coop.[25] The better Mexican schools were of wood-frame construction while the Anglo schools were of brick or block masonry.[26] There was wide variation of land and building values between the La Habra Mexican and Anglo schools. In 1924 the Mexican West Side School enrolled 189 pupils, covered 1.44 acres, and had buildings valued at $28,000. The Anglo Lincoln School enrolled 190, covered 4 acres, and had buildings valued at $80,000.[27] The marked variation was a fact of life, symbolizing the economic and social relations of society in the citrus region.

However, the La Jolla School was an exception to the general run-down condition of village Mexican schools. When first constructed it was, in some respects, as modern, well constructed, and roomy as the Anglo schools of most districts. The school even had an assembly room capable of being converted into a gym, an asset few schools of the region could claim. On the surface, this anomaly is puzzling. Why would a district devote significant funding to a group expected to drop out of school between the eighth and the tenth grade? Mexican students were certainly expected to finish their formal education at the end of junior high school. A former teacher at La Jolla School, Bert Valadez, offered his assessment. The decision to build a school above the average for Mexican schools was partly political on the part of the school board. The strictly segregationist board contended that the Mexican villagers would accept a segregated school more readily if instruction was imparted in a competent plant that had sufficient equipment and grounds.[28] That political ploy was not consistently applied. The La Jolla ex-principal Chester Whitten recalled that as the school population grew

> they moved in all old buildings, all the old wooden shacks that they could move in and although we did get a few of the portable bungalows . . . some of the other schools had them too, but not to the extent that we [the La Jolla School] had them. And if they got rid of the furniture it was shipped down to us. After it didn't look good in the Anglo school, they would ship it down and we had no other say than to take what we were given. I was never glad to have it but we had to use it anyway.[29]

Not all of the villagers accepted the schools; some reacted with dismay and anger. According to the former principal, "many times . . . our youngsters would say to me 'The reason they do it is because we're Mexicans.' The parents felt that way too."[30] Nevertheless, the La Jolla curriculum placed great stress on industrial education, paralleling that of the fourteen Mexican schools of the county. Furthermore, it applied a general policy ending the education of Mexican children at the end of junior high school level.[31]

Not only the physical plant of the schools, but the quality of teachers, their pay level, and their status in the district differed in Mexican and in Anglo schools. Teachers at Mexican schools were usually novices waiting for a promotion to an Anglo school. At La Habra Lincoln and Washington schools, teachers earned an average of $1544 annually, slightly above the Mexican Wilson schoolteachers' salary of $1450 annually.[32] Moreover, within districts professional esteem divided along school lines; teachers at Mexican schools were accorded significantly less respect from their colleagues. Ex-principal Chester Whitten of the La Jolla School remembered that a spirit of inferiority surrounded the Mexican school. District teachers in general considered the Mexican school an anomaly, and although that attitude did not exist within the La Jolla faculty, teachers in Anglo schools thought that Mexican schoolteachers were inferior and that to be assigned to a Mexican school meant a demotion.[33]

It was easier to construct separate schools than to mold a pedagogy to the specifics of the alleged Mexican abilities and intellectual qualities. In pursuit of a separate pedagogy, schoolteachers and administrators shared information, experiences, successes, and proposed and debated measures for the effective resolution of the "Mexican educational problem" in local and countywide meetings. Schoolteachers from Mexican schools bonded into a subgroup, eventually meeting professionally on a regular basis to discuss the education of their pupils.[34] The La Habra Wilson schoolteachers originated "the idea of a Mexican Teaching Group" and upon their initiative the group expanded to include teachers from districts throughout the county. Over sixty teachers from fifteen schools, gathering at La Habra in 1932 for the first intermeetings, listened to educators from across the county. Americanization teacher Druzilla Mackey discussed the purported cultural progress within the villages that she felt had resulted from Americanization. She noted that Mexican homes had become more sanitary and physically appealing, and, she concluded, "They have learned to serve dainty, well-appointed luncheons."[35]

Mrs. Edith Ritter of the Santa Ana schools offered glimpses of her experiences in the Santa Ana Americanization program and from them drew lessons for effective instruction. According to a news reporter present at the proceedings, she described "how she has tried to cultivate a taste for American foods by serving them at lunches. The whole Mexican family never sat down together at a meal, she said . . . so the lunches were good social training. The school savings have formed thrift habits."[36]

Following the presentations, there were discussions among the delegates, concluding with a list of key objectives for the teachers of Mexican children, among them "cleanliness in thought and body," "love for the fine arts," and "train [for] tastes for music, art, shop, dramatics, science."[37] The El Modena district selected to serve as the host for the next meeting. By the mid-1930s, administrators and teachers were meeting regularly to improve technique "especially adapted to the personality of the Mexican child," as the principal of the El Modena Mexican school stated.[38]

The Placentia School District hosted the 1939 conference, which brought more than forty teachers and administrators to the three village schools. Participants observed the organization of schools, curriculum, methods, and actual classroom instruction in the morning. After lunch at the La Jolla cafeteria, three groups formed to discuss issues relevant to their work; a final general conference with the assistant county superintendent recapitulated long-standing thinking on the education of Mexican children.[39]

Not only was the curriculum limited to vocational subjects, junior high was considered the terminal schooling for the vast majority of Mexican children. A general rule, administrators, teachers, and counselors maintained that only an exceptional Mexican was high school material, and for boys exceptional meant proficiency at football and/or vocational subjects, for girls outstanding performance in home economics and for both, English proficiency. Only a handful attended the Anglo high school during the 1920s and 1930s.[40]

Most districts followed a strict segregationist policy, but some sympathetic educators felt that deserving Mexican children merited enrollment in an Anglo school. Principal Treff of Wilson School surveyed the policy of the Mexican school administrators and found that "in some districts . . . only the brighter pupils are permitted to enroll in American schools."[41] In spite of some variation, seldom did a teacher "encourage any Mexican to attend the Anglo school, and they did everything to discourage us," as Placentia's first Mexican American educator explained in reference to the possibility of enrollment of a Mexican student in an Anglo school.[42] Thus, when a handful of Campo Colorado/Corona Mexican children attended the Anglo Lincoln School, authorities monitored the situation "rather carefully," noting in particular, Mexican pupils "home conditions and background before . . . [they were] allowed the privilege of attending Lincoln School."[43] The general attendance rule in every district administering a Mexican school mandated that enrollment in an Anglo school required board approval. Some districts, such as La Habra, Anaheim, and Westminster were flexible (with the conditions noted above), while others, such as Stanton, Magnolia, and Placentia, leaned toward separatism. However, in all other respects, especially regarding their conception of the learning abilities of Mexican children, and in their curricula, uniformity rather than diversity characterized the village schools.

More than conventional instruction took place in the segregated schools, as shower stalls were a common feature in the village school. For the children, the teacher's regular morning inspection often resulted in a shower bath. At Wilson School at Campo Colorado the first activity of the day was the listing on the blackboard of those needing a shower—to the embarrassment of the child. If their clothes were judged too dirty, an emergency loan from the clothing cupboard replaced the offending dress or overalls.

Teachers were not unanimously opposed to all academic instruction, but only little evidence indicates that much beyond vocational course work was given. Schools somewhat differed in their involvement in extracurricular activities, which often were of a community welfare nature. Chester Whitten, principal of the La Jolla School, regularly drove an ill child, with her or his parents, to the county hospital. He formulated a school program that functioned as a community center, so that when formal adult Americanization instruction terminated in 1936, the school provided space for village groups to meet, plan and sponsor fund-raisers. In the evenings, the school offered courses for adults. The course work emphasized, as it had in the past, Americanization and English instruction, and also included shop classes and music courses.[44] On the other hand, the Atwood school appears to have been little interested in community adult education.[45]

Until the Placentia Board of Education took a most unusual step and hired Bert Valadez in 1937, no Mexican American had taught in the county. Because of the lobbying of a YMCA administrator, the board changed hiring policy—signaling a partial shift in attitude—toward the Mexican community. Consequently, the La Jolla School hired Bert Valadez, and, a year or so later, Mary Ann González. The two were indeed privileged and rarities. They were considered by the dominant community to be examples of the "different" Mexican, not to be confused with the uncultured laborer, his family, and neighbors. Valadez recalls that at the time Mexicans were considered to be, and treated as, ignorant,and that most districts recoiled at the thought of hiring a Mexican American teacher.[46] Through back room maneuverings the local YMCA, which was at the time involved in youth work among Mexicans, engineered the hiring. Ms. González attracted townspeople's attention because of her supposed ability "to understand her own people and [her deep] interest in their problems."[47] Mr. Valadez and Ms. González were touted in the local newspaper as role models, as providing a "fine example and an 'inspiration,'" to the pupils of La Jolla School. Evidently their presence assured the board greater success in the realization of the district's objectives vis-a-vis Mexican children. Little of the school's curriculum was changed by their presence. In fact, La Jolla School remained an exclusively Mexican industrial school well into the 1950s.

Extracurricular Emphases

Apart from the marked emphasis on language transition, vocational training, and bathing and clothing inspections, schools performed the regular functions of the Anglo schools. Parent-teacher associations organized athletics, "Public Schools Week," Christmas parties, and parents' nights, plays—all rounded out the schools activities. At the Wilson School, the PTA boasted 100 percent enrollment in the 1930s, but whether or not all mothers participated, most Mexican schools had an active PTA, parents joining (some probably ambivalently) with faculty and administrators in traditional PTA functions.

For one event, the Wilson PTA participated in the first countywide Mexican schoolteachers' meeting in 1932 by cooking and serving "a Spanish dinner" [sic]. A handful of "high school girls from the Mexican camp" served the meal. One of the preparers, Mrs. Pablo Gusman, would, six years later, feel the wrath of the school board when her husband, a school janitor, was fired by the district for supporting the picker strike (see chapter 7). PTAs raised funds for school and community use through a variety of functions such as bazaars and dinners.[48] They funded organizational activities such as Christmas programs, or hosted dinners to raise funds for the needy. From time to time, the organization served as a link between school and parents. On the occasion of a community assembly for discussing school issues, the PTA easily brought the villagers to the community hall or meeting room. Often PTA meetings were opportunities for school principals to address parents on school matters, or to invite guest speakers who generally spoke on themes relating to an aspect of segregated schools, for example, the need for mutual understanding between Anglo and Mexican or the benefits of industrial education.[49] Generally PTA functions were very well attended, dinners for two to three hundred persons were not uncommon and indicates the importance villages placed upon what they considered "their" schools.[50]

Curriculum and extracurricular activities utilized aspects of the national culture of the children. On Mexican patriotic days and during Christmas and Easter, schools incorporated Mexican songs, dances, skits, and oratory that to some degree reflected the culture of the villagers. Quite often the affairs were a chaotic mixture of American, Americanized-Mexican, and Mexican forms. The program of 1937, the Cinco de Mayo celebration at Wilson School, included "Danish Dance of Greeting," "Did You Ever See Lassie," a "Hansel and Gretel Fandango," the Mexican songs *"La Golondrina," "La Paloma,"* and *"Jesucita"* and ended with a Maypole dance. At the Anaheim La Palma Mexican school, a group of county Americanization teachers was entertained by the schools' students. A pastiche of Christmas carols, Mexican traditional songs, and poems in English was capped by a chorus singing "America." There was also an exhibition of pupil art, sewing, and woodwork. The program and exhibition provided teachers with an interesting, if incongruous, testimony to the accomplishments of both students and teachers.[51]

On parents' nights or evenings capping a "School's Week," a school program presented each class's proficiencies. A patriotic exercise traditionally opened the event, followed by examples of the students' expertise in English through skits, poems, and songs. Exhibits of work done in shop, art, and domestic science classes attested further to the peculiar abilities of Mexican children. The 1930 end-of-the-year celebration at the three Placentia Mexican schools corresponded with the region's method of organizing and expressing the school's work. The local paper praised the programs for "splendid art exhibits," dances and plays (some in Mexican costume). A "Spanish playlet" at the Richfield School displayed tumbling acts and a "Toreador" reflected the odd choice of a Spanish theme intended as a Mexican play. At the Placentia Baker Street School, an "exhibit of art work [provided] all . . . an opportunity to see the unusually good work of the Mexican children in the first six grades." The exhibit included posters, block prints, wooden models, and studies in line and technique."[52] The 1931 fete exhibited an "unusually attractive" handwork display featuring articles made in art, home economics, and manual training. Baskets, candy, cookies, towels, pillow cases, aprons, braided rugs, and dresses complimented the usual song, dance, and dramatic presentations on American, Mexican and, by way of mistake, Spanish themes.[53] Similarly, festivals such as May Day were opportunities to display the accomplishments of the teachers as well as the students. The first priority in learning English skills, appears to have dominated the programs. The 1924 Wilson School May Day illustrates: songs, recitations, drills, and processionals all displayed the use of English followed by the usual exhibits of shop and domestic science work.[54]

Educators and popular opinion held the musical and artistic abilities of Mexicans in such high esteem that school children often entertained at civic club meetings. As an example, Wilson School pupils entertained the La Habra Women's Club twice in 1925. Kindergartners sang, danced, and whistled tunes, a "young lad" gave a harmonica solo, and two others danced in costume. A recitation taken from the play Los Pastores by "a lad in costume" was notable for being "very funny"; a chorus sang "The Swallow" followed by two singers accompanied by a guitar.[55]

Achievement

Enrollment reached the 95 percent range—on the whole very satisfactory—but attendance was something different. Families migrated seasonally to different areas, some for local walnut picking, others for Navel harvest to the North, and the remainder for fruit and vegetable picking in the central valleys. Schools recognized and accepted the migration, scheduled the opening and closing of the school year to the seasonal cycle, and in several cases, adjusted the length of the school day during the walnut harvest. The La Habra and Santa Ana school districts, for example, opened their Mexican schools at 7:30 A.M., closing at 12:30 P.M. to allow children to accompany their parents to the groves. The Placentia District Board of Education attendance policy placed employers' labor needs equal with the child's right to an education. Accordingly, in an effort "to cooperate with the walnut growers" the three Mexican schools in the district operated on half-day sessions during the walnut harvest.[56]

The many children arriving for school in October and leaving in May were, according to state law, "student-farmers" and therefore eligible to "privileges" such as "special class hours." In a disingenuous interpretation of the law, State Attorney General U. S. Webb (who advised that segregation of Mexican children was legal and educationally sound) allowed county school superintendents a legal basis for establishing a schedule for individual Mexican students, as well as for a Mexican school as a whole.[57]

Girls not only harvested but also cared for their younger siblings. The size of the family especially affected girls, and in large families they attended school very irregularly. The educational experience of Teresa Vásquez of La Jolla exemplifies the limited schooling of many girls. Each winter her family migrated to Lindsay for the Navel harvest—her father and brothers picked and her mother provided board for pickers. She recalls a difficult youth, "It was hard for me, so many children to help my mother with that I missed a lot of school because I was the oldest."[58] She never graduated from the eighth grade and married as a teenager. "In those days," she recounted, "girls got married young."

Lack of normal school progress considerably handicapped Mexican children, as evidenced by the substantial number of children who repeated grades at La Habra's Wilson School. In the 1930 school year, 41 of 86 district pupils repeating grades were from the Mexican school. The 41 represented nearly a quarter of the Wilson School's enrollment. On the other hand, at the two Anglo schools, less than 6 percent repeated grades.[59] The retention rate dropped to 15 percent in the first six grades in 1932, so that the La Habra district's 1932 official report indicated "there are more Mexicans completing the eighth grade (or intermediate school) than ever before."[60] Yet of 245 pupils enrolled in first through sixth grades, only 13 were in the sixth year compared to 39 in the first. Two years later only 16 pupils attended the sixth grade, while 85 enrolled in the first. The figures remained constant throughout the 1930s, indicating an extremely high dropout rate in the elementary years.

Enrollment figures for both integrated and segregated junior high schools indicate that in junior high school, Mexican students were winnowed from continuing to high school. In 1934, 4,037 Spanish-surnamed students enrolled in the county elementary schools, but only 187 were eighth graders and only 165 attended high school. Of the 165 high school students, 77 were freshman, 48 tenth graders, 25 were eleventh graders, and 15 were seniors.[61] Similarly, less than 1 percent of the La Habra area Mexican children, about 250, enrolled in high school in 1934, and, of the total La Habra Mexican population of about 1500, only 32 completed the eighth grade.[62] Although Mexican children composed over 57 percent of the Placentia district's enrollment in 1936, only 6 out of a class of 48 (14 percent) graduated from the district's high school four years later. In 1940, out of a total 530 enrolled in all grades, a mere 13 graduated from the La Jolla Junior High.[63] Thus, not only were tenth graders a distinct minority among students, but so were elementary school graduates.

The former principal of the La Jolla School, Chester Whitten, offered an explanation for the low number of high school graduates:

[the junior high] was more of a terminal in those days. It was a school, I feel sure, to keep the youngsters out of high school because there were many people in the community, especially the wealthy class, who didn't want this mixing of the races or of the nationalities. I think they created this especially for this purpose and then they bussed children out of Placentia, out of Atwood to our school that could have gone to Valencia High School just as well . . . the leading citizens of our community were among the very people who wanted to maintain this thing.[64]

No wonder, then, that the high school graduate was singled out by the townspeople as the "exceptional" Mexican, and celebrated by editors, Americanizers, and civic groups. When Isabel Martínez graduated from Fullerton High School in 1931, the *Placentia Courier* headlined "the first student of Mexican parentage who has graduated from the high school."[65] Nevertheless, in spite of the excitement, little progress occurred. Six years later the numbers of Placentia students graduating numbered but six, less than 2 percent of Mexican students enrolled in all grades.

Graduation for the few assumed a serious mien for students, parents, and especially the school administrators. But in the same fashion that schooling segmented the curriculum according to nationality, so did administrators differentiate between a Mexican school graduation and an Anglo school graduation. The Placentia School District combined the graduation ceremonies of their three Mexican schools into one large affair, while the Anglo schools had their individual ceremonies. The Anglo schools invited only Anglo commencement speakers, while Mexican schools generally, but not always, had a Mexican American speaker.[66] The program for the Mexican schools underscored the content of instruction exemplified in the 1936 Richfield School program featuring students speaking on homemaking, thrift, culture, citizenship and character—main themes in the education of Mexicans.

Some attempts to encourage Mexican children to continue to high school did appear from time to time, but seldom was this the work of the school district. As exception, the La Habra schools, underscored the value of continuing education by touring Wilson eighth graders through the local high school. On other occasions Anglo high school students were invited to speak to the Wilson School pupils. Americanization supervisor for the Fullerton-La Habra-Placentia area Druzilla Mackey encouraged secondary schooling. At one event observing the 1932 "School Week" in La Habra, Mackey "gave an inspirational talk urging Mexican eighth graders to enter Fullerton High School."[67] Selected role models who appeared on the same program included Isabel Martínez, the first Mexican graduate of Fullerton High; her sister, a Fullerton High student; and a Mexican-American nurse at the Orange County Hospital. Each discussed the advantages gained through the high school diploma.

In keeping with that strategy for change, two other speakers shared the podium during observance of La Habra's Schools Week, one spoke on the necessity for thrift and cleanliness, the other stressed law observance and "complimented the Mexican residents on the low percentage of offenders from the La Habra colony in comparison to other Mexican groups in Orange County."[68] At every turn, even in the snippets of encouragement of education, the Mexican community was reminded of its inadequacies. Such encouragement strongly suggested a dose of medicinal education to overcome those deficiencies. Many educators felt that for Mexicans to be accepted in the Anglo world, they must be raised to the Anglo's cultural level. The cultural divide between the two communities could be closed; but the difference was to be overcome by a cultural change within the Mexican community, a change based ultimately upon a design drafted by the dominant community.

Across the board, Mexican children achieved comparatively poorly in schools. And even when a student was fortunate enough to receive a high school diploma there was no guarantee of employment beyond those occupations limited to the Mexican community. Many a resident of the village remembers the restrictions placed on a graduation certificate if one was a Mexican. In not a few cases, high school graduates picked oranges alongside their lesser educated companions.[69]

In the educator's mind, high school for Mexican children did not imply a freedom to branch into course work beyond vocational arts. "The high school," counseled Wilson School Principal Warren Mendenhall, "can take care of the [Mexican] children who have the ability and are interested in the professional aspects of these vocational courses."[70] In the final analysis, vocational education followed the Mexican student, from kindergarten through, if fortunate, the twelfth grade, maintaining, rather than changing, the social and economic distinction between communities.

Community-sponsored education was offered from time to time in many of the villages; the most prominent case occurred at La Habra's Campo Colorado. Juan Figueroa, a high school student, held classes for elementary school-age children on a voluntary basis in the 1930s. A letter published in the *La Habra Star,* written by a village resident in rebuttal of the local Mexican school principal's allegations of Mexican cultural inferiority, included a description of the enterprise: "Right here in camp, during the summer months, we have a sort of 'summer school' conducted for the benefit of all children, to teach them the fundamentals of the Spanish language. It may be surprising to note that the teacher's services are free. Surely, one that is unselfish enough to do this for nothing must be rewarded for his efforts by knowing that his pupils are learning."[71]

Perhaps the more prevalent form of village education, apart from the cultural activities that had a significant impact on the shared information of the village, were parental attempts to instruct their children. Numerous accounts tell of a childhood learning the rudiments of the Spanish language, Mexican history, or religious doctrine in the home.[72] As noble as these attempts were, they probably left a lesser impression than the education received in the segregated public schools.

Isabel Ruiz, reared in the Manzanillo village in Garden Grove, vividly remembers her father's lessons. Ruiz's father enjoyed the evening hours listening to classical music, reciting poetry or Shakespeare to his children. He emphasized pride in their ancestral past, "the magnificent civilization the Aztecs had. He would tell us that they had engineers, that they had accountants," but then, she recalls, "I would go to a segregated school in the morning."[73]

· 5 ·

Americanizing Village Adults

The frenzy to Americanize the immigrant sweeping across the United States as the nation entered the First World War did not sidestep the Southwest and affected the Mexican immigrant. Americanization programs were based on modern social theories that warned of the potential for political disorder in a hierarchical industrial society.[1] That theory premised that a major threat to order emanated from the immigrants' distinctive national cultures, which allegedly made them susceptible to a class consciousness and radical political action. The prescribed remedy incorporated a cultural transformation as the political antidote that best suited immigrants. Logically then, the course of action dictated a public policy for the elimination of class consciousness and class conflict through eliminating national cultural distinctions. Social theorists were not without some foundation for their claims as the immigrants were most of America's industrial working class and were often involved in strikes resulting in sharp conflict.[2] This is not surprising, since nineteenth-century immigrants and their descendants comprised three-quarters of the population of the industrial Northeast.[3] However, in the southwestern economy, to paraphrase Paul S. Taylor, development meant Mexicans.

Soon after the great influx of Mexican families and their settlement, focused adult Americanization programs were applied to them. State-directed Americanization, with the backing and codirection of private enterprise, civic organizations, and local government, entered into the community experience of the villagers. An examination of the state-sponsored program launched in 1913 to Americanize California's immigrant population illustrates the inclusion of the Mexican population into national political designs. Indeed, the national political matrix significantly affected their cultural history. More than local and regional interests and public policy worked their way into the villages. National efforts to standardize both education and the politicocultural tenor of society, conducted via Americanization, deeply affected the regionally concentrated minority. An analysis of the Americanization ventures in the villages provides insights into the state's continual endeavors to realign the culture, particularly the political culture, of the adult village population (citizen or not) into conformity with the culture of the dominant nationality. Whereas the Americanization programs in the local villages appear unique, in reality they reflected a generalized expression for the eradication of national cultural differentiation across the United States.

Generating Americanization: The Commission of Immigration and Housing

The immediate impetus to dissolve California's cultural heterogeneity stemmed from the Wheatland Riot of 1913, in which two sheriff's deputies and two strikers were killed after what had begun as a peaceful demonstration to protest wretched camp conditions became violent.[4] An alarmed legislature, responding to the demands of the public and employers, established a special state agency, the Commission of Immigration and Housing, to ameliorate the living and working conditions of the state's immigrants. Indeed, the large numbers of foreign-born and second generation in the state (some 50 percent of the population in 1920), the sizable role played by them in the economy, and their appalling living conditions compelled the state to take the lead in promoting improved housing and effective immigrant socialization.

The ameliorative goal behind the housing emphasis rested on the conviction that poor living and working conditions led to discontent, thence to an imagined class consciousness, and finally to political anarchy and rebellion.[5] The maintenance of the social order required the immediate raising of housing standards for immigrants across the state; thus, the commission inspected housing, cited violations, and recommended tenement and labor camp legislation. The commission, as the state authority on housing, claimed to have significantly altered housing conditions and eliminated the original causes for concern. The 1923 commission report found a considerable lessening of the "just grievances of workers" thereby diffusing the "causes of labor unrest and trouble."[6] Whether this was the case was certainly debatable, and ample evidence from the 1930s demonstrates a continuing pattern of wretched conditions in rural labor camps. It appears in retrospect that industries employing Mexican labor took an activist approach toward the commission seeking to work with it and very nearly within it, which may explain the persistence of shoddy housing. For example, the American Latin League, an organization of employers of Mexican labor—representing the citrus, sugar, railroad, and cement industries—regularly conferred with the commission over a range of issues that included labor-management relations, housing, Americanization, and immigration legislation. In most fundamentals, the League and the commission enjoyed cordial relations and most disagreements were resolved through compromise pleasing to both parties.[7]

That matters of wages did not interest the commission (except when illegally withheld) is not surprising, nor is their disinterest in deliberate segregation and restrictive covenants. The origins of immigrant settlements were perceived as the natural consequence of a cultural preference on the part of immigrants to be with their fellow countrymen, reinforced by economic limitations that made low-rent areas attractive.[8] It is within this idea of an inevitable and natural segregating process—a process that in and of itself did not create conditions needing remedy—that the commission sought relief. The commission largely ignored matters of private housing, that is, workers living in their own homes. Thus, the commission excluded from its purview the citrus districts, where many a home was owned or rented by its residents, and where extreme financial limitations compelled the construction of small and often barely hospitable dwellings. Often, the intervention of the city, county, or state affected the quality of housing in a few villages. Although commission agents made a few inspections and noted regulation violations in the Campo Pomona, Campo Colorado, and Bastanchury camps, the housing quality remained fundamentally similar for camp dwellers, renters, and homeowners and changed little over the years. In the El Modena *colonia,* made up of renter shacks, few if any improvements were ever made. On the contrary, conditions worsened with time.[9]

The commission's charge extended beyond housing into the problem of immigrant education—or Americanization. In the view of the commission, not only did poor housing wreak havoc on law and order, the nonacculturated immigrant, one who spoke only his or her native language and remained a noncitizen, similarly posed a substantial threat to political stability. Consequently, the commission established a Department of Immigrant Education within its operation in 1914, and successfully lobbied the passage of the Home Teachers Act of 1915. The act enabled school districts with a large foreign-born population to employ special teachers "whose educational work should lie among the immigrant women." Indeed, Americanization focused on the immigrant women rather than men. The reasoning was simple: privileged males moved freely into an Americanizing atmosphere, while the mother remained isolated behind doors, reproducing a culture and a family neither American nor foreign, and which soon degenerated into disorder and conflict. From this family-based cultural maelstrom emerged delinquency, charity cases, immorality, and class warfare. "Crime among the immigrants," reported the commission, "points back to the un-Americanized mother."[10] Responding to the immediate political hazard similarly required that "American influences would have to reach the home, reach the mother."[11]

Home teachers served as a neighborhood role model, as well as cultural teacher, social worker, and, when necessary, as friend and advisor. However, the purpose of home instruction was the teaching of English, "the most important step in the assimilation of the immigrant."[12] The immigrant's acquisition of English ensured a barrier to "professional agitators" who preyed upon "distrust and disloyalty"[13] that was rooted in a foreign language that sustained a consciousness and loyalty to the mother country. Much of the basis for the commission's objectives rested on a simple theory of political stability, that is, nonacculturated immigrants were threats to the social order. If left to practice his or her own national culture the immigrant would become "a man without a country," vulnerable to labor and political agitators.[14]

The commission extended its mandate beyond housing and education issues and actively intervened in labor disputes involving immigrant workers. Several examples illustrate the commission's commitment to maintaining cooperative labor/capital relations across the state. In a number of instances, the commission sent bilingual agents to settle what were essentially labor/management matters. One action among discontented Slovenian lumber workers resulted in a significant reduction of tension and a return of workers to the mills. In a second such action, an agent "delegated to work among the Spanish-speaking people of the State" was sent at the behest of a "large fruit company . . . interested in preserving a friendly feeling among the Mexicans."[15] The agents' success prompted the company to telegram their appreciation to the commission "for bettering our relations with the Spanish [sic] element" and asked if the said agent could be present "for a part of the fruit season." He instills, continued the telegram, "a friendly sentiment" among the agricultural laborers.[16]

On another occasion, the commission assisted growers to break the labor monopoly of Japanese workers in the Sacramento Delta. Agents advised the growers on the type of camp that would be attractive to American labor; soon new camps, distinct from the "Oriental type," promised, according to the commission's report, "the Americanization of the Oriental Delta district."[17]

The commission served as the cutting edge of Americanization, suggesting programs, forming committees, and coordinating private and public efforts. The California Committee of Public Agencies for Americanization was one such organization, coordinating the State Board of Education, the University of California, and the commission in order to prevent duplication of work. The commission also collaborated with civic and professional groups interested in Americanization, especially the California Federation of Women's Clubs.

The commission found its most willing partner for the Americanization of the Mexican people in the California Fruit Growers Exchange. As in the case of association housing (discussed in chapter 1), the Exchange considered Americanization an insurance toward maintaining a cooperative, efficient, and low cost work force. Thus housing and Americanization emerged as a dual program for integrating the work force more efficiently into the productive process. As in the guidelines elaborated by the commission, Americanization in the citrus camps and villages emphasized the woman. According to George Hodgkin, an official of the California Fruit Growers Exchange, the Americanization of women and the costs for picking labor were directly related. Americanization, he contended, rooted the picker into a healthier and happier atmosphere, attracting and holding them so that he "will think twice before leaving" and simultaneously would "increase the physical and mental capacity of the workers for doing more work."[18] Such education, he contended, would "make the labor camp pay. . . . make it produce the desired workers . . ." and moreover, would serve to "enforce desired standards" among the camp dwellers. Clearly, their economic interests were primary in motivating the California Fruit Growers Exchange's, and its affiliates, expression of support for Americanization. Without Americanization, warned Hodgkin, "there will be a surprisingly small number of good workers."[19]

In some respects Americanization in the citrus areas paralleled the settlement houses of the urban centers. Both, for example, utilized the concept of community service centers that sponsored education, health clinics, consumer awareness, naturalization classes, and recreation. Obvious differences were the rural, small-town, quality of the centers in the citrus region, the direct intervention of employers, and in some villages, notably Campo Colorado and Campo Pomona, the utilization of a resident home teacher as Americanization worker. Further, a single small house, not unlike the homes of the people, built by an association, served as the home for the teacher, and the villages under the supervision of the citrus industry and boards of education assumed a variety of projects, including recreation and social clubs, sewing and cooking classes, English and etiquette instruction, home care and child rearing, drama and festivals, and more.

George Hodgkin, director of the Industrial Relations Department of the Central Exchange, assumed, while leading the campaign for picker housing, the task of convincing the local associations of the need for the Americanization. By the late teens, the California Fruit Growers Exchange eagerly participated in the statewide campaign for Americanization. And when the state legislature contemplated terminating Americanization support in 1923, the Exchange sent a lobbyist to Sacramento to urge the program's continuation.[20] By the late 1920s Americanization reached into practically all the villages of the citrus region, in great measure the California Citrus Growers Exchange can be credited with its widespread implementation.[21]

The first Americanization teacher in the Orange County area, Druzilla Mackey, had several years' experience as a home teacher among Los Angeles Mexican residents when she was recruited in 1919 by George Hodgkin to do similar work among Mexicans in the La Habra Citrus Growers Association "model camp," Campo Colorado.[22] That the Exchange selected Mackey directly was not unusual, it was understood by the state's Department of Immigrant Education that a cooperative venture between employers, school districts, and civic groups was the desired approach to establishing an Americanization program. According to the La Habra school district superintendent, the "impetus that placed the whole program in motion came from the La Habra Citrus Association," furthermore the association, not the school district initially hired Mackey. Under George Hodgkin's guidance, Americanization evolved into a coordinated effort between the Fullerton Union High School District, the La Habra Grammar School District and the La Habra Citrus Association. The cooperative effort, in the words of Druzilla Mackey, was led by the "labor employers."[23]

Americanization teachers engaged key people and groups from the towns in establishing their projects. Of course, the teachers' most important connections were with the growers. From the ranks of the growers came the main political figures shaping public policy in the local and regional arena (with significant impact on the state and national levels). Americanization did not function without their decisive input; for it was a fact that growers' approval was absolutely necessary before initiating programs. Moreover, growers associations partly funded Americanization, and growers commonly served on boards of education administering the programs. Accordingly, Americanization teachers were considered a joint employee of the board and the associations.[24] Thus, when Druzilla Mackey assumed a supervisorial position in 1922 and Eleanor Hazen of Los Angeles replaced her to work at Campo Colorado, the La Habra Board of Education was careful to hire Miss Hazen "providing the La Habra Citrus Association approve her."[25] Americanizers also kept a watchful eye on villages, reporting unusual activities that might not be to the liking of the association. Arletta Kelly, for example, worked the Bastanchury and Campo Pomona villages for many years and part of her task was to "keep closer track of the Mexican residents because that was part of my responsibility to the packinghouse."[26]

The Fullerton Union High School Americanization Department communicated regularly and amicably with the Placentia Orange Growers Association regarding a wide range of matters, including curriculum, activities, and funding. Often the association directors were invited guests at Americanization functions.[27] Thus at one of the first functions at the Campo Colorado Americanization center, a dinner cooked by the village women, the guest list included George B. Hodgkin, and W. C. Roberts, the chief county welfare officer.[28] Americanization practitioners, then, knew who held power and acquiesced to it.

Civic Boosterism and Americanization

In the early years of the Americanization program, the dominant community, especially the growers associations, displayed a steady interest that bordered on boosterism for Americanization. Simultaneous with efforts to establish Mexican settlements, meetings chaired by leading citizens were held to interest the community in, and inform it about the fledgling Americanization program. One such affair, hosted by the La Habra Citrus Association at Fullerton High School, sponsored such guest speakers as the ubiquitous George Hodgkin, Ethel Richardson, assistant state superintendent of education, and C. L. Crumrine, manager of the La Habra Citrus Association. Each spoke warmly of the Americanization work and of the positive changes occurring within the Mexican community. Finally, the speakers agreed, the work at La Habra's Campos Colorado and Corona was a "model" to be emulated across the state. Indeed, George Hodgkin commented that although similar work is being done elsewhere, he had not seen "a camp to equal the one in La Habra."[29] Druzilla Mackey was credited with having created "model" citizens within three years. According to manager Crumrine, much more than model citizens were molded by Mackey's projects, the camp residents became permanent dwellers rather than drifters moving in and out of town. In the view of the growers, Americanization maintained a reliable labor pool. But for the villagers, Americanization distinguished them as an identifiable target for cultural transformation.

Another booster meeting, this one at the Anaheim Elks Club, was attended by two hundred citizens who also listened to Druzilla Mackey recite the successes in Americanizing Mexicans. She buttressed her remarks with slides of the several villages capturing "before-and-after" affects and Americanization influences in the villages. Other speakers expressed the firm belief that "Americanization of the Mexican population would be an important step toward [Anaheim's] advancement."[30] The meeting concluded with a resolution calling for every effort to be made for the Americanization of the villages.

The bandwagon atmosphere snared a wide number of community groups. The Anaheim PTA, in conjunction with the Anaheim High School Americanization Department, sponsored an ambitious weekly lecture series to arouse the public to support Americanization. Eight speakers addressed various issues, one of whom spoke on Mexican national history and the origins of Mexican culture. Another reviewed the attitudes of the Anglo-American majority toward Mexicans and urged a receptive and sympathetic frame of mind. The series was enthusiastically received. From the chamber of commerce, school superintendent, and the county PTA came a chorus of applause.[31]

Despite the surge of public support, the *Anaheim Gazette* reflected considerable public opinion shortly after the booster meetings in an editorial noting that the "state has [a serious problem in] too many Mexicans."[32] The chief of the county's health department, Dr. V. G. Presson, echoed the editorial, contending that only through immigration restriction can the Mexican "situation" be resolved.[33] Further, newspapers freely utilized racial invective in reporting on the Mexican community. If a Mexican allegedly committed a transgression, that person was identified (and highlighted) as "Mex" for the benefit of readers.[34] Newsworthy items were published on a consistent basis that related to Mexican unemployment, welfare, illness and disease, accidents, and law violations. Occasionally articles defended Mexicans from their critics, offering a limited counterbalance to the views that Mexicans were welfare burdens, criminally prone, or lazy. A partial exception to the general discourse was the *Placentia Courier,* which emphasized the achievements of Mexican children in schools. Nevertheless, its editor, Frank Rospow, defended the segregation of Mexican children. His defense was based on the "separate but equal" doctrine. But his belief in racial separation and inequality did not preclude a belief in the need to educate Mexicans to their ability. The *Placentia Courier* thus reported each week on events in the Mexican community, in a column titled "Americanization Notes." The paper also gave sizable positive coverage to the patriotic festivities.

The *La Habra Star* devoted a weekly column to the Mexican communities, generally touting the villages as "different" from other Mexican communities, due according to the editors, to the Americanization program. But more often than not, articles in the citrus belt's newspapers recapitulated prevalent views of the period, buttressing rather than undermining a host of negative myths concerning Mexican intelligence, birth rate, ambition, work ethic, propensity to illness, and violent behavior. The reporter's scales weighed heavily against the potential for equality, as this typical article, which appeared in the *La Habra Star* in November of 1929, demonstrates: "More Mexican storks, bearing brown-skinned infants, skim through the California heavens, swoop down to over-populated Mexican slums each year. Thousands of wee dusky babes are annually deposited in sordid homes where they are none too welcome; soon die as a result of ignorant care, filthy surroundings, improper feeding."[35] The contradiction between articles like the above and those that underscored the achievements of "camp residents," seemingly escaped notice by editors, reporters, and readers.

Moreover, suspicion underlay police-village relations, resulting in several nighttime raids on numerous villages over the years. The raid on Campo Colorado/Corona in January 1928 is illustrative. Seven deputy sheriffs and three local policemen arrived near midnight as part of a "county-wide clean-up" and, without notice or warrants, officers "made a thorough search of the camps, every house being visited."[36] Newspapers reported that "little evidence of unlawful activities of any kind was found," and took the occasion to laud the villages as "a very well behaved place all things considered." Law enforcement—on the other hand, in this case and in every other case reported on, whether they involved Mexicans or not—remained free of published criticism.[37]

Such an outsider's image of the village, simultaneously receptive and rejecting, mirrored the tension the townspeople experienced: they disliked the villagers and distanced themselves socially but Mexicans proved economically indispensable. Within this conflict, Americanization programs became the employers' shield to counter the fears of many that Mexicans were an insoluble racial problem. As long as Mexicans were economically indispensable, Americanization would cleanse them of those undesirable traits the majority found offensive. The consequence of this recognition was the Americanization campaign largely orchestrated by the California Fruit Growers Exchange.

The Americanization Center Program

Through the village center's activities, undesirable Mexican traits were expected to dissolve into the mainstream culture. The director of Americanization in one county school district compared attitudes toward labor of Anglo-Americans and Mexicans, contending that the former were "active and energetic" while a Mexican "wants labor only when he wants it, in amounts and intensity to suit his poetic soul."[38] Louis E. Plummer, superintendent of the Fullerton High School District during Mackey's tenure, staunchly supported Americanization because in his view the persistence of "Little Italys, Little Chinas, Little Mexicos" stifled the development of a "homogeneous people." In particular, the failure of Mexicans to live in a "model way" or as "first class citizens," which was produced by a "hangover of lazy independence" made it imperative that rather than merely learning skills, Mexicans had to learn and live within the fundamental cultural norms of the United States.[39] His perspective summarized much of the Americanization spirit in the larger community.

In the Orange County Americanization effort, Druzilla Mackey was considered the leader in the field. So effective was her work at Campo Colorado/Corona that she was elevated to the Director of Americanization for the Fullerton Union High School District, which covered the La Habra-Fullerton-Placentia area. Her responsibilities expanded from La Habra's Campo Colorado/Corona into the several villages on the Bastanchury Ranch, the Fullerton *colonia,* Campo Pomona, and the three villages in and around Placentia. By the end of the decade Mackey supervised six Americanization centers, which served eight villages, staffed by her and five other teachers, all committed to erasing rather than bridging the cultural gulf that divided the Mexican from the English-speaking community.[40] Independent but parallel undertakings appeared in the surrounding areas of Anaheim's La Palma and La Fabrica, Independencia, Stanton, Orange, Santa Ana, and El Modena, all under the general supervision of the county director of Americanization. During the 1920s, the concentrated effort to socialize the Mexican population, children and adults, brought forward a host of educators dedicated to a specialized professional objective. They in turn formed a special organization of county educators to work among the Mexican population, and within that organization, several smaller groups. The countywide organization met from time to time, but local groups met regularly, discussing problems and issues related to educating and Americanizing the Mexican population.

Americanization did not ignore social assistance for the villagers. Teachers attended many real needs, and some that they only imagined. Aside from English instruction, Americanization teachers taught women modern methods of disease prevention, sanitation, and health care. Americanization centers sponsored free health clinics, offering vaccinations, free general health examinations, and instruction in the care of infants. Modern methods of health care were not always understood by the villagers and was a main focus of center activity. The sympathetic eye of a La Jolla school principal captured the tension between the old and the new. Hospitals were poorly regarded by the villagers, he recalled. "So many times they would not permit their kids to go to a hospital. . . . Once the [county health officials] came and got this boy [infected with TB] . . . it was a free for all fight. The parents were fighting and the officers were fighting. Well, they took the boy anyway. . . . In those days many of the people were very superstitious."[41] Social activities rounded out the program. Centers provided a meeting place for community-organized self-help lodges and groups, religious, and patriotic functions; and they sponsored village clubs and societies.

In fulfilling their mandate, Americanization centers deliberately sought community leadership and organization. The Americanization program was successful to the extent that these centers seized an opportunity to perform social service that the villagers, and especially the women, saw as beneficial and rewarding. As a consequence, Americanization successfully elicited village participation. In 1932, After thirteen years of Americanization effort, Druzilla Mackey happily announced that five hundred adults enrolled at the six centers for courses in "home making, cooking, sewing and gardening, health instruction and care of babies" and English classes.[42] Indeed, learning to read, write and speak English was neither unnecessary nor unwanted. Most villagers had little schooling, nearly half were illiterate, and the center was their first opportunity for formal education. For this chance they were appreciative and eagerly sought to participate in the community centers.

Moreover, for the majority of students, the Americanization teacher was their first sympathetic contact with the English-speaking world. For example, Druzilla Mackey, like her successors Eleanor Hazen and Arletta Kelly, went beyond home teacher duties and settled into a "cottage" where each resided for a substantial period. Mackey so impressed the villagers that they secretly arranged neighborly aid. Neighbors brought milk, eggs, and treated her to daily "delicious" dinners.[43]

Mackey fondly remembered journeying to the Bastanchury villages, where she was "always met with a cordial welcome." From isolated introductions to the women, first one mother then another, Mackey soon coordinated a good deal of the community's social and cultural activities. Even more effectively in the late 1920s she worked with the Commission on Immigration and Housing "to secure better homes" to replace the villagers' hovels and a community hall in part to replace teaching in a village home. Unfortunately, the hall "was much too small to accommodate the audiences assembled for entertainments and community meetings."[44] Nevertheless, within two years the Bastanchury community center sponsored English instruction, lodge meetings, and an orchestra; held community dinners, sewing classes; ran health clinics; and presented dramatic and musical events. The center's centerpiece was the formation of a mutual aid society "for education and social betterment," and which "paid part of the expense of a well-baby clinic."[45] Meanwhile, housekeeping and sanitation habits were being altered, so that, for example, the villagers stored their garbage for weekly collection rather than tossing it in a distant field as they had, and livestock was moved into especially constructed corrals and stables.

In 1924, the Americanization spread from Campo Colorado/Corona and the Bastanchury villages into the Placentia area. In anticipation of a Placentia Americanization center, local Americanization supporters, Mrs. John C. Tuffree and Mrs. Thomas L. McFadden (wives of prominent growers), came before the Board of Directors of the Placentia Mutual Orange Growers Association (PMOG) and, according to the association *Minutes,* "outlined a plan for Americanization work among the local Mexicans."[46] Both the Placentia Orange Growers Association and the Placentia Mutual Orange Growers Association cooperated with the Americanization Department. The PMOG donated $300.00 to the construction of the Americanization center and over the years both associations contributed matching funds to help defray the center's expenses.

The first Americanization classes in Placentia were taught in an abandoned restaurant, which was renovated and cleaned by the villagers in order to provide a place for English instruction. The high school district supplied chairs and a blackboard, the local Round Table Club paid the rent,[47] and Mrs. John Tuffree, head of the Americanization work of the Women's Christian Temperance Union, donated sewing instruction.[48] A community volunteer, Mrs. Clemence Allec Melton (also a growers' wife), "dispensed English across the lunch counter three evenings a week to a full house."[49] A year later, under the leadership of a major grower and political figure, C. C. Chapman, and with the cooperation of three citrus associations and the high school district, a formal Americanization center was built. Much of the labor was furnished by the men of the Placentia village and because of this help the villagers considered the center an integral part of their community.

In due time all the Americanization centers in the region entered into the village organization, culturally and physically. Village residents appropriated the center for numerous community activities, many of which were sponsored through the Americanization program, but many others of which were strictly village affairs—baptism celebrations, wedding parties, patriotic, or religious events, and other celebrations. The Placentia Americanization center emerged as one of the Mexican community's main meeting places, and although the sponsors intended thereby to Americanize the villagers, in many respects the center secured rather than shortened the distance between cultures. Here "classes, dances, parties and patriotic celebrations" were held. When the pickers were not in the groves, they assembled at the center to chat, play cards and pass the time. When working conditions became intolerable workers discussed possible methods to organize for redress of their grievances. Women "came in groups to make quilts and comforters." When particular matters needed sorting out, such as how to purchase a home, the teacher secured a volunteer to lecture on the rudiments of buying a home.[50]

To their credit, the centers often brought entertainment otherwise not easily accessible in the remote villages. Before the era of the "talkies," silent films were popular in the evening at Bastanchury when a "two reel picture of the Essex automobile, showing its manufacturer" was shown to an audience of twenty-eight at the small center in 1923. The same film was shown at Placentia and Campo Pomona.[51] Later that year, the film *Bear Facts* was shown around the circuit.

On other occasions, the centers served as the village assembly hall for consulate-sponsored programs. In the early 1920s, at Campo Pomona consul Garza Leal arranged the showing of two three reel silent films, the first was about the excavations at Teotihuacan, the second about the City of Mexico. The evening was entirely a Mexican affair, rounded out by traditional music on the psalter and guitar, and songs and dances, all by local residents.[52]

English classes were the axis around which the activities of the center orbited, although men and women seldom attended English classes together. Men labored during the day and attended night courses; women accompanied by their children, assisted at afternoon classes. English instruction was functional to their roles in the division of labor. English classes for men were designed to enable them to work more effectively in the groves. Lesson plans emphasized picking functions, thus the men learned the verbs "to pick," "to prune," "to snip," and "to lift"; and the nouns, "scissors," "box," and "gloves." Women, on the other hand, were taught an English that related to their domestic responsibilities, including shopping for staples. In addition, English classes were meant to be a mechanism for eliciting cultural transformations; thus etiquette, table manners, grooming, and house care were taught through English instruction. Whether significant language transformation occurred is not known, but if the language proficiency of the surviving immigrant villagers is any indication of language transition, then little substantial change occurred.

Nevertheless, Anglos' perceptions evolved with the centers' development. Many referred to the local village as "our Mexican camp."[53] Camp entertainments were often attended by civic officials, or representatives of town clubs and societies. In turn, active villagers were invited guests at civic group functions, some performing dances or musical numbers for the assembly. The Americanization center emerged as the locus of social interaction between Spanish- and English-speakers, serving as a social and cultural frontier, one expected to eventually disappear once Americanization truly occurred.

Americanization teachers, then, often organized events with an eye to breaking through the gulf between respective communities. Teachers regularly arranged community entertainment—incorporating skits, songs, instrumentals, poetry—and dances, and townspeople performed on the program. On one such evening at Campo Pomona, the program was divided between villagers and Anglo performers. To cap the evening, the audience sang "America" while "Miss Georgia Bernal impersonated America."[54] On an evening in February 1926, the Fullerton Union High School invited the villagers and the Anglo community to listen to two addresses by Mexican residents, one given in English, the other in Spanish. The first spoke in English on Benito Juarez and was heartily applauded several times. The second addressed the audience in Spanish on Abraham Lincoln and was reported to be "well received."[55] A skit *La Sorpresa de Isadora* by a local dramatic group, La Sociedad Teatral, closed the evening.

Americanization on Display

Throughout the Americanization era the Americanization center was the single most important point for social interaction between dominant and minority communities. The "model" Campo Colorado was held in high esteem by local growers and civic organizations. Every opportunity was taken to open the village to outsiders, especially during village celebrations. Thus the camp's Christmas and patriotic celebrations often had invited guests present to view the Americanization work. During the 1924 Christmas season, Americanization teacher Eleanor Hazen invited "a number of celebrities from Los Angeles and Fullerton" to enjoy an afternoon of tea and a "review of the Christmas program put on by camp talent."[56]

Motoring to the "camp" to view particular Americanization projects occurred frequently. Usually such outings were sponsored by a local women's group or a civic club and coordinated by the Americanization teacher. One example of a widely practiced activity sponsored by the dominant community through the Americanization centers was "Better Homes Week." The event encouraged villagers to beautify their homes through, among other things, lessons on vegetable gardening and flower culture taught in English classes. According to the *La Habra Star* the 1925 campaign "showed decisively the value to the aliens of encouragement in the beautifying of their homes."[57] Contests were held to select the best gardens in the villages, and apparently a spirited competition stirred.

The final activity at the 1928 Atwood Better Homes Week brought an audience of two hundred from both communities to the school auditorium in a common observance. The evening opened with the singing of "My Country 'tis of Thee" and closed with "Home Sweet Home," sung by the Fullerton Union High School Glee Club. The evening's entertainment included musical numbers by the Anglo and Mexican performers. Among the honored guests were the packinghouse manager and the president of the board of the Yorba Linda Foothill Groves Association. The president of the local chamber of commerce "complimented the students for their good work," and a school board member urged a "closer understanding amongst the American people and Mexicans." Americanization teachers Alma Tucker and Druzilla Mackey appealed for "Better Homes in America," and villagers provided translation.

"Better Homes Week," like many functions, offered an opportunity to demonstrate to townspeople the effectiveness of Americanization. Accordingly, open invitations were extended to "the citizens of La Habra and vicinity . . . to inspect some of the pretty homes" during the events.[58] Generally "the citizens" attended such functions only when they were personally invited and accompanied by someone associated with Americanization work. Nevertheless, Americanization workers consistently opened the village doors to the townspeople, and the villagers generally cooperated. Those few Anglo-Americans who circulated through the villages to view a particular event, or perhaps even to march in a religious procession or to deliver a short talk on the 16 de Septiembre, rarely had an opportunity or a reason to return except when invited. The cultural and social gulf separating village and town held firm in spite of the popularity of the center with both villagers and townspeople.

Townspeople held their festivals and celebrations without much thought given to the possible participation of villagers. Annual packinghouse picnics, for example, did not as a rule include pickers. Similarly, town celebrations, such as those for Christmas or Easter, had few, if any, village participants. In the displays of the district associations' annual Valencia fairs, little note was made of the pickers role in the production process; other areas of production, such as the packinghouse, were highlighted instead.[59] The town and the village, although interdependent, were separate communities.

Not surprisingly, when Americanization events were held outside the village, Mexicans commonly did not attend. When Eleanor Hazen decided not to leave La Habra to accept a position in Los Angeles, a dinner hosted by leading growers and civic figures paid tribute to her success in the village. Speakers expressed appreciation for her work, one of whom "paid a compliment to the well-kept appearance of the new camp." Rousing cheers and a final toast celebrating her work closed "a most successful and happy evening."[60] Although the meal consisted of a "four course Spanish [sic] dinner" cooked by a Mrs. Cervantes, and an exhibit of art made by the villages graced the room, no Spanish surname could be found on the guest list. Within the village, usually only invited Anglo guests were present—the majority and minority generally stood well apart in spite of some attempts to bridge the chasm. Many a surviving village resident has not forgotten that in their youth the "Anglos never wanted to have anything to do with us except that we pick their oranges."[61] Such was the nature of the dominant contours in the Mexican and Anglo social relations in the citrus towns.

Nevertheless, several forms of outreach brought village artwork into stores and schools of the town. One such exhibition arranged by Francisco Espana, the highly skilled Campo Colorado artist, and displayed La Habra's Hilbert Department Store, consisted of "dresses, underwear, aprons . . . kimonas, fancy work in table spreads, napkins, etc."; that had been made by students at the Campo Colorado community center. Another on permanent exhibit at the Fullerton High School Department of Americanization Office consisted of posters by village artists. The posters expressed a common theme in Americanization practice, scenes of the village before-and-after Americanization. Another example of village artistry on display as manifestations of Americanization were the exhibits displayed over the years at the county fair. The 1925 fair unveiled wax figures of the Christ child, a dancing girl, a candy vendor, and roses, along with rag dolls that a local newspaper described as having been made with "features and even fingers on the hand" that only Mexicans are able to do.[62] Various first place prizes were awarded to the contributors.

In addition to adult instruction, youth and adult clubs were sponsored and met regularly. At Campo Pomona, La Jolla, and Placentia, The Happy Circle girls clubs were formed, aimed at creating "friendship . . . goodwill," and staging social events as fund-raisers. Placentia women, under the direction of the Americanization teacher, organized "El Club Benificio Mexicano." The club sponsored, among other things, evenings of variety entertainment performed by local amateur musicians, singers, and actors—a small admission fee raised funds to help needy families and individuals in the community.[63]

At Placentia, Independencia, and other villages, the Women's Christian Temperance Union supported and actively participated in Americanization work. At their meetings, WCTU members regularly heard teachers describe their work, as when the county director of Americanization spoke to the membership on the philosophy of Americanization.[64] The WCTU involved itself with the centers directly, as in sponsorship of the "Loyal Temperance Legion in Placentia . . . among the Mexican boys and girls."[65] The Legion, a statewide organization, also utilized the Placentia center for its lecture series. On a December evening in 1929, a Miss Mary Johnson lectured, with stereopticon, on "Fire Eaters" for the Mexican residents of the community.[66] The Protestant mission networked with the WCTU through Reverend J. Raymond Janeway, who was in charge of the local Legion and was pastor of the Placentia Mexican Baptist Mission.[67] An enthusiastic supporter of Americanization, the WCTU established a Department of Americanization under the direction of Mrs. John C. Tuffree. (Earlier Mrs. Tuffree had taught the first English course in Placentia.) Annual essay contests open only to students at Americanization centers were also sponsored by the union.[68]

Villagers who had attended a course regularly were rewarded with certificates of merit at graduation ceremonies. The Campo Colorado/Corona graduation ceremonies were an annual highlight, bringing invited townspeople to observe. At the 1921 ceremony a dozen graduates assembled about a table filled with miniature beds, stoves, and other home items. Each graduate came to the table, picked up an object, and spoke about it in English. Then in unison they sang songs in English, proving to their audience that learning, or, better, Americanization, had in fact taken place. Among the observers were officials of the California Fruit Growers Exchange, local merchants, and the directors of the La Habra Citrus Association.[69]

Americanization centers in Orange County were touted throughout the state as models of the kind, regularly hosting entourages of teachers, students, diplomats, scholars, and state and industrial officials. School teachers earning Americanization certificates awarded by the State Department of Education eagerly made the rounds of the villages, "inspecting homes and gardens" observing classes, usually topped with a meal prepared by a center's students.[70] The Mexican consul appeared as a guest from time to time, sometimes at a special patriotic program sponsored by the center. On other occasions, a Mexican consul brought touring Mexican educators to the Americanization centers, which were generally praised by them. The *La Habra Star* reported a visit to an Americanization center by Carmen Ramos, "a noted writer from Mexico City." According to the article, "she was especially enthusiastic over the facts that the Americanization teachers are not only teaching American history, and the standards of good American citizenship, but they are also endeavoring to preserve the best of the legends and the history of Mexico."[71] Two years later, Dr. Gabino Palma, "a prominent educator from Mexico," visited the Campo Colorado/Corona center. The local newspaper covered the tour, calling attention to Dr. Palma's "deep sense of gratitude in behalf of his countrymen for the educational and social work which is being done for them by the La Habra Citrus Association and the union high school district."[72] That international recognition was spreading to Europe is evidenced by the visit of a "Dr. R. Duncan of the University of Edinburgh, Scotland." The eminent Berkeley economist Paul S. Taylor had informed Duncan of the Orange County program, suggesting a visit as part of Duncan's ongoing research project on "social educational work in the United States."[73]

Separate cultural identities never established an impregnable barrier between the two groups. The strong Mexicanismo seldom, if ever, led to a definition of the Anglo-American as an implacable foe. The Mexican's ethnic identity manifested enough flexibility to accommodate participation in Americanization programs, public schooling, and welcome Anglo-Americans into their villages. Unlike the French-Canadian immigrants in Rhode Island, who held steadfast to French-Canadian culture fifty years after their initial arrival, Mexicans expressed willingness to enter the culture of the Anglo-American world. However, that willingness to accommodate did not imply a desire to abandon the culture of the homeland. The villagers merely stopped short of drawing a line on the cultural sand.

Did Americanization promote a backlash or at least serve to fracture the villagers into conflicting groups? No evidence demonstrating a backlash or internal contentiousness toward Americanization appeared in the interviews or written materials. Both Americanizers and villagers seemed satisfied with the enterprise. Moreover, the consul nodded approval manifested through the customary invitations extended to "leading citizens" from the town to participate in the annual patriotic festivities. Americanization raised no strong village objections, but neither did it stimulate an enduring intercourse between the two communities. Rather, Americanization steadied a social pattern begun when Mexicans were first employed as pickers.

Constrasting Rural and Urban Americanization

Village Americanization differed substantially from similar programs in urban centers, Los Angeles, for example. Los Angeles Mexican immigrants settled into both ethnically homogeneous and heterogeneous settlements. The Watts area contained three distinct barrios alongside a predominantly African American ghetto. On the east and southeast sides of Los Angeles, various immigrant groups including Mexicans rubbed shoulders. The historian Richard Romo noted the cultural tableaux on the eastside: "In addition to becoming the site of the Jewish settlement, Boyle Heights became an immigrant community where Italians, White Russians, Poles and Mexicans lived side by side."[74] In the area known as the Flats, on the eastside, Russian Molokans settled and purchased rental properties and Mexicans became their main renters. Later, Mexicans supplanted the Molokans, a transitional process that was repeated in several areas of Los Angeles such as in Lincoln Heights, where Mexicans replaced Italians during the 1940s.[75] Nevertheless, even in the principal Mexican settlement, the Plaza area near downtown Los Angeles, over twenty ethnic groups comprised the population although Mexicans and Italians formed three-quarters of the population. This ethnic diversity contrasted sharply with the simple ethnic division found in rural settlements: on the one side, Mexicans, and on the other, Anglo-Americans. It is doubtful that a clear cut separation dividing Anglo-American and Mexican immigrant and their contact stood in bold relief as it did in the rural areas. Urban immigrant dwellers, such as the Chicagoans described in the study by Lizabeth Cohen, often interfaced with several intervening layers of ethnic groups before relating directly with the Anglo-American community.[76]

Urban Americanization programs consequently required a nonethnic specific version of that program practiced in rural regions. The concepts of community center, home teacher, neighborhood cottage, English instruction—all components of the Americanization process—were adapted to a multilingual *and* occupationally varied population. Americanization in the cities never focused exclusively on one nationality as was the case in the citrus areas. In Los Angeles, Mexicans, Italians, Russians and others sat alongside one another. The Americanization course at the Twenty-eighth Street School in Los Angeles illustrates this diversity. In 1926, sixty-seven men and women enrolled in the course but they represented eleven different language groups.[77]

There are other distinctions as well which separate the urban from rural Americanization. In the exclusively Mexican sections of Los Angeles the immense size of the largest *colonia* with a population of thirty-five thousand prevented the centers from reaching more than a handful of the community. This contrasts with the rural experience in which the Americanization center was but a short walk away from the whole *colonia* and therefore the programs touched a far greater proportion of the population.

Occupational diversity, greater in the cities, inevitably affected the design of the Americanization program. In Los Angeles, Mexican labor became an "industrial asset," working primarily as common laborers in a wide variety of enterprises including textile, food processing, laundries, cement, construction, masonry, carpentry, glass, furniture, steel, road street repair, and much more.[78] Immigrant education classes at the Maple Avenue School, in the heart of the Mexican *colonia,* reflected that occupational diversity and offered, among others, simple courses in electricity, plumbing, vulcanizing, and welding incorporated into an Americanization goal.[79]

Administration of Americanization differed between the two contexts as well. Americanization in the villages was directly accountable to a specific economic sector: the grower associations, who held the reins of power on the boards of education. In the urban centers, Los Angeles or Pasadena as examples, the local school boards initiated, developed, and supervised Americanization programs within general policy guidelines usually drawn up with the general support of a variety of organizations, including the chambers of commerce, women's clubs, and churches. Urban school boards nevertheless exercised sole authority over the Americanization centers. Americanization in the citrus town, as we have seen, operated within the oversight of the local grower associations. However, unlike the case in the industrial Northeast of the United States, Americanization was not particularly encouraged by the Catholic church. The church preferred a neutral stand and neither opposed nor actively supported Americanization, although it founded missions to serve the villagers exclusively.

Denouement

Over the life of the Americanization centers, a number of organizations cooperatively interacted to sustain and develop the Americanization program. Among them were Protestant churches, the WCTU, women's clubs, growers associations, boards of education, county and state governments, and the Commission of Immigration and Housing. The key connection, and by far the most significant in the promotion of Americanization, came from two sources: the state government, through the Commission of Immigration and Housing, and the citrus industry, through the California Fruit

Exchange and its local affiliates. These two led the way, enlisting the support, or being joined by, other groups along the way. If conflict or contentiousness divided them, no evidence has surfaced in the wide range of materials that document the initiation, development and eventual termination of a concerted program to Americanize Mexican villagers.

However, this cooperation could not sustain the programs, and after thirteen years' effort, Americanization was dealt a debilitating blow by the Depression. Instead of protecting unrestricted entry of Mexican labor, civic groups and county officials saw benefits in the return of Mexicans to Mexico. Rather than adhering to the line that Mexican labor was ideal for picking—and for cheap labor generally—discussion shifted to the viability of employing native American white labor for picking. The proud display of the results of Americanization, the generalized paternal attitude toward the villagers ("our Mexicans"), and the networking among civic groups to support and bolster Americanization dissolved. Americanization centers accepted a new and strange role, no longer would they perform the function of acculturating Mexicans into American society. The centers that had sponsored classes purporting to teach illiterates to read and write, women to purchase economically, and families to live on meager wages assumed a vastly distinct function. Americanization centers, wrote Druzilla Mackey,

> were now used for calling together assemblages in which county welfare workers explained to bewildered audiences that their small jobs would now be taken over by the white men, that they were no longer needed nor wanted in these United States. They explained that the Welfare Department no longer had money to aid them during times of unemployment, but would furnish them a free trip back to Mexico. And so—one morning we saw nine trainloads of our dear friends roll away back to the windowless, dirt-floored homes we had taught them to despise.[80]

In all, two thousand Orange County Mexicans were repatriated. Some one hundred pickers and their families from the Bastanchury Ranch alone, unemployed and homeless, returned to their native land.[81] The depiction of Mexicans as quaint, artistic, simple folk—imbued with a rich history and culture—was overshadowed by a resuscitated image that Mexicans were a financial burden and a social problem. It is interesting to note the attitude of the Mexican government. Rather than critique or oppose the drive to return their compatriots, the consuls acquiesced to it. Local consulate representatives assisted the return, sometimes boarding the trains to accompany the repatriated to the border. Once in Mexico, however, the repatriated were very much on their own, and often endured extreme difficulties. It is said that because of their inability to eke out much of a living in Mexico, many, if not most, returned to the United States.[82] Even the great poverty they experienced in the United States was better than their lives in Mexico—better, even if not by much.

Meanwhile, boards of education scrambled to cut costs and the citrus industry examined its expenditures carefully. Together with the townspeople, they lost faith in the potential of, or the need for, Americanization. In 1932 the Fullerton Union High School Board of Education voted to terminate its Department of Americanization. Although the six centers remained open on a limited schedule, only the supervisor, Druzilla Mackey would officially conduct the program (the Campo Corona/Colorado center remained open and functioning with part-time staff). Scaled down, the Americanization program operated formally for only four more years, when finally Druzilla Mackey resigned because of health problems. No one replaced her, the interest in Americanization had disappeared, engulfed by overriding concern to effectively maintain the economy.[83]

In retrospect, Americanization raised a subtle dividing barrier rather than effecting a lasting integration. Some seventeen years after having been hired by the Exchange, Druzilla Mackey, who was still involved in Americanization in the north county, doubted that anything of lasting value came from Americanization, *"Quien sabe?"* (who knows), she sadly summarized. It is within this strained context, when wages declined to levels preventing "even a Mexican to support a family," that the pickers organized the first large-scale strike to hit the citrus industry.[84] The strike raised to the surface social hostilities that had been untouched and unaffected by Americanization, and heated them to class warfare. The effectiveness of Americanization can be measured upon analysis of the citrus picker's strike of 1936.

· 6 ·

Unionization and
the 1936 Strike

On June 11, 1936, nearly three thousand citrus pickers declared the largest strike ever to affect the industry, disrupting the growers' image of a contented work force.[1] The strike was more than a workers' revolt against employers. The organization of work and society dictated that the employees and their communities as well should take up the workers' cause. Union locals originated from within the community's culture and organization so that many of the union leaders were prominent patriotic committee members as well. Moreover, the union's organizational structure assumed the pattern of the *colonia* system, rather than that of packinghouse employment. The strike, like the cultural life of the village, was a community affair thereby accentuating existing sharp social divisions and submerged hostilities separating the villagers from the dominant community. The grim social reality in the citrus belt—the tragic poverty of life in the villages, and moreover, the political domination over the villagers—appeared in bold relief. Inevitably, the strike assumed ethnic, economic, and cultural dimensions. Class warfare and ethnic rivalry shattered the industrial peace that had long rested on the myth of contented Mexican labor.

Historians have neglected this important strike although it was one of the most violently suppressed in California's intense labor-capital relations of the 1930s.[2] Moreover, according to Stuart Jameison, the strike proved "a turning point in agricultural relations in California," resulting in the resuscitation of the "powerful anti-union Associated Farmers of California."[3] The strike also brought into relief internal picker union struggles between radicals and the conservative consulate. That conflict resulted in a bitter and permanent split between the Mexican labor union, known as CUCOM (or Confederación de Campesinos y Obreros Mexicanos) and the Mexican consulate.

The citrus industry demonstrated a staunch opposition to unions over the years. Sporadic strikes in the 1910s and 1920s, and the growers' determination to control all union activity, indicated a profound incompatibility between labor and the growers.[4] The tumultuous agricultural labor struggles of the early 1930s brought forth a bitter statewide antiunion campaign directed by the Associated Farmers of California. The California Fruit Growers Exchange, more than merely keeping step with that campaign, provided major funding, leadership and policy direction.[5] During the mid-1930s lapse in union activity, the Associated Farmers was largely inactive, creating an offensive vacuum. During the 1936 strike, the Orange County District Exchanges filled that void by reviving the county Associated Farmers and, going one step further, by establishing the Orange County Protective Association, presided over by a Placentia packinghouse manager, J. A. Prizer.[6] The OCPA was modeled on the organization of the district exchanges, each local association elected one representative to the districtwide OCPA. The OCPA looked after the interests of its members principally by hiring guards "to convoy orange pickers to and from the groves during the strike."[7] All legal liabilities incurred by sheriffs, police, highway patrolmen, or any other deputized law enforcement official would be shouldered by the organization rather than any individual or local grower association. The OCPA also acted as the employers' representative in negotiating with the picker's union, and lobbied with local and county governments to pass ordinances, such as antipicketing laws, that were favorable to growers. Finally, the OCPA collaborated with law enforcement, civic officials, and the media, to oppose the union. Four years after the strike the spokesperson for the OCPA, the extremely conservative Stuart Strathman, served as field secretary for the revived Associated Farmers of California. Obviously the citrus pickers of Orange County challenged seasoned veterans of California class warfare.

The dominant community strongly supported the Associated Farmers and the OCPA (both were comprised of the same members).[8] Newspapers, radio, county and city governments, boards of education, and patriotic and civic groups in unison backed the growers. It is clear in retrospect that the battle lines had formed long before the strike was called, long before Mexicans became the predominant picking and packing force. The roots of the conflict run deep in the nature of California agriculture, an enterprise that over the previous century had institutionalized a structured dependence on cheap and exploited foreign labor.[9]

Again the active leadership of the consulate is of critical concern to the analysis. The high profile displayed by Consul Ricardo Hill and his county representative Lucas Lucio must not be discounted. While the vast majority of pickers held the consul in high esteem, contemporary observers and labor activists' analyses indicated a consul acting not entirely in defense of the workers interests, intervening directly in defining union objectives, and ultimately gaining control of union leadership. It is of great importance to weigh the consular contributions to the striker's cause, to ask whether the consul represented the workers interests or the policies of the Mexican government toward labor. The two may not have been identical.

There are indications that the consul operated from an agenda apart from that of the pickers. At the same time that the consul busily engaged in picker union activity, the president of Mexico, Lázaro Cárdenas, broke a railway strike, and the Confederation of Mexican Workers, in protest of Cárdenas's labor policies, called a general strike. The Cárdenas government and that of his postrevolution predecessors instituted corporatist controls over the labor movement and consistently adhered to a policy that no union would be tolerated if their goals and practices fall outside the general political and economic objectives established by the ruling party. Moreover, the Mexican government feared a class-conscious, organized, and independent labor union. A key labor policy enforced by the Cárdenas government (inherited from previous administrations) brought government-sponsored labor unions into the structure of the ruling political party and therefore into the government bureaucracy. Professor Gregg Andrews's compelling study of United States Mexico relations in the 1910–24 period is revealing in this regard. He concludes that the Mexican governments "promoted policies in the 1920s that laid the basis for institutionalizing corporatist controls over the labor movement in the 1930s."[10] The Cárdenas era is better known for its land distribution program, which established *ejidos* (peasant communes), and the nationalization of the oil industry. However, the Cárdenas administration should equally be credited with institutionalizing a highly centralized, authoritarian, one-party state—a unique political organization incorporating workers, peasants, landowners, and the middle to upper classes into a single bureaucratic corporatist system. Cárdenas fashioned a structure that ensured political stability in Mexico but did not fundamentally restructure the agrarian feudal landholding system that had been constructed under Spanish colonialism. Except for extensions of relatively unproductive lands distributed in *ejidos,* the large landholding pattern, the centerpiece of the agrarian economy, remained. The resistance to change by Mexico's agrarian-based economy maintained the utility of a corresponding traditional political culture, one in which the government, ultimately in the person of the president, was accorded the role of protector of the well-being of the individual. The government, or the president, was a powerful *patron* who could be implored to fulfill a personal request, accessible to even the poorest.

That corresponding value system, fostering reliance on the authority of the government patron persisted, to varying degrees, among Mexican immigrants in the United States, a condition that the Mexican government utilized to seek leadership in the Mexican labor movement in the United

States. The possible return of the migrants, who had learned in the United States a political independence that was in contradiction to the political consciousness desired by the Mexican government, could conceivably undermine stability in Mexico. To stave off that possibility, the Mexican government vigorously participated in the California Mexican labor movement. In so doing, the consul and the citrus associations shared similar views, the former toward its political constituency, the latter, toward its work force. Indeed, one is not sure which of the two opposed union radicalism more.

The presence of the consul stimulated, or at least assisted, the formation of unions but simultaneously helped contain the union's political definition. In so doing the Mexican State's intervention via the consul paralleled in remarkable ways the labor policies of the U.S. federal government in the 1930s. The actions of both resulted, on the one hand, in the right of labor to organize, and on the other, the channeling of labor unions onto politically acceptable grounds. In the instant labor-capital conflict, state intervention into Mexican unions occurred largely, if not exclusively, via the representative of the Mexican State. This stands in contrast to the state intervention described by Linda C. Majka and Theo J. Majka, who underscore the role of the U.S. federal government in containing California's agricultural labor movement.[11] However, regardless of whether the United States or Mexico intervened, both aimed at guaranteeing the short-term interests of labor while securing the long-term interests of capital.

Mexican Labor Unionism in the County

The beginning of union activity in the Orange county preceded the citrus strike by several years, when, in 1928, county Mexican laborers participated in the formation of the early labor union, the Confederación de Uniones Obreras Mexicanas (or CUOM). The CUOM founding conference, organized in Los Angeles, brought together delegates representing twenty-three local labor organizations from Los Angeles, Orange, and Riverside counties. Fourteen Orange County delegates attended from the communities of Delhi, El Modena, Buena Park, Orange, La Jolla, Richfield (Atwood), Placentia, Fullerton, and other points.[12]

The CUOM, like Mexican unions formed in later years, featured the active presence of the Mexican consulate. The resolution calling for the formation of the union issued by the Federation of Mexican Societies was signed by eight organizers—one of them F. Alfonso Pesquiera, the Mexican consul. The first CUOM manifesto set forth eight general principles, one of which illustrates the close ties the CUOM held with the Mexican government and the government-controlled union, the Confederación Regional Obrero Mexicano (or CROM). The manifesto proclaimed the need to equalize the rights of Mexican and American workers and "to establish . . . solid relations" with CROM. The document also clearly separated the union from leftist, and in particular, radical "agitators," opting instead to work entirely within the legal framework of the United States. Finally, the manifesto urged a prominent role for the Mexican-consulate-controlled patriotic committees. Ideologically, the union posed no threat to the established institutions of the United States or Mexico, and in many ways it reflected the position of the Mexican government policy towards labor-capital relations.[13]

The Mexican government recognized the inevitability of unions and the right of workers to organize, it did not, however, respect the right to union independence. The legitimate grievances and the just need for an organization of labor brought forth the determined action of the Mexican government to cosponsor CUOM and to participate in a highly visible manner in that organization. Indeed, so close did the newly formed CUOM work with the Mexican government's CROM that the latter's delegate to the convention, Emilio Mujica "did more than observe as he remained in Los Angeles for about a month . . . and helped organize the Mexican unions in southern California."[14] The constitution hammered-out at the first convention included phrases like "class struggle," and "complete liberalization [of the proletariat] from capitalist tyranny" (in much the same demagogic styled language as that used in the documents of government controlled unions and organizations in Mexico).[15] However, closer analysis reveals the fundamentally conservative nature of the organization. The CUOM documents affirm allegiance to the capitalist system and furthermore, a firm respect for the laws of the United States for defining the parameters of union activities.[16]

Neither the leadership nor the rank and file appear to have been concerned over the presence and influence of the consulate and the CROM. On the contrary, between two thousand and three thousand workers joined the CUOM soon after it was founded. The majority of these were seasonal workers in the Los Angeles and Orange county areas. Orange county's presence in that initial drive was impressive—of the twenty affiliated locals, fourteen were in Orange County. However, the effort's success was short-lived. Membership fluctuated according to the availability of seasonal work, and dwindled to two hundred within a year. Scattered locals remained active in various areas in spite of the decline of the CUOM on the eve of the Depression.

The economic collapse of the 1930s decimated the already precarious standard of living of agricultural workers, causing a surge of intense union activity across the state's agricultural regions, where 140 strikes by 127,176 workers continually disrupted production. In 1933 and 1934, the leadership of the Cannery and Agricultural Workers Industrial Union (C&AWIU) made successful inroads among Mexican workers across California, demonstrating that there was, among Mexican labor, a receptivity to leftist organizing. Leftist-led unions were in many cases in the vanguard of the union movement; the consulates remained active but not consistently in a leadership position. Mexican workers were the most active participants in the strikes, invariably affiliating or cooperating with leftist and communist party-led unions. Consequently Mexican labor faced the contradictory ideological principles—on the one side, of the radicals and leftists and, on the other, the conservative and antiradical consulate. Conflicts between the two sides arose at Dinuba, El Monte, Guadalupe, Santa Maria, Oxnard, Tulare, Pomona, and Redlands among other sites.[17] In one instance, that of an impending Imperial Valley strike, growers negotiated an agreement with the consulate-led Union of Mexican Field Workers to undermine the efforts of the C&AWIU. The consul eventually lost leadership, among the rank and file, to the C&AWIU, allowing the latter to lead one of the most violently suppressed strikes in California history. Later, the Mexican consul, encouraged by the growers, organized a Mexican union under the name Asociacion Mexicana del Valle Imperial, soon regaining leadership from the C&AWIU. In great measure the failure of the C&AWIU to maintain organizational leadership in the valley was due to the collusion of the growers and the consulate. Federal mediator General Pelham Glassford observed that the Mexican union organized by the consul was "a company union because it was encouraged by growers who refused jobs to anyone but its members."[18]

Notwithstanding antagonisms between contending leaderships, the "most effective agricultural labor unions . . . were those organized among Mexicans."[19] The major force in this activity was the second Mexican union, the independent Confederación de Uniones y Obreros Mexicanos del Estado de California (CUCOM) founded in Los Angeles and Orange counties in 1933, and by 1934 "claimed as many as 10,000 members."[20] Under the leadership of the IWW-style radical Guillermo Velarde, CUCOM led the most significant agricultural labor struggles of the mid-1930s. CUCOM had no fear of, nor any antagonism toward, the C&AWIU as did the Mexican consul (illustrated by the united front the two unions formed when several hundred Los Angeles county citrus pickers and packing shed workers struck in 1933). The left-wing of the labor movement understandably "placed their main support behind the CUCOM and [through Velarde] ultimately assumed control of it."[21] CUCOM leaders recognized the honor accorded the consul by the immigrant community and the depth of Mexicanismo harbored by the expatriates. To exclude the consul invited alienation of the very workers expected to join the union. On the other hand, the consulate understood well that a Mexican tradition of labor unions including an anarchistic tendency had long existed.[22] Attacking the union broadside could conceivably distance the immigrant community from the consul. The consulate and CUCOM then entered into a delicately balanced united front, although CUCOM generally maintained a measure of independence from consular leadership. The 1936 vegetable worker strike in Los Angeles county illustrates this relationship. Withering police and grower tactics to break the month-long strike by five thousand workers proved fruitless, while CUCOM leadership successfully limited the consul to an intermediary role in ending the strike. We shall see a considerably different relationship in the case of the Orange County citrus picker strike.[23]

CUCOM first appeared in Orange County in 1933, when 125 vegetable workers demanding 30 cents per hour started a spontaneous Laguna Beach strike that then spread throughout the county. Their success attracted attention to CUCOM, leading to the formation of CUCOM locals in several vegetable worker villages, under a county-wide organizational structure led by Esteban Muñiz. Over the next two years, Orange County CUCOM, based in the Delhi village, organized a series of successful strikes in celery, squash, peas and lettuce crops. Not only were Mexican workers involved, in 1935, white and Filipino workers each with their own national unions joined with CUCOM for a month-long strike gaining significant pay increases.

CUCOM's initial county organizing remained limited to vegetable workers, but by 1935 conditions in the citrus groves provoked spontaneous walkouts, accompanied by the usual presentation of a list of grievances. From a small eruption in Villa Park in 1935, the call to organize spread rapidly through the citrus villages. At least one old CUOM local revived while in the majority of villages new CUCOM locals formed. Their natural allies were the existing CUCOM locals of vegetable workers with which the citrus locals immediately affiliated. Mexican labor in the county in 1935–36 stood completely within the ranks of CUCOM.

Picker Grievances

Four institutionalized citrus industry practices, low wages, the bonus system, charges for transportation and equipment, and abusive foremen rallied pickers to the union cause. Much of the conflict revolved around the issue of abusive foremen, most of whom were former pickers living in the same communities as the pickers. The citrus industry preferred to make foremen responsible for the selection of crews rather than to hire a labor contractor to recruit and hire workers independently.[24] The packinghouse manager decided the wage rates, labor standards, and the type of pick; and foremen carried out the manager's policies. A field boss reporting to the packinghouse manager supervised the foremen. Although the packinghouse manager reviewed the foremen's selections, foremen were given wide leeway to choose their crews. Methods of selecting crews were hardly uniform in the industry, foremen could if they wished express preferences for a relative or friend over a stranger, regardless of their abilities. Employment possibilities were frequently sweetened with bribes, gifts, or some satisfactory form of extralegal payment, such as selling jobs to the highest bidder. Personal relations, bribes, the outright selling of jobs, and sometimes extortion were therefore of significance in the selection of the crews.

Wage rate systems and work standards were fairly uniform in the industry, as was the practice of charging the picker for transportation costs to the groves, for equipment (such as sacks, clippers, and gloves), and sometimes for drinking water.[25] Pickers alleged that on many occasions the cost of a day's transportation alone was greater than the amount earned. Several factors easily resulted in a net loss to pickers. Transportation on a foremen's truck was obligatory, and whether the picker used it or not, a charge of 15 cents to 20 cents to his earnings was made nevertheless. Not infrequently groves were worked for only two to three hours or less, due to factors such as moisture, wind, or rain, low orders, a difficult grove to pick, or one that had already been picked nearly bare. In such cases, the picker could become, and often was, indebted to the employer at the end of the day.[26]

Foremen refined other methods of siphoning off pickers' earnings. One was the practice of hiring many more crewmen than were necessary, especially on a day when orders were low, yet charging them the same for transportation reducing already meager wages. Thus if a thousand field boxes was the order for the day and if thirty instead of fifteen or twenty men were hired, the workers' pay was less while the portion owed to the foremen rose proportionately.[27] Foremen received 1 cent per box, whether ten or a hundred men worked, skimming the extra proceeds for transportation, a racket that sorely aggravated pickers. If that was not enough, pickers often charged that filled boxes were often lost to pilfering foremen. Further, foremen were not above extortion, threatening dismissal that a few dollars would prevent. These practices occurred often enough for it to be a major item on the union's grievance list.[28]

Strikers' grievances included more than extortion, bribery, racketeering, transportation, and costs for equipment. A bonus was customarily paid at the end of the season only if the picker worked through to the end of the harvest. If the picker left for better wages elsewhere, the bonus was lost and went to the grower's profits. A kind of indentured labor system prevailed discouraging pickers from seeking employment with other employers. In spite of the loss, pickers frequently left a crew to pick in other areas promising better pay. The seasonal migration to Navel picking fattened the coffers of the growers estimated by pickers at about $20.00 on the average.[29] In such cases the "bonus" returned to the grower a fraction of picker labor uncompensated and directly appropriated by the employer.

Finally, the pay itself, regardless of skimming, insured poverty for the picker's family. A picker did exceedingly well if he earned $15.00 per week, but often earned only $5.00 or less. As noted above, a packer earned, on the average, $423.00 annually and pickers earned somewhat less than that. According to two studies the average family income (including income from spouse and children) varied from $600 to $800 per year.[30] Declining living and working conditions during the Depression finally affected the value that pickers' and the communities' placed on work, and their high esteem for the working person. Some unionists compared the citrus ranch to the southern plantation, contending that they labored more as slaves than as free men.[31] For many villagers, citrus work was antithetical to their deeply ingrained respect for work. In the mid-1930s refusing in an organized fashion to work became more important than accepting work. The high cultural value placed on labor did not apply under these circumstances.

A Preview of 1936

Throughout the citrus era, localized spurts of revolt seemed to characterize the extent of the organization of pickers. The Anaheim CUOM local survived into the 1930s but there is no evidence it held a significant role in the labor force.[32] Small independent negotiations sometimes by an individual, at other times by one or several crews, generally ended without significant implications locally or regionally. This same process emerged during the 1935 harvest in Orange County. However, in this instance the process led to a concerted organization rather than a repetition of separate minor labor-management conflicts having no significance outside the immediate area.

The first stirrings of a citrus picker organization did not appear until 1935 and then only in isolated cases at several scattered points. In late September, throughout October, and into November, the growers fought localized independent stabs at resolving long-standing grievances. At Villa Park a crew of twenty-five were required at one particular grove to haul filled field boxes onto a waiting truck, a distance of one hundred yards, without additional pay. The disgruntled crew demanded a higher rate of pay because the hauling shortened their picking time considerably. Spontaneously, the crew sat out, discussed among themselves courses of action, and from their ranks selected Pablo Alcántar to negotiate with the field boss. The field boss responded that either the crews work at the set rate or get fired. For Alcántar no such choice was offered, he was promptly fired and blacklisted by the Associated Farmers throughout the county.[33]

Shortly thereafter, a strike at the Santiago Hills Orange Grower Association packinghouse did not end well either. Striking workers were met by sheriff's officers who "tried to force them to work"[34] through sheriff patrols and arbitrary stops and searches, causing some of the workers to return. Tensions increased and a mass meeting at the Orange *colonia* gathered 50 strikers plus another 250 concerned supporters. There was one instance when workers' grievances were satisfactorily addressed, the Tustin Hills packinghouse granted workers a ½ cent per box pay increase. The small victory encouraged pickers elsewhere to follow suit in airing their grievances to growers, but rather than negotiate immediately, they retained the county's consulate representative Lucas Lucio to act as spokesperson and negotiator—a role he had first performed eight years earlier in a dispute between vegetable pickers and labor contractors.[35] Early on, Lucio determined that militancy among the workers needed to be checked and channeled. Soon, he was attacking "radicals" and "outside agitators," warning them to stay clear of the deepening conflict.

Inevitably, Mexican consul Ricardo Hill was brought into the dispute, and on October 11 he addressed a mass protest of over 2,000 pickers and their supporters at an Anaheim park, urging them not to strike and, moreover, not to engage in radicalism or violent tactics. He also announced a plan for the organization of a pickers' union and urged negotiation with growers the next season. The consulate had clearly taken a leading position within the county's union movement.

The 1935 situation continued to deteriorate when some 450 pickers struck in the north county area in early November. Mexican villages stirred in this augur of things to come. Eleven El Modena women, led by Herminia Valencia, were reported "in the fields of Orange County attempting to influence" Mexican scabs from the Pomona area to leave their jobs.[36] In spite of the community action, the ten-day-old strike ended, like other incidents, without resolution.

The response from the growers and their supporters was by late October well rehearsed and predictable. The Orange County Farm Bureau issued a resolution requesting the State Farm Bureau to "work for the dismissal of any foreign representative [that is, the Mexican consul] who attempts to incite trouble among workers in the United States."[37] Stuart Strathman, a Placentia packinghouse manager and an activist in the county Associated Farmers, was selected by the county growers association as their representative in labor disputes issued detailed statements to the press. Strathman's prepared releases consistently ignored workers' legitimate grievances; moreover, from the associations' perspective growers not only paid well, but cannot possibly pay more. "No justification," argued Strathman, "can be found for the attempted strikes from the standpoint of workers' pay."[38] Moreover, he would continually reiterate the theme that growers would never negotiate with a union, especially one allegedly led by communists. Meanwhile, the county sheriff provided assurances that he would send in armed guards when requested. And journalists reflected the growers' opinions of each picker disturbance, labeling strikers reds and outside agitators. The 1935 picking season ended with ominous warnings of future labor conflict. Not one picker grievance was resolved. Growers responded with dismissals, blacklists, the threat of force, outright refusal to negotiate, and accusations of communist influence.

A revolt simmering beneath the surface gathered force in the off-season. By then the presence of the Mexican consul, in the person of his representative Lucas Lucio, in the emerging picker rebellion was crystallizing. Still, the pickers' daily more obvious militant attitude alarmed Lucio, who consistently espoused negotiation over striking, warning workers to utilize only legal and accepted methods to realize their objectives. At one point Lucio spoke over a Spanish-language radio broadcast, cautioning pickers to stay within the legal process.

The pickers' spontaneous and individualized actions soon merged into a unified course of action. From the scattered defeats of 1935, the citrus picker union was born—shortly to be baptized in the fire of the citrus industry.

Organizing the Strike

The spark to organize was limited by the dispersed settlement pattern and by the seasonal nature of picking. Many pickers migrated or worked in neighboring counties during the off-season, and this presented a formidable hurdle to organization. The year before, CUCOM representatives, accompanied by the consul, had approached the pickers, offering to assist them in forming a union. Shortly before the season began, a mass meeting at Orange elected Celso Medina of El Modena a chief organizer for a countywide pickers union to be affiliated with CUCOM. With a clear mandate, the proconsul Medina assumed the task of organizing a union from the ground up.

Medina, accompanied by either Guillermo Velarde, Esteban Muñiz, Consul Hill, or Nicolás Avila (a CUCOM organizer), "stumped" the county in a rusted worn-out Dodge, visiting each picker village. Flyers crafted on a donated mimeograph, calling for union meetings were handed out in pool halls, homes, or on street corners. Medina and his companions delivered an impassioned call to organize, which was enthusiastically received by assembled workers and their families. The times were right to call for a

union. Within several weeks each of the fourteen villages had elected its
union representative. The isolated villages previously connected only
through informal links and the consulate's *comisiones,* now shared a common worker cause.

During the organization process attempts to negotiate a settlement proceeded. At this early point in the developing storm, Lucio was placed somewhat into the background while the radical Velarde and the moderate Muñiz
shared negotiations. The union boiled down their negotiating agenda to
union recognition; the termination of the bonus system; the termination of
transportation and equipment costs to pickers; a base pay increase from 27
cents per hour to 40 cents and 7 cents per box over the minimum of 30;
and the termination of foremen abuses and the firing of twenty-three abusive foremen.[39]

The first union petition submitted to the growers was signed by Velarde,
representing the CUCOM Executive Committee; Lillian Monroe, head of
the State Council of the newly formed Federation of Agricultural Unions
of America (a loose front of national minorities and native American agricultural unions), and by the moderate Muñiz, head of the Orange County
CUCOM federation. Both Velarde and Monroe were acknowledged radicals, the former from the IWW tradition, and Monroe an ex-member of the
Communist party. This situation prevailed in March of 1936, a month before the harvest. Leadership, however, was far from having decided how
to proceed.

Meanwhile, the consul began a "harder line" toward radicals, advising
workers not "to mingle with any un-American groups."[40] For several years,
Lucio had busied himself with publishing *El Nuevo Mundo,* a publication
that proclaimed the consulate line and was delivered weekly to each of the
villages. Lucio used the newspaper to reiterate the danger of radicalism,
urging workers to reject radical leadership, urging negotiation mediated by
federal agencies. The contention of forces had not created a serious rupture in the ranks, but cracks were appearing.[41] A second petition was prepared in late April, this time signed only by Velarde and Muñiz and, in a
significant move, delivered by Lucio and Muñiz. Growers responded neg-
atively to both petitions.

Two tendencies had by then emerged in the ranks of labor. The dominant wing, conservative and antiradical, operated under the leadership of
the consul and his representative Lucio. The second faction, militant and
radical, or at least sympathetic to radical doctrines, challenged the conservatives. The radicals and their sympathizers appear not to have a dominant
leader within their ranks, although various elements consistently espousing a harder line at union meetings generally supported Guillermo Velarde.
The political divisions in the pickers union, a continuation of the nearly
decade long power struggle between the conservative consulate and mili-

tant union leaders, would eventually share center stage with the struggle between the union and the growers.[42]

The unions' first two calls for the growers to negotiate with them fell on deaf ears. Instead of listening, the growers stepped up their red-scare tactics, accusing the unions of communist tendencies and "beef squad" tactics. Strathman warned citizens that the American way of life, private property, and the means of livelihood of the growers of Orange County were dangerously threatened. By early June, when a strike appeared unavoidable, the "red-scare" proved successful, bringing responses from several quarters including an "emergency call to all American Legion and Veterans of Foreign War members of Anaheim to organize for the protection of life and property." At a meeting arranged by the county sheriff, forty-two patriotic veterans met at Anaheim on June 10, promising their full cooperation to police and sheriff's officers.[43]

Sheriff Logan Jackson (himself a citrus rancher) assured the growers and the citizenry that preparations were being made to maintain "life and property" in the event of a strike. Sheriff Jackson warned the union that he would strictly enforce the law and was prepared to "call 500 special deputies into action at a moment's notice."[44] In a show of force immediately preceding the strike, citrus pickers throughout the county were "escorted to and from work." "We are patrolling the settlements where the pickers reside" commented the Sheriff, "only to protect the pickers who wish to work and to live quietly."[45] Local police patrols also rode through the villages taking stock of any union or unionlike activity. On June 10, officers questioned assembling pickers and truck drivers in the early dawn, and reported El Modena "all quiet and OK" and "no talk of or sign of apparent strike." Sheriff's deputies also patrolled the packinghouses in Anaheim and "then to the La Jolla Mexican camp where they escorted pickers to their work . . . reporting no agitators."[46]

The call to strike did not materialize until six weeks into the 1936 season. The two months of off-season organizing clearly were not sufficient to construct a solid union, but workers, in desperate straits, and incensed at the past defeats, were in no mood to continue working. The unanimous feeling for a strike could not be restrained. Efforts by the union to negotiate through two petitions, presented in April and May, had failed, leaving the bitter and wounded union membership no other alternative than to strike. The call to strike was announced on June 11. Flyers handed out in *colonias* throughout the county to announce the strike call read: "Strike Fellow Workmen! The moment has arrived . . . For some time our complaints . . . have not been given a dignified answer. This has to have an end and the end is the strike."[47] A strike committee composed of ten members assumed leadership. Jesús Caldera, a radical sympathizer, was elected to head the strike committee. Each committee member assumed responsibility for a particular strike operation. Among other responsibilities, a head of patrols received information on scabs and sent pickets to rout them; a press secretary issued news and information to newspapers and radio; and a treasurer secured donations and collections from individuals, groups, and unions.

Reports vary as to the number of pickers who refused to work. Strathman reported 750 (itself a fairly small number), but Celso Medina, the union's organizer, recalls that no one except scabbing foremen broke the picket lines.[48] Throughout the strike Strathman would say the strike was ineffective, that strikers were a minority and failed to cut production. Yet a former foreman at the Placentia Orange Growers Association, Joe Raya, testified that the strike cut deeply into production at a tremendous loss to the growers, a fact the association never publicly acknowledged.[49] Several days into the strike the Placentia Orange Growers Association recorded a sharp decline in boxes picked, from a prestrike level approximately seven thousand per day to thirty-three hundred.[50] And several former packers recalled that their work was sharply curtailed during the strike. "There weren't any oranges," they said.[51]

Strathman, the sheriff's department, the police departments, and newspapers continually depicted the union as infested by radicals and teeming with outside agitators. The ever-present Lucio and the consul responded to the allegations by issuing statements that radicals were persona non grata to the union cause, and that radicals were eliminated from the leadership whenever possible.[52] As a consequence of Lucio and the consul's position, Guillermo Velarde had to struggle to gain a leading role in the union and influence its strategy. He encountered both willing unionists, and conservatives under the influence of the consul and Lucio. Ultimately, Velarde and his radical colleagues, Lillian Monroe and José Espinoza, did provide leadership to some members of the strike committee, most notably to Jesús Caldera, the head of the committee. Pablo Alcántar, "head of patrols" on the strike committee, recalled that Velarde and Monroe gave solid advice concerning picketing the groves and tactics in general. Alcantar credited Velarde with helping to design the union's antiscab tactics, and with offering useful suggestions such as, for example, that no union orders for demonstrations or picketing be put in writing.[53] Velarde participated on a limited basis throughout the strike, given that Los Angeles was his primary residence. Nevertheless he rented a room near the Orange strike headquarters, where he resided on weekends.

Growers had prepared for an eventual strike, planning to hire Mexican laborers from Los Angeles and Riverside counties, luring them by doubling the per-box pay rate.[54] Scabs were trucked in each morning and transported back at the end of the day under police protection. At least one federal agency cooperated with growers, the National Re-employment Service under the Department of Labor, furnishing an estimated 100 to 150 strike breakers. The local administrator justified sending workers to the packing-houses, contending "there is no strike."[55] Growers also recruited high school and junior college students. Boards of Education and school administrators cooperated by permitting flyers and posters in school buildings advertising employment on the ranches.[56] One newspaper reported "scores of youth . . . taking the place of pickers," and "schools are being contacted throughout the county 'to save the citrus crop.' "[57] Extensive advertising and recruitment resulted in a work force with extremely wide variation in ability, from experienced scabs to young bumbling novices. The latter never performed satisfactorily, picking good and bad fruit indiscriminately and often injuring the good. Yet the fact that they were widely employed testified to the sharp drop in the number of Mexican pickers.[58]

Law Enforcement Used to Defeat the Union

It was the head of patrol's responsibility to identify groves being scabbed and to send out crews of pickets either to convince or force the scabs to drop their equipment and join the strike. On June 12, the second day of the strike, newspapers reported "numerous Mexicans . . . urging pickers to leave their jobs." Sheriff Jackson reacted to the deployment of unionists with a counterstrategy dividing the county into three semimilitary zones, "each with sub-divisions for efficient patrolling . . . furnishing escorts of workers to and from the orchards."[59] Twenty highway patrolmen, veterans of the violent Imperial Valley labor strikes, responded to Sheriff Jackson's requests for reinforcements and assigned to patrolling the groves. In addition "two movable police radio sets" were secretly installed, and "100 special deputies on duty guarding workers in the orchards [increased] to nearly 200 by the end of the strike."[60]

The Sheriff procured a large-scale map of the citrus areas, which identified the location of the groves. Daily he pinpointed each grove being picked, the exact location of radio patrol cars, and the areas of striker activity. The militaristic deployment of forces had an effect on both sides, assuring growers of support by force, and as well demonstrating to the strikers that they were facing a determined, armed, and technologically advanced opponent.[61]

Obviously, Jackson did not design a neutral strategy. The *Los Angeles Times* reported that "plans were mapped out for controlling the situation" during meetings between packinghouse managers, Sheriff Jackson, and the District Attorney's office.[62] The *Orange Daily News* revealed an ongoing coordination between growers and law enforcement, reporting weekly meetings between Sheriff Jackson, Highway Patrol Captain Henry C.

Mecham, and packinghouse managers of the Orange County Fruit Exchange.[63] Whenever possible, the sheriff attended packinghouse meetings to discuss the strike situation "generally assuring them of his full cooperation."[64] Sheriff's deputies and police officers made daily and nightly rounds of the villages, submitting reports to the growers and noting all unusual activities.[65] That strategy included spies at the nightly union meetings held at each of the villages, tipping off authorities and growers of striker's plans. When spying and counterstrategies appeared not to work, outright threats of arrest or bodily harm were selectively applied.[66]

Notwithstanding the firepower mustered by the growers, the strike continued, with picketing the order of the day. On June 14, two hundred women in the Anaheim area took up positions on the village street corners where crews assembled, stopping trucks and crying out to the scabs that "if they insisted on working their homes would be burned and they would be beaten up."[67] The *Fullerton Daily Tribune* reported "women working in gangs throughout the county sought to keep pickers who wished to work from entering the orchards." Twenty officers were dispatched to "quell the disturbance led by the women."[68] Meanwhile, gangs of pickets appeared in the Brea and other areas of the county. Police patrols rode through eight villages on the night of June 18, "finding all quiet." Daytime picketing by numerous small groups of men and women "continued regularly . . . chiefly in the Mexican colonies."[69]

Growers gradually raised the level of suppression. Immigration authorities announced inquiries into the legal status of strikers and stated that any found to be illegally residing in the United States would be deported.[70] In addition, as early as June 12 unionists at Campo Pomona were told to vacate the premises. Later in the strike some fifty families would be evicted from Campo Colorado, the model camp of the citrus industry.[71] In spite of all of the threats, agitation, and potential for violence; relative calm characterized the first few weeks of the strike. Newspaper headlines reemphasized what Strathman had been saying all along—there was neither union nor strike, consequently there would be no negotiation.[72]

Nevertheless, support for the strikers came from all sides. CUCOM, of course, pledged its full support to its Orange County comrades, and Mexican organizations throughout southern California collected funds for striker's families and sent volunteer pickets.[73] Local Mexican store owners donated food and extended credit, and unions in the region collected food, clothing, and other items for the strikers and their families.[74] Rallies at the Los Angeles Placita (the heart of the Mexican district) and fund-raisers at private homes and union locals raised cash donations.

Pledges of support also arrived from Mexico's labor central, the Confederación de Trabajadores Mexicanos (at the time engaged in a national strike against Cardenas' labor policies). Union president Lombardo Toledano sent representatives to investigate "persecution and injustices" against pickers.[75] The Los Angeles Communist party's International Labor Defense organization announced its complete cooperation for the legal protection of arrested strikers. The American Federation of Labor and the California State Federation of Labor extended organizational support. Fred West, vice president of the state federation, "called upon trade unionists and sympathisers to support" the union cause, and visited the county to assess the situation firsthand (where he was promptly arrested for "vagrancy").[76]

Union songs captured the swirling intensity of the period. Emilio Martínez, arrested for picketing, composed the "Corrido de la Huelga" in the county jail, and the song proved quite popular at rallies and picket lines. Its lyrics proclaim:

> Good-bye, California, Good-bye
> state of flowers
> Long-live the unionists
> death to the scabs.
>
> . . . .
>
> Much has been said these days
> that the strikers are communists
> don't believe what they say
> these are phrases of the capitalists.[77]
>
> Adiós, California, Adiós
> el estado de las flores
> Que vivan los unionistas
> y que mueren los esquiroles.
>
> . . . .
>
> Mucho, mucho se ha dicho estos días
> que estos muchachos son comunistas
> no se crean de lo que dicen
> son frases de los capitalistas.

Notwithstanding the forces arrayed, a stalemate emerged at the end of June—the union seemed to drift rather than lead the growers to the bargaining table. Anger, resentment, and talk of stronger tactics filled the air. Militants, grasping the opportunity, put forward a more vigorous strategy. Reports filtered out of strikers "advocating violence," and in fact, sporadic spontaneous acts of violence did occur. The younger tough unionists, the "muchachos," assumed the call for such duty. Sometimes their activities included smashing scab crew cars, or stoning scabs being transported to the groves. At Campo Colorado some sixty pickets ambushed a "truck load of Mexican orange pickers . . . injuring two men and severely damaging the truck."[78] At Anaheim, a scab found his "car windows and windshield smashed." Gangs of pickets did more than harass scabs, entering the groves to chase and beat pickers or overturn filled boxes. Increased incidence of beatings or threats of beatings from around the county alarmed growers. Immediately Sheriff Jackson deputized 170 additional officers (generally growers or their employees) who, in his words, "will protect, to the limit, every picking crew and packinghouse in the county."[79] Strathman was close to pushing the panic button, describing the emerging situation "no longer a strike . . . but a 'warfare' waged by agitators."[80]

Meanwhile Lucio busily promoted an antiradical union image, exhorting workers to refrain from strong-arm tactics. At one point Lucio arbitrarily eliminated union recognition from the list of union demands, the single most important union objective, and the critical issue for growers. Lucio made explicit the existence of arbitrary consular intervention when he publicly announced "the chief trouble was favoritism shown by field bosses."[81] Lucio proposed a different goal, the amelioration of harsh working conditions and higher pay, the union reduced to a secondary concern. That maneuver by Lucio alarmed many unionists eliciting a correction reported in the *Santa Ana Register.* While Lucio's "chief complaint is against the 'racketeering' system," stated the strike update, "a striker's committee, following a meeting in Orange, attended by scores of Mexicans, said that was not the only objection . . . [union] recognition [is] also wanted."[82]

Law enforcement let it be widely known that they planned "wholesale arrests of citrus strike agitators who violate technical provisions of the state traffic laws."[83] This was not an idle threat. Trumped-up arrests for vagrancy, driving without proper ID, or on the wrong side of the road, jaywalking, disturbing the peace, and drunkenness, harassed and temporarily deterred not only the pickets but all villagers as well. Any union activity, peaceful, legal, or otherwise, became pretext for detention. This is illustrated by the apprehension and detention of five Anaheim unionists for soliciting donations for the strike fund.[84] One unionist recalls that "the strike was difficult for the workers because they had to fight the bosses and the authorities—the police, the sheriff—and many of us were afraid to leave our homes. As for me the only action I got involved in was to drive my car to Los Angeles and bring back bread and groceries. I was never caught but had I, I would have been beaten; many were beaten."[85]

Not a few of those arrested on flimsy charges were handed out stiff sentences, as happened to pickets Virginia Torres of Placentia and Epifania Marques of La Jolla, sentenced to the county jail for sixty and thirty days, respectively, for "disturbing the peace."[86] During the course of the strike, four hundred men and women were arrested, almost all on the vaguest of charges. Clemente Hernández was stopped for a broken taillight, the car searched, and officers "uncovered" a tire-iron, which was confiscated as an illegal weapon.[87] Like many of those arrested, he remained in jail a month before being brought to trial. On the evening of June 27, twelve men were arrested, most for not having proper ID. Luis Valencia of La Jolla, for example, had no driver's license and was arrested and sentenced to thirty days. Andrew Leos of Anaheim and Merced Torres of Anaheim were similarly charged, both were handed $500.00 bails by the court.

Arbitrary questioning and searches, usually followed by an arrest if they inadvertently offered the slightest hint of "suspicious" behavior, affected all Mexicans, unionist or not. Many pickers and their supporters thought the extended mass jailing with enormous bails was a version of hostage taking. Families went without means of support while fathers and husbands languished in the county jail. As it turned out, jailed strikers were not released until the strike ended. The exaggerated bails for minor violations (most of which were trumped-up) were used as a leverage to break the strike.

Newspaper reports of nightly union meetings in the villages appeared regularly throughout the strike. California highway patrolmen, sheriff's deputies, police, and paid spies kept track of union meetings, participants at the meetings, their residence, and their relationship to the union. One news report illustrates the objectives of surveillance and the continual mention of "outsiders" and "agitators": "Last night a striker's meeting in Orange with the 'striker's committee' was reported to have brought 1000 Mexicans out. A complete checkup of all parked cars in the vicinity of the meeting place on North Cypress Street by California Highway patrolmen, revealed license plates from a score of places outside of the county and it was believed these plates were registered to some of the allegedly imported agitators.[88] And at another union meeting held that same evening at Campo Corona, Sheriff Jackson "made a check to determine how many of 27 Mexicans present were aliens." Given his objectives, the endeavor was productive. He reported "all but one were never naturalized," a fact well known and perfectly acceptable during periods of labor peace, but brought to the public's attention during the strike.[89]

Peace officers and growers representative Stuart Strathman adhered to a specious and narrow characterization of the strike. Accordingly, they alleged that the union, led by reds, outsiders, and aliens, tricked or forced the rank and file, "who don't even know what the strike is about" into a strike.[90] In a sharp reversal of attitude concerning Mexican villagers, authorities often portrayed strikers in stereotypical terms: "armed with knives" was a favorite line for describing pickets.[91] Not surprisingly, Santa Ana merchants were contacted by that city's police chief and were requested not to sell ammunition "to any Mexicans during . . . the strike."[92] Images of a Mexican revolutionary army engaged the imagination of some authorities, prompting Strathman to characterize union leadership as Cárdenas's followers, "staging something of a revolution right here in Orange County."[93] Such talk and actions no doubt alarmed the dominant community, serving to alienate public discussion from the substance of worker grievances.

With tensions and violence rising, the Consul made an attempt to separate the consulate from the violent confrontations. In late June, Hill declared that he and Lucas "no longer have any connection with the strike in any way and will not be responsible for any violence in the future."[94] He ascribed the violence to "communists or persons of similar ilk." Lucas Lucio similarly alleged that outsiders gathered a following among local Mexicans and were responsible for the violence.[95] Their disclaimers, however, did not prevent them from continuing their efforts to influence union strategy. Publicly they separated themselves from the strike, but covertly they wrestled for union leadership. Their stand, however, did not deter strikers from continuing a confrontational strategy.

The Apogee

The *Placentia Courier* headlined that "the worst outbreak of the month old citrus strike . . . brought shooting, beating and slugging to armed guards and ranch owners."[96] In coordinated forays at exactly 2:00 P.M. on Monday, July 6, caravans of pickets descended on strike breakers at several locations, charging into the groves, pulling down ladders, upsetting orange boxes, physically routing strike breakers, and engaging in battles with armed deputized foremen and growers. At no time were pickets armed, and, although shooting occurred, most of the injured were scabs and guards. At least one guard at Tustin Hill was severely beaten. Four hundred police, highway patrol, and sheriff's deputies sped to the conflicts, chasing, clubbing, and arresting strikers in wild melees. As the battle zone quieted, some two hundred unionists found themselves arrested and jailed, fifty-five cars were confiscated in what the *Los Angeles Times* described as a "miniature civil war."[97]

The strike had taken a major turn toward increasing violence. Sheriff Jackson further inflamed the conflict by issuing orders for armed guards to "shoot to kill" and declaring: "This is no fight between orchardists and pickers. . . . It is a fight between the entire population of Orange County and a bunch of communists."[98] The County Board of Supervisors immediately authorized Jackson "to purchase additional arms and ammunition"[99] for the 175 deputized guards previously armed with shotguns.[100] Strike breakers received clubs, and truck drivers were "equipped with side arms and shotguns."[101]

In spite of the armament buildup, the intensified union campaign continued on Tuesday as strikers intercepted a foremen's bus in La Jolla, smashing and burning it. Individual strike breakers also reported that they were sporadically attacked and their cars burned.[102] Meanwhile, mass meetings were held in the various *colonias* to discuss possible courses of action, and, high on the agenda, freeing the jailed strikers. In previous weeks, law officers had spied on or patrolled meetings; but as the strike intensified armed vigilante groups intent on disruption—and in some cases, the destruction of meeting places—found meetings to be fair game. Thus on July 10, at a Placentia handball court, an assembly of 150 unionists was "suddenly confronted by 30 or 40" vigilantes, who armed with guns, clubs and tear gas, and who, in the words of the *Los Angeles Times,* "nearly demolished a rendezvous," sending one man to the hospital. The unionists responded with rocks, breaking the windows of several of the getaway cars.[103] On the same night, another band of "night riders" attacked an Anaheim *colonia* grocery store used as a union meeting place, ransacking "the place, smashing benches, windows and equipment."[104]

Later in the week a La Jolla strikers' meeting was surrounded by a hundred men "armed with black jacks, billy clubs and new white axe-handles." The vigilantes identified in one news report as "sons of grove owners," and in another as law enforcement officers, threatened the assembly for a quarter of an hour but left after the chief of police interceded.[105] The *Santa Ana Register* strike coverage reported two simultaneous attacks that did not end as peacefully. "Stepping from automobiles which glided up to the fronts of striker's meeting places in Anaheim and El Modena last night, white men non-chalantly pushed their way through the crowds and tossed tear gas bombs into the halls. Then they stepped back into their cars and drove away as the strikers scattered."[106] None of the vigilantes was ever arrested, although the *Santa Ana Register* reported that the Placentia raiders were apprehended by police but allowed to go free.[107] Moreover, that they used tear gas, had clubs and shotguns, weapons only the Sheriff could have provided, strongly implicates the participation of the sheriff and police authorities.

Despite the violence, the stalemate between the two opposing groups seemed nowhere near resolution. The pace toward settlement, however, appeared to hasten in mid-July, although "Mexican strikers and sympathizers continued to ride about the groves . . . shouting threats at workers."[108] Reports of possible negotiations between the two sides appeared simultaneously with the preliminary hearing of 115 strikers who had been arrested on July 6 on riot charges. Following a motion by the district attorney, James L. Davies, the presiding judge granted a continuance on the basis of a thawing in the conflict and a potential for settlement. In the view of contemporary observers, the jailed might be exchanged for a future propitious striker negotiation.

In early July the constant jockeying between the radicals and the consulate-led conservatives eventually debilitated the union but did not immediately destroy a unity of purpose. However, over time the strain proved too great and a rupture occurred about the second week of July. The divided union did not come asunder; the consulate assumed leadership. Although not eliminated, Velarde and his group had been pushed to one side. With the clarification of leadership, the conservatives sent out feelers for a negotiated settlement. The growers, not surprisingly, responded favorably.

In mid-July Consul Ricardo Hill, as well as a special negotiator sent by the Mexican government, former president Adolfo de la Huerta, chief of the consulate bureau in Mexico City, and Lucio met at Fullerton with thirty-eight packinghouse representatives, reaching a tentative agreement for the strikers.[109] Reports filtered that union recognition would be withheld although a pay increase, and all union demands concerning transportation, bonuses, and equipment would be granted by growers.[110]

Guillermo Velarde and the few radicals on the strike committee did not capitulate, describing the proposed settlement as a sell out to growers, and swung into action. Whereas Hill, Lucio and de la Huerta urged ratification of the agreement, Velarde made the rounds of *colonias* urging rejection, demanding that union recognition be of highest priority, that strikers be reemployed immediately, and that pickers now working be discharged.

Velarde and the union's radical faction composed the one force in opposition to settlement of the strike. With a simple elimination of Velarde, the settlement might be reached. Law enforcement swung into action, in this case benefiting both sides in the negotiations. On July 15, police arrested Velarde at the Fullerton *colonia* on the preposterous charge of vagrancy (he operated a grocery store in Los Angeles), jailed him, and set an exorbitant bail at $1000.00. His bail was raised by the California Labor Federation and after two days in jail, he was released and ordered "to leave the country." Clearly the trumped up charges, arrest, jailing, and orders to leave were an attempt to eliminate Velarde as an influence on or participant in the negotiations.

Nevertheless, Velarde defied the "orders of Sheriff Jackson . . . making the rounds of Mexican picking camps and urging strikers to continue fighting for a 40-cent hourly wage and union recognition."[111] Velarde surprised everyone when he appeared at Gonzalez Hall in Santa Ana at a July 17 meeting of the *colonia* union representatives called by Hill. Velarde openly accused the consul and Lucio of attempts to "trick the Mexicans into a settlement and argued that only the union can negotiate union matters, not the consulate."[112]

Efforts to reach agreement lagged as Velarde convinced several members of the strike committee to reject the proposals. Meanwhile, consular officials "made the rounds of eleven pickers colonies" on July 18, "testing the sentiment to end the strike."[113] The growers were satisfied with the agreement as were Consul Hill, de la Huerta, Lucio, and at least half of the strike committee. The other half followed Velarde. On July 20, in an effort completely to dislodge Velarde from influencing the strikers or the strike committee, Jackson issued an arrest order for Velarde, in effect forcing Velarde to go underground. On July 21, a settlement had still not been reached; the radical Velarde and the conservative consulate struggled for leadership over the issue of union recognition. Meetings in the *colonias* discussed the pros and cons of each side. Nevertheless on July 24 the outcome of the discussions, were a vote to be taken, remained uncertain.[114]

A sizable group of unionists held out to continue the strike, as is evidenced by several reports of the burning of foremen's cars and attacks on scabs. At a Placentia striker's meeting, a "tall woman spoke . . . urging them to fight on and to continue demands for union recognition."[115] The opposition to Hill, de la Huerta, and Lucio was apparently not out of the picture, and both growers and the consul-led faction recognized the necessity to eliminate Velarde if the settlement they desired was to be reached.

Hardliners remained active as late as July 25, when three carloads of unionists "descended upon a crowd" of East Los Angeles scabs who were awaiting transportation to Fullerton, beating them with "clubs, iron bars, and chains."[116] Velarde claimed "we're not licked." But with "every peace officer . . . actively engaged in a hunt for Velarde," forcing him underground, the pendulum swung toward Hill.[117] Meetings in several communities voiced approval of the settlement placing Hill and his group in a position of strength. In one last attempt to reclaim victory, two carloads of strikers surrounded eight nonstriking pickers, seriously injuring several of the victims.[118] Such attempts to extend the strike proved futile, the mood of the majority was in favor of settlement. The consul succeeded in steering the union toward the settlement, and on July 27 the strike officially ended. In the strike's aftermath the radicals were dealt another blow. Growers negotiated on the condition that all radicals be expelled from the union ranks. And in compliance Hill and Vice-consul Romero promised "to use their best efforts to clean out radical and red elements, particularly Velarde and his union group from the ranks of the Mexican pickers."[119]

The agreement signed by the strike committee, Consul Hill, and, for the growers, Stuart Strathman, essentially denied the obligation of growers to negotiate with a union and in that regard reaffirmed the status quo ante. Nonetheless, the strike resulted in the termination of the seasonal bonus and costs for transport and equipment, and it provided a pay scale of 20 cents per hour and 3 cents per box, without penalty for poor picks—in sum, providing a higher wage. This settlement, of course, was encouraging to, and a partial victory for, the workers. However, the sixth clause of the agreement re-established the traditional ad hoc mode of picker-grower relations. It read as follows: "The growers agree to meet with representatives of workers through committees of one or two individuals of a crew or a packinghouse provided they are selected by the workers at the site. . . . if no agreement is reached . . . a committee formed by each of the signatories and presided over by a neutral party shall arbitrate."[120] The clause did not obligate growers to arbitrate grievances with the union, nor did it guarantee anything other than a growers promise. There was no legal or binding contract with the picker; the union was given no recognition. Thus the strike ended after a year of bitter and open antagonism, its grievance not wholly resolved. Inevitably, recriminations followed.

Many radicals or suspected radicals were denied jobs even years later.[121] A janitor at the Wilson Mexican school in La Habra was fired because he rented a small building to the local unionists for meetings.[122] At the La Jolla School, Bert Valadez was warned by Principal Whitten to be wary of physical assaults by supporters of the growers from the town.[123] The paternalistic attitude of the dominant community toward the villagers waned considerably.[124] The apparent harmony between the dominant and subordinate societies proved to have been built on sand; a good jarring brought it tumbling down. In the past, growers' donations had supported village celebrations and recreational activities. Not so in the aftermath of the strike. The Placentia associations had had an usually good relationship with the village patriotic committees, having assisted with donations of money and materials. After the strike, petitions for support for the Independence Day celebrations went the way of the union petition—even several years later they were simply ignored.[125] And within the picker communities the "latent antagonisms" between foremen and pickers surfaced. At times violently, as in Campo Colorado where a foreman was threatened numerous times, finally shot at by an assailant attempting to kill him. An Orange strike breaker who was killed by an angered unionist was not as lucky.[126]

The county had spared no expense in countering the union, incurring a $25,000 bill covering tear gas, shot guns, pistols, ammunition, two-way radios, extra officers salary, court costs, and food and medical expenses for the jailed.[127] The same budget-minded officials who had cut education and relief funding, and had sought to repatriate Mexicans because they were a financial burden, felt confident in expending thousands of dollars of the public's money to fight the union. As such the government acted not only on behalf of the growers association, but as a party directly involved in countering the strike. In effect, the picker's union had called a strike that had challenged the state as well as the growers.

It was appropriate, then, that the Orange County Protective Association hosted a barbecue for all law enforcement officials in appreciation of their cooperation during the strike. Meanwhile, the Associated Farmers circulated a blacklist of alleged radicals and agitators, some 60 individuals who now had to make a living in other ways than picking oranges.[128]

Upon the return of strikers to work, the 115 unionists who had been jailed in early July were freed. Of this number, 13 had faced serious charges and in the end ten served prison sentences. The eviction notices at Campo Colorado and Campo Pomona were rescinded, allowing some 75 families to continue to live in their homes.

In the following decade, the union movement among citrus workers declined, although several locals existed. Some remained with CUCOM, others were affiliated with the CIO, but most were affiliated with the AF of L. The CIO's United Cannery, Agricultural, Packing and Allied Workers of America or UCAPAWA attracted one wing of the CUCOM some two hundred citrus pickers. The AF of L on the other hand pulled the majority group. Thus in the late 1930s, the CUCOM picker union separated into distinct unions, the AF of L, however, had the largest membership among the pickers.[129] Within the ranks jurisdictional divisions emerged. The strategic decision of the AF of L to focus organizing upon the packinghouses placed the pickers, a harder lot to organize, into the background. The pickers of Orange County never again achieved the union strength they had displayed in June and July of 1936.

As for CUCOM, the executive leadership eventually voted against cooperation in union matters with the Mexican consulate. Not surprisingly, the citrus strike was one of the last labor disputes in which the Mexican consulate engaged. When the next big citrus strike occurred at Ventura County in 1941 the consul was nowhere in sight. Future union embroilments involving Mexican labor engaged the AF of L and the CIO, and not the Mexican consulate—a sharp departure from earlier Mexican agricultural disputes. The presence of the consul had hindered and split the picker union rather than assisting in uniting to realize its goals. That Mexican labor organization would in the future wrestle principally, if not exclusively, with the political realities of the American labor movement was a major step toward direct participation in the national political process, rather than being shackled by Mexican domestic politics that were unconnected with the conditions facing Mexican workers in the United States.

Finally, notice was served to growers that their 'locals' were not the ideal labor supply as once thought. The editor of the *Placentia Courier* voiced the concerns of the area's growers when he wrote that "too much dependence has been placed on Mexican labor" creating a serious weakness "in the present structure of the industry."[130] Twenty years earlier the President of the California Fruit Growers Exchange, Charles C. Teague, described Mexicans as 'natural' agricultural workers, "loyal and faithful . . . good natured and happy."[131] The strike transformed these myths such that the local Mexican emerged undependable and disloyal—in short, expendable if a better supply could be secured. The second World War secured the conditions for substituting a new source of labor, the Mexican contract laborer, or bracero, thus eliminating the growers dependence upon local Mexican workers. This would have a profound impact upon the villages and contribute to its transition to a blue collar barrio.

· 7 ·

World War II: The Decline of the Citrus Picker Village, the Rise of the *Barrio*

The establishment of the first *colonias* resulted in a form of community destined to last less than two generations. The second form to appear, the contemporary barrio, entered the county scene during the 1940s. A host of changing conditions: economic, social, political, and cultural, emanating from a national and international configuration of forces, eliminated the older *colonia,* replacing it with a nascent suburban and urban barrio. Between 1940 and 1950, a combination of circumstances reshaped the villages and so reshaped village life and its economic and social relations with the dominant society. As the decade ended, the barrio remained an economically subordinated ethnic enclave, a characteristic that survived the transition from *colonia* to barrio.

Breaking Grower's Dependence upon Village Labor: Contract Labor

In the interwar period agriculture was able to protect its labor force from the competition of urban industry and manufacturing. With the outbreak of hostilities and the spawning of defense plants and increases in production across the board, the relative security of rural labor lessened. The growing demand for labor and military personnel reached into the remotest rural pockets, and as it did, agriculture came into a bidding war with urban employers causing wages to rise.

The price of labor was not the lone factor as the resident labor force came to learn the ways of the working class and thus formed active unions. Labor, no longer the tractable labor supply, came to understand the difference between good and bad working conditions, wages, and treatment. In a period of rising wages and labor shortages, the market advantage swung to the employee. Wages, wrote Dr. Ernesto Galarza, were breaking "from their old moorings."[1] Indeed, 1942 picker wages rose to 61 cents an hour in Orange County—a startling and unacceptable situation growers faced.

The first stirrings of change reverberated through the citrus industry in the Fall of 1941. Growers associations reported a scarcity of pickers and, as the season wound down, at least one alleged a considerable slowing of shipments because of a shortage of pickers.[2] The growers asserted a number of causes for the shortage. The most widely held (and most plausible) contention was that wartime industry competed with agriculture, pulling local pickers into the industrial mainstream. But other reasons were mixed in as well, consisting of alleged laziness, drunkenness, disinterest, and disloyalty, leading to the loss of "many man-hours." "Much criticism," wrote C. J. Marks, editor of the county *Farm Bureau News,* "has been heard of the half-way efforts that are being expended in the fields . . . by . . . Mexican workers."[3] Charles C. Teague laid similar arguments before the U.S. Senate Special Committee on western farm labor. The "inefficiency of the agricultural labor that is left," argued Teague, was a direct result of the competition for better workers from defense plants paying higher wages. In addition, the agriculture industry was forced into paying higher wages than before, and for labor of allegedly poorer quality.[4] Several associations charged that opportunistic pickers were taking advantage of growers by moving to higher paying areas before the end of harvest, and, when working did so at their own pace and under conditions of their choosing. Growers accused pickers of dictating pay rates and working conditions, a situation that growers had managed to avoid in the past. The sum of these charges went beyond the scarcity of local labor to the independence of the work force as well as their off-duty recreational habits. The labor problem involved more than the labor shortage to include the manageability, and hence the desirability, of the existing work force. The combination of shortage, inefficiency, and manageability argued not for enlarging the local force but rather for replacing it as much as possible. However, the exaggerated claims of inefficiency were largely a political window dressing highlighting the need for a return to the era of a tractable work force.

The acute labor situation prompted growers to resolve the dilemma by recruiting pickers from among high school students and women, and through the YMCA. In the 1943 season, cooperation between associations and the YMCA partially alleviated the situation, but the scope of the problem was much too large for novices to have much impact. YMCA pickers were required to labor 8 hours a day at a guaranteed 40 cents per hour with a "minimum" of boxes to be picked. Associations always understood that high school labor supplied only half their actual needs and that it was therefore only a short-term solution. Nevertheless, at Placentia, Orange, San Juan Capistrano, Tustin and Fullerton, schools and other buildings were transformed into barracks to house several hundred young men sixteen years of age or over, working throughout the area.[5] Despite good wages and working conditions, workers such as these were inefficient. The original 150 recruits at Placentia wilted in the heat and by midsummer dwindled to 90; and the only report of YMCA recruits utilized after 1943 came from the Anaheim Growers Association, which employed 200.[6]

Within the campaign to solve the labor crises, modes of addressing the issue varied. The Yorba Linda Citrus Association purchased an old school bus that made the rounds of citrus towns in the surrounding area in the 1942 harvest, "picking up pickers and packers who are available for work."[7] The association hired children as young as twelve (providing they had work permits) expecting them to "pick a minimum of five boxes a day" and earning an average of $2.00.[8]

Such short-term measures as these had mixed results. Naturally, inexperience, lack of skill, and lack of physical size lessened the new workers' productivity. Although they were better than no workers at all, the industry realized that a longer term solution was needed. Again, as they had in the early part of the century, growers looked toward Mexico not to complement the existing work force but to supplant it as far as possible. It is within this context that village pickers were en masse pushed from the picking force.

Stopgap measures by individual growers associations evolved into an industrywide campaign to import laborers from Mexico. Rumblings about the labor shortage were immediately communicated to the appropriate agencies in Washington. The agencies responded by forging a labor agreement with the Mexican government in 1942. In the past, migratory movements had been largely unplanned and unsupervised. But in the face of this labor "crisis," an organized importation of contract workers (or braceros) from a number of points in Mexico to the United States was used to alleviate the situation. Interestingly, or perhaps ironically, the pre-existing organizations, the Associated Farmers and the Agricultural Producers Labor Committee—both dedicated principally to systematically reducing the power of unions and isolating their labor from unions—assumed a key role in the importation, allocation, and management of Mexican contract workers in the county.[9]

Grower associations participated actively in the Associated Farmers and the Agricultural Producers Labor Committee over the years and paid sizable yearly dues to each. The two organizations generally opposed unionization in somewhat different ways. The Associated Farmers was a "watchdog" agency, issuing reports on labor organizations and organizers, their activities, and areas in which they operated. It also lobbied for state and local legislation favorable to its views. The Agricultural Producers Labor Committee had made its first appearance during a labor conflict in the late 1930s that involved packinghouse workers. The committee's goals included limiting federal intervention into agriculture—in particular "to check the National Labor Relations Board's decisions" and to control possible "encroachment of the new Wage and Hour Administration onto the farm." The committee sought to "procure exemptions for agricultural and allied workers from the jurisdiction of the Social Security Board."[10] In 1943, the Agricultural Producers Labor Committee metamorphosed into the Citrus Emergency Harvest, Inc., a statewide agency for rationalizing the bracero program within California's citrus industry.

George A. Graham, though not a grower, was serving as the secretary for the Associated Farmers of Orange County when he assumed the duties as director of Citrus Growers, Incorporated, a consortium of forty-five county packinghouses. Citrus Growers, Inc. rationalized the importation, allocation, housing, and feeding of contract labor in the county and served to negotiate directly with Citrus Emergency Harvest, Inc. Clearly the old organizations that prepared for class warfare assumed an entirely new function to meet the distinct wartime demands placed on the growers. In place of antiunionism, the Associated Farmers, the most visible growers' organization apart from the Exchange itself, took charge for the administration of the bracero program within the county's citrus industry. From 1943 until the termination of the contract program some twenty years later, the Citrus Growers, Inc., under George A. Graham, ministered to the industry's labor needs.[11]

Braceros were contracted to work a specific period of time, after which they either returned to Mexico or agreed to another contract (if a need for their labor could be established). Wages were to be set at the prevailing rates and all transportation and housing was furnished free; workers paid only for their board and personal necessities. A rather small first contingent of workers arrived in 1942, but none in Orange county until the summer of 1943. By then private organizations, such as grower associations, were allowed to arrange for the importation of braceros. However, the more important amendment to the original agreement emerged from discussions between the National Council of Farmers Cooperatives, presided over by Charles C. Teague (President of the California Fruit Growers Exchange) several agricultural organizations, and the federal government. That agreement placed individuals favored by the grower lobbying groups into key administrative positions. For example, the administration of agricultural labor matters was taken out of the hands of the secretary of labor, which initially handled the bracero program, and delegated to Lt. Col. Jay Taylor, owner "of a number of ranches" and a favorite of growers.[12] Following the reorganization of the Department of Labor, a plan formulated by the National Council of Growers for "a new recruitment agency" directly responsible for the importation of braceros was instituted and administered by another favorite of the industry, citrus rancher Thomas Robertson of Simi, California.[13]

When the administration of the contract labor program was placed largely in the hands of individuals directly representing agricultural interests the citrus industry tapped into the Mexican labor pool on a scale not seen since the 1920s. By the summer of 1943, a radically distinct form of Mexican labor, large-scale importation of temporary single-male laborers, branched into every section of agriculture throughout the Southwest. In California, that labor flowed overwhelmingly into the citrus areas of Southern California. The charge that "local Mexicans . . . are not plentiful and often not satisfactory in general attitude" was eventually balanced by "Mexican nationals . . . anxious to work" and "under control." Temporary passports made deportation of those found "unsatisfactory because of quarrelsome nature . . . or other factors" relatively easy.[14] Employers found an ideal labor supply: tractable, flexible, inexpensive, acquiescent, experienced, but with "no distractions to keep them from doing good work."[15] From the perspective of the antiunion grower associations, a bracero was the ultimate laborer—easily employed, highly productive, easily terminated.

With the 1943 harvest pending, county growers requested 1,650 men to pick the crop. Citrus Growers, Inc. communicated the need to the statewide agency, Citrus Emergency Harvest, which then placed the order with the federal agency. Placing an order was the simple part, the more complex matter involved housing. Two key problems arose: first, the cost, which Citrus Growers, Inc. solved through raising $100,000 from its members to cover housing; and second, and this was the trickier issue, was where to place the housing. The choice of those associations to which had been allotted a supply of braceros was to place them within, or next to, picker villages, or on the rural outskirts of towns.

In deference to the opinions of the townspeople, the seven new bracero housing projects called "camps," as had been the *colonias* in Orange County, were located in outlying districts away from the towns. Several camps were converted from existing buildings, including the county insectary and an abandoned Mexican school building (which had been condemned in 1939 because of the 1933 Long Beach earthquake) in the Atwood Mexican village.[16] Most of the camps were converted army bunkhouses. Four were placed within or next to a Mexican village. Bunkhouses were placed in Campo Pomona and La Jolla, and another in Delhi. In spite of the distant placement of the bracero camps, fears among the townspeople remained. In one instance a Yorba Linda association elected to house their supply of braceros within the Placentia city limits, but a hue and cry from Placentia townspeople forced the Yorba Lindans to withdraw their proposal.

The American Legion spearheaded the opposition, not only against the Yorba Linda group, "but against anyone housing a large number of men in the city."[17] The image—already stereotyped, of single men, dark complexioned, and poor—raised a sense of unease. To quiet fears and allay anxiety, uniformed sheriff's deputy "on duty at all camps . . . were put there to eliminate trouble." According to the Orange County sheriff, the deputies' main task was to keep outsiders "out of the camps."[18]

Growers did their best to create a favorable impression of the bracero—in a campaign somewhat similar to that employed for 1920s Americanization campaign. News releases reiterated that comfortable accommodations, large mess halls, nutritious and satisfying meals, entertainment, and recreational facilities were bestowed upon the braceros. At least one journal was founded to do nothing other than to construct a favorable image of the bracero and disseminate it widely.[19] Local growers, especially boards of directors of associations, like the Americanization teachers before them, often motored to a camp for a "Spanish dinner." On these occasions guests included journalists, civic organizations such as Rotarians, and chamber of commerce officials.[20]

Once the campsites had been established, there was a yearly cycle of arrival of braceros for the season, leaving at its termination. From 1943 to 1958, approximately seventy thousand braceros were transported to Orange County, the majority of whom were transported back to Mexico at federal government expense, therefore at no cost either to the county or to growers.[21] Some remained to work as year-round ranch labor, and some never returned to Mexico. Each year a sizable number simply "jumped" their contracts, to filter into the economic mainstream and join the village as permanent residents. According to Eduardo Negrete, assistant to the Mexican consulate in matters relating to the braceros, many chose to stay illegally. Growers never distinguished between legals and illegals, and no employers were punished for using illegals.[22]

Throughout the war and into the postwar period, temporary contract labor of various sorts further stabilized the labor supply for the industry. Jamaicans, Navajos, wartime refugees, and German prisoners of war entered the picking force. In 1945 some 750 German prisoners of war, 1,300 Jamaicans, an unknown number of Navajos, and about 1,600 braceros—together with pickers from the villages brought the total picking force to 5,400, the largest ever assembled in the county. All of the temporary labor was administered and managed by the Citrus Growers, Inc.

The Jamaicans' insistence on familiar meals, their outgoing demeanor, and their independent work habits disappointed the growers. They were quickly sent back soon after the season and never returned.[23] The German prisoners of war were inexperienced and performed far less productively than did the braceros.[24] Of all the labor available to growers during the war, only the braceros seemed to satisfy the major requirements of the managers and foremen: speed, efficiency, reliability, and a willingness to work under a wide spectrum of conditions. The annual reports of the Villa Park Orchards Association had many kind things to say of their braceros, as is reflected by this excerpt from its 1947 report: "More than one hundred Mexican workers were housed and fed in our Villa Park Camp during the season. Most of these men proved themselves to be good reliable workers and are a very desirable source of labor for the harvesting of our food crops."[25]

Where it was feasible, citrus ranchers stopped using already resident Mexican villagers as pickers and replaced them with temporary-status braceros. By 1945, 65 percent of southern California picking labor were Mexican braceros.[26] Many pickers charged that the bracero program did more than answer to a labor shortage, it also arbitrarily reduced employment of resident Mexican labor.[27] The trend continued so that one year later over 80 percent of its picker supply were braceros; the industry had largely divested itself of local Mexican laborers.[28] Their elimination of the use of resident Mexicans as pickers meant that Orange County growers employed the lion's share of bracero labor in southern California. In 1944, 67,860 braceros arrived to work in 21 states, of these 8,246, or 12.2 percent, were sent to California citrus growers. Of the 8,246, the largest share, 2,698, went to Orange county, nearly double that of the Los Angeles County bracero force of 1,954. Records for 1943 and 1945–47 reveal a continuing imbalance in the placement of braceros throughout the citrus areas.[29] Clearly, Orange County savored a privileged status in the citrus industry.

This disproportion was understandable given that Charles C. Teague, President of the California Fruit Growers Exchange and chair of the statewide Agricultural Producers Labor Committee, represented agricultural interests in contract labor in Washington. Nevertheless, growers associations were never satisfied with the numbers of braceros allocated and consistently requested more than they received. But those that did arrive became the "nucleus around which the picking crews . . . performed."[30] Indeed, George A. Graham, secretary of Citrus Growers, Inc. concluded that only 12 percent of Orange county's picking crews were assembled from local sources, that is, from the picker villages. From the perspective of the grower, an ideal labor situation was spun-off from the wartime labor shortage—the practical elimination of locals from the crews.[31] Some associations went so far as to direct their managers to hire "imported workers . . . exclusively in the field if possible."[32] Most associations probably had an overwhelming presence of braceros in the groves, illustrated by the splitting of labor in the Anaheim Cooperative Orange Association's picking force, which comprised 43 braceros and 25 local Mexicans.[33] The 1944 records of the Placentia Orange Growers Association show an even greater disproportion, a total of 190 pickers were employed but only about 40 came from the local villages.[34]

Growers found it "much simpler to order [braceros] from a camp manager than to search through communities for workers"[35] causing many local pickers to sour on picking, preferring to wait until an opportunity arose in industrial or defense plants. But those who chose to remain in the force found themselves gradually squeezed out and many eventually chose unemployment relief.[36] The local picking force underwent a socioeconomic transition that the Japanese working in agriculture in the United States had experienced in the early decades of the century, and for many of the same reasons. Mexican citrus pickers had learned the need for organization, adopted the necessary skills for collective bargaining, and, when necessary, had launched strikes. In the minds of growers, resident Mexican pickers, like the Japanese before them, teemed with agitators and had grown independent and disloyal. "Our Mexican camp," emerged from the 1936 strike a liability rather than an asset, so their replacement by braceros, German POWs, Navajos, Jamaicans, and others brought a sigh of relief from growers. Once again, associations had found a dependable labor supply to supplant one that had learned the benefits of organization. Many growers would say that the braceros "saved the crops," however, they might more accurately have said that "braceros saved the industry from unionism."

The village felt the effects of several more changes in its occupational structure. Women villagers entered into the packinghouses in greater numbers so that by the end of the war they were the majority of packers. Few records reveal their precise number, but former packers generally recall that the war offered increased job opportunities for them, in the packinghouses as in defense industries.[37] A wider variety of occupational opportunities was placed before the men and women of the villages, and many took advantage of it.[38]

Naturally the war called hundreds of village youths into the armed forces, and in some towns they formed a sizable percentage of those summoned to serve. The March 1943 Placentia call, for example, inducted twenty-one from the area to duty. Fourteen villagers came from Atwood, La Jolla, and the Placentia villages.[39] A Placentia resident thought that probably 90 percent of all young Mexican men served in the military.[40] The large number of Mexican servicemen and their heroic exploits garnered a substantial degree of press coverage in some town newspapers. The *Placentia Courier* published numerous accounts of local village servicemen, and went as far as to publish a flattering editorial entitled "Our Latin Heroes." Villagers were keen to point out that many of the old neighborhood's windows had multiple insignias indicating a household member in the armed services. By the war's end, several villages endured the loss of at least one of its own, and in such cases the display of the proper insignias allowed the family to share its sorrow with friends and relatives.[41] Ironically, while newspaper articles praised Mexican servicemen, the employers of their fathers, brothers, and relatives were loathe to hire them. And segregation remained—in schools, parks, theaters, residence, and restaurants. But change was in the air.

Challenging Segregation: The Mexican American Generation

A new political consciousness and organization emerging from a generation educated in the United States and acculturated to the mainstream political culture appeared in the county during the war years. Three principal organizations surfaced, the Mexican American Movement (MAM), and the Latin American Organization (LAO), later evolving into the League of United Latin American Citizens (LULAC). Composed primarily of American-born Mexicans, many of whom were returned veterans, these organizations addressed issues and problems rooted in their experience within the United States. An earlier village cultural practice in the form of allegiance to Mexico, Mexican patriotism, and Dieciséis de Septiembre celebrations, was outside the major concerns or themes in the accelerating civil rights movement.

The key issues confronted by the organizations included the obvious inequality separating majority from minority, the lack of educational achievement, and the enforced legal segregation that maintained socioeconomic inequality. Their ideological outlook like that of the second generation of other immigrant groups across the United States was of a piece with New Deal liberalism; that is, rather than exerting pressure radically to uproot and alter the basic institutions of society, these organizations sought state action to remove imposed barriers to the achievement of their ethnic group and thereby to the individual.[42] In so doing, these organizations adhered to the belief that individualism unfettered by segregation was in the final analysis the ultimate objective of their civil rights activities. The path to achieve this democratic goal differed somewhat among the organizations, but the general objective, to raise the socioeconomic level of the Mexican community on a par with that of the Anglo community, remained constant.

These shared political goals caused these organizations to connect, either formally or informally, with the statewide as well as the national civil rights network campaigning to remove racial discrimination across society. Two characteristics of this network's political consciousness strongly indicate the acculturation of the second generation. First, their consciousness was in part woven from their status as a second-class citizenry. Second, their intense dissatisfaction with the consequences of discriminatory social controls led them toward New Deal liberalism, a major political trend expressing an agenda to overcome such discrimination.

Even before the second generation had sided with New Deal Democrats, village immigrants had made President Roosevelt into a hero. The belief that an expanded government role was necessary to offset the disadvantages placed in the second generation's path was based on an ideology not altogether different from that of their parents.

Mexican immigrants placed considerable trust into their own government and its representative, the consulate, for protection within a society filled with uncertainties—and one of the main government actions was the defense (albeit conditional) of the right of workers to organize unions. The policy parallels between those of the home country and the New Deal was sufficient to allow the second generation to accommodate easily to New Deal liberalism. No great ideological leap of faith was involved when the second generation assumed political maturity.

MAM, the first group to appear, emerged from annual YMCA-sponsored Mexican Youth Conferences in the Los Angeles area of the 1930s, which were dedicated to developing "leadership and fellowship among Mexican American youth."[43] MAM was formed in 1942, an independent organization "planned and directed by Mexican American leaders."[44] In 1945 the organization was formally incorporated with six Southern California councils, three of which were in citrus districts; two of these were from Orange County—Placentia and Anaheim.[45] Orange County citrus villagers were prominent among these founding leaders and included Gualberto Valadez, Mary Ann Chavolla, Lionel Magaña, Ted Durán, Luis Sandoval, and Ross Chavolla.

The ideology of MAM reflected the thinking of one sector of the community, primarily educated, professional, and, in the eyes of their community, successful individuals. MAM proposed that these leaders "encourage and inspire higher educational achievements among Mexican Americans as a means of overcoming the problems of prejudice, segregation, discrimination, social inequality, and inferiority complex."[46] The general goal of the Movement was the socioeconomic "betterment of our people," through an education gradually altering the community and thereby equalizing relations with the dominant society. "We believe," stated the MAM *Handbook*, "that this effort must come from within this group."

With these modest liberal goals and philosophy as guidelines, the two MAM councils in the county entered into the political affairs of a wide scattering of villages—Placentia, Atwood, La Jolla, Campo Pomona, Fullerton, La Palma, and La Fabrica. In these settings, MAM sought to encourage youth to prepare for the "competitive American life" by way of several activities aimed at interesting youth in the value of education.[47] The

Placentia council planned for a "recreation center where Mexican children might spend their after school hours . . . so that character building stressed by schools in the daytime might not be spoiled by evenings spent in beer and dance spots."[48] In pursuit of that objective, council members organized youth clubs. The club for first through sixth graders was called the "Friendly Indians." Older boys might join a "Y" Pioneer Club, and high school age youth were encouraged to join the Hi-Y. Shortly, a Boy Scout troop and a Girls Service Club were formed.[49]

During the immediate postwar period, the Placentia MAM maintained good relations with the dominant community, entering into the institutions of the town. Meetings were held at the city hall. The Boy Scout troop used the American Legion Hall, and the various sports activities used school facilities. MAM raised funds through benefit dances much as their fathers on the patriotic committees had done before them. Monies raised at the June 1946 dance were applied to college scholarships for a Mexican American student.[50] The Placentia council raised enough funds the following year to carry out its extensive recreational activities plus "awarding two $100 scholarships" to local high school graduates planning to enter college.[51]

The Anaheim council, like the Placentia and Fullerton councils, focused on recreation and scholarships and actively participated in MAM regional and interstate activities involving councils in Arizona, New Mexico, and Texas.[52] Anaheim's MAM "organized a very large following" of "approximately 80 members" and accomplished substantial success in youth recreation such as the Hi-Y and others.[53]

MAM was relatively well received by the townspeople—no indications of opposition from civic or grower organizations, nor of bad publicity, surfaced. On the contrary, educators and city officials seemed to welcome MAM leaders, allowing them use of public school rooms for meetings and playgrounds for MAM youth work. Such a cooperative spirit is illustrated by the choice of the guest speaker at the 1945 La Jolla Junior High School commencement exercises, MAM president Paul Coronel.[54] The annual Orange County regional MAM conference was hosted in La Jolla in 1946 and heard speakers from Los Angeles, Pasadena, Anaheim, and East Los Angeles and received favorable publicity in newspapers.

The record of MAM's impact on the villages and social relations with the dominant community is obscure. Highly visible in the north county area until 1949, MAM increased the recreational opportunities for youth and awarded a number of scholarships to college-bound youth, yet there is no evidence that MAM entered the political sphere, nor that it significantly challenged the social relations of the area.[55] The leadership in Anaheim opposed segregated schools claiming that such schools resulted in school failure. However, its successes were achieved through integrating the public plunge and the local theater.[56] MAM also brought an awareness to the

Mexican communities that an organization led by their own was prepared to work to change things for the better. If nothing else, MAM symbolized the dissatisfaction and the desire to eliminate the barriers to social and economic equality. Still MAM expressed a firm conviction that if equal educational opportunities can be secured, significant social changes would unquestionably appear. However, MAM contended that change must first come from within the group, gradually reaching outward to touch the larger society.

A second civil rights group formed in the mid-1940s, the countywide Latin American Organization. LAO was founded in Santa Ana and shortly was joined by members, primarily veterans, from surrounding villages. The organization emphasized the need for equality, especially in educational opportunity but perceived the segregated educational system as the key barrier to social change. Although not much is known about the organization, since it left no records of any kind, it did have a significant role in the process leading to the filing of a successful lawsuit against the county to terminate the practice of segregating Mexican children. By 1943 parents and individuals in Santa Ana, Garden Grove, La Habra, El Modena, and Westminster demanded an end to segregated schooling and supported the right to equal access to schools. From small aggressive outbursts challenging local boards of education a concerted effort was launched on a countywide basis. The Latin American Organization emanated from this ground swell of spontaneous activity and began to coordinate the separate efforts in 1944–45. Their long-range goals were to terminate the practice of segregation and to equalize educational opportunity. To achieve these ends, the group cooperated with parents to file a lawsuit in the district federal court against Orange County arguing that their constitutional rights, in particular the Fourteenth Amendment guarantees of due process, were violated. Parents and the LAO contacted a lawyer, David Marcus (who had previously acted as counsel in the desegregation of San Bernardino swimming pools), who agreed to prepare the case.

On March 2, 1945, the suit Mendez vs. Westminster was heard by Judge Paul J. McCormick, who ruled in favor of the plaintiffs.[57] The defendants in the Mendez case, the Orange County Board of Education, appealed the district court's decision, and not until June, 1947 did the Appellate Court uphold the district court's finding while severely reprimanding the county. The ruling went beyond a narrow interpretation of the Fourteenth Amendment, and delved into and cast doubt on the separate-but-equal doctrine. Physical equality, argued McCormick, does not guarantee social equality, and moreover, the constitution requires that the American public school system guarantee social equality. "It must be open to all," stated McCormick, "regardless of lineage."

During the appellate process, LAO voted to join the League of United

Latin American Citizens (LULAC), which was to be the third county civil rights organization, and established a Santa Ana chapter, the first in California, followed by Placentia and El Modena chapters. Formed mainly from returning veterans groups, LAO, and individuals from MAM groups,[58] LULAC continued the court challenge at the Appellate level which eventually sustained the lower court's ruling. As in the MAM organization, leadership and support came from the middle sector of the community: high school graduates, proprietors of small businesses, and professionals. Hector Tarango, a photographer; Manuel Vega, undertaker; Cruz Barrios, grocery store owner; Tony Luna, locksmith; and Fred Aguirre, mason, among others, at various times provided leadership. LAO and LULAC efforts attracted wide attention, not only locally but nationally. The Council on Race Relations sent Fred Ross, one of its most highly skilled community organizers, first to assist LAO then LULAC in their antisegregation struggle. Ross espoused grass roots community organizing in the radical tradition of Saul Alinsky. In the future, Ross's participation would alarm the county establishment. The political power of the county, challenged once again by the Mexican community, emerged the loser in the Mendez case, but not without continuing the fight on a different level.

The Associated Farmers of Orange County took the political baton from the Board of Supervisors and launched a stinging red-baiting campaign against the civil rights activities of the Mexican communities. With Ross's participation LULAC engaged in voter registration drives throughout the county and during the November 1946 statewide election launched a campaign supporting Proposition 11, the Fair Employment Practices Act. The Act barred employers from hiring according to race, religion, or nationality and authorized a statewide commission to enforce the act. Apart from the November election, LULAC chapters went door to door to register voters in order to more effectively deal with local issues, such as civic improvements, services, and political participation. The Placentia chapter was so successful, registering nearly three hundred voters in the latter part of the 1940s, that the Mexican community held the swing vote in local elections determining which candidate would emerge victorious. In Placentia, activists gradually redefined the village's political relations with the town, so that by the early 1950s LULAC placed their candidate on the city council.

Meanwhile, El Modena activists, with the support of Fred Ross, organized a voter registration drive in 1946 to elect their candidate to the segregationist board of education. The board, recognizing a stiff election challenge on the horizon, ordered voting booths to close at 2:00 P.M. rather than the customary 7:00 P.M. Incumbents expected a Mexican community preference for work and wages rather than to vote. In assessing the political will of the Mexican community the board veered wide of the mark. The opposition Mexican American candidate won by a large majority thereby defeating the staunch segregationist candidate.[59] The potential for electoral success and the possibility that it may be repeated elsewhere sent the county's political guardians into action.

At the urging of the Associated Farmers, in the spring of 1947 the district attorney gathered together LULAC leadership for a special meeting to discuss a favorite topic of the agriculturalists: communist influence within the Mexican American organization. Subsequent to the meeting, at which LULAC's leadership was once again warned of the dangers of communism, a letter from the Associated Farmers was sent to the leadership. The letter contained a series of implied accusations that LULAC was an unwitting associate of the far left. The letter claimed that the American Council on Race Relations (one of three organizations LULAC was alleged to have contact with) was "so infiltrated with communists and fellow travelers that now rather than functioning as organizations for the promotion of better race relations [they] have become subservient to the aims and purposes of the communist party."[60] The letter continued, "we suggest that it would be in the best interests of your splendid organization to refrain from any association" with the American Council on Race Relations as well as any other communistic groups. The seed of discontent had now been planted, but more was in store. The Associated Farmers contacted parish priests, informing them of their allegations, urged them to seek out LULAC leaders, and suggested ousting Fred Ross and any others of similar thinking.[61] If LULAC did not take the bait, the priests did. The parish priest of the LULAC president (the president was a devout Catholic) called him onto the rectory's carpet and told him in no uncertain terms that Ross must go. The stage was set for a regression in the intensity of civil rights activities.[62] Although no specific action was taken by LULAC, a weakening of support for Ross indicated that it was best for him to leave. Ross then went to Los Angeles and helped to establish the Community Service Organization, which played a critical role in the election of Edward Roybal to the Los Angeles city council. Tony Luna and Hector Tarango, both in the leadership of the Orange County civil rights movement at the time, felt that Ross had performed an invaluable service for the community, moreover, his loss stilled the momentum gathered in the mid-1940s. Los Angeles's gain was Orange County's loss.

In spite of later stalling, LAO and LULAC added a dimension of social change, one that had repercussions beyond the county, to the state, the Southwest and the nation. Indeed, the Mendez case attracted national attention and is considered a precursor to the 1954 Supreme Court decision overturning the heinous practice of racial segregation. The American Council on Race Relations affirmed the Mendez case "signaled the opening of a legal campaign to have segregation declared unconstitutional per se."[63]

One legal commentator wrote that the Mendez decision "breaks sharply" with the Plessy Doctrine and finds that the Fourteenth Amendment requires "social equality" rather than "equal facilities."[64] Another suggested that "this case must be ranked among the vanguard of those making a frontal attack upon the "equal but separate" canon of interpretation of the equal protection clause. While not decided solely on the basis of this constitutional guarantee, the instant case foreshadows a far-reaching possibility that the precedent of 1896 may not be vested with permanence."[65] NAACP legal defense attorneys Thurgood Marshall and Robert C. Carter followed the case closely and filed amicus curiae briefs for the Appellate Court. Indeed, Robert C. Carter considered these briefs as the "dry runs for the future" that established an argumentative precedent for the Brown Decision, which was to follow seven years later.

LULAC continued to struggle for a more just society in its own way, and individuals involved with LULAC forged independent efforts. Hector Tarango, a Ross supporter who had appeared with Fred Ross before the Santa Ana Board of Education in 1946 to demand compliance with the district court's ruling, published a weekly newspaper, the *Latin American,* devoting substantial space to civil rights issues. He exhorted the Mexican American community to become politically involved, lamented and criticized the lack of participation from the community, and warned against complacency in matters concerning civil rights. In one of the last editions of the paper, Tarango urged his readers to take the time to join LULAC so that "intolerance, prejudice, segregation, etc." will be eliminated.[66] Nonetheless, in the years that followed social relations in the county remained much as they had been—the most dramatic change had taken place through the Mendez case. Thereafter, in Tarango's words, social relations improved for many individuals, but for the most part the Mexican community continued in a subordinate position.

Meanwhile, the old guard, the group that had formed the patriotic committees of the 1920s and 1930s, continued its traditional role in the community through self-help lodges, religious organizations, and the county central patriotic committee. The county Comité Central de Festejos Patrios, founded in 1940, continued its patriotic mission and remained under the tutelage of the consul. Sponsoring the traditional Dieciséis de Septiembre celebrations, the *comité,* itself a historic link with the first settlers, encountered less and less enthusiasm as the years progressed. The Mexican communities seemed disinterested, or so it appeared to *comité* president Emilio Martínez, who noted that "patriotism is disappearing with giant strides."[67] In search for a revived Mexicanismo the *comité* published its own journal *NOVEDAD,* broadcasting *comité* functions, meetings, celebrations and generally emphasizing "respect and adherence" for the consul general.[68]

Two types of community action emerged in the 1940s. One type comprised the traditionalists and celebrated Mexican patriotism and national culture. The other comprised the newer groups, which concentrated on community organizing, political unity, and the extension of legal protections to the Mexican American community. The two groups appeared to have separate constituencies: the former composed of immigrants; the second, their children. Yet this distinction, while generally true, does not reflect the support that the older generation gave to the civil rights movement. For example, Eduardo Negrete, guest speaker at the 1931 Placentia Dieciséis de Septiembre celebration, donated funds to the desegregation campaign.[69] Generally, the old guard welcomed the new political organization although it did not join it. One reason offered by Negrete was that most immigrants never learned English well enough to participate in LULAC meetings, which were, in accordance with its by-laws, held in English. Further, membership was open only to citizens—thus the name, League of United Latin American *Citizens.*

Interestingly, the difference between the two groups within the community can be detected in their respective newspapers. The older generation read *El Acción,* a countywide weekly founded in 1942 by Francisco Moreno and based in Fullerton, or the Los Angeles daily *La Opinion,* both printed exclusively in Spanish. News items in *Acción* were cultural in nature, often consisting of whimsical chatter from the villages, from time to time delving into social or political matters involving relations between Mexican and Anglo society. The second generation's the *Latin American,* on the other hand, was published principally in English and on occasion published Spanish language articles. From time to time the paper presented a bilingual image; at other times, it was an English language sheet, but never did it publish exclusively in Spanish. Moreover, the issues that it addressed and to which it devoted substantial space included civil rights affecting not only the county but also the United States as a whole.

If one can find a critical distinction between the two groups, it is that the old guard continued to orient its organizations toward Mexico. The newer political organizations tended toward involvement in political processes in the United States as they concerned issues of social equality. This distinction is borne out by the continual contact between the Comité Central de Festejos Patrios and the Mexican consul. There is no record indicating ongoing contact between the Mexican American Movement, the Latin American Organization, or LULAC with the Mexican consulate.

The simultaneous political trend away from the leadership of the consul and toward political action against segregation was not a localized phenomenon. It occurred throughout the southern California region—and in some areas the move to jettison consul leadership was deliberate. Ignacio Lopez, founder of the politically active Unity Leagues in San Gabriel

Valley citrus towns, noted with some disdain the role of the consulates in fomenting Mexicanismo.[70] However, in Orange County the consulate was simply left in the wake of the activists of a new political vanguard.

Indeed, when the Placentia LULAC chapter engaged in a voter registration drive in the late 1940s, and registered several hundred residents, very few of those registered were of the immigrant group due to extremely low naturalization rates. Naturally, the success of the Placentia chapter translated into a new balance of power in the small community. The victory of Fred Aguirre in the mid-1950s, the first Mexican American elected to the Placentia city council, resulted more from the goals and objectives of the immigrants' sons and daughters than those of the immigrants themselves, the first settlers in the villages. "We were all in our twenties," noted Hector Tarango, and truly the activity of the era mirrored a youthful idealism and belief in American liberalism.

The Disappearing Village, an Emerging Barrio

The influx of braceros, the wartime labor shortage, and the rise of the second generation had several significant social effects on the villages. First, beginning in the 1940s, a four-tiered community emerged composed of the old immigrant group; the second generation; the new immigrants, braceros; and "illegals" (either braceros who jumped their contracts or undocumented immigrants). During the war and in the postwar period, the four groups fairly well joined together and adjusted to each other, expanding the community's boundaries while increasing its population.[71] Intermarriage between villagers and braceros was not uncommon, all groups worshiped at the same churches, and came together for patriotic and cultural observances. In addition, the villages served a valued purpose as far as the growers were concerned; they acted as an existing social structure into which the new imported laborers would be placed. Growers, then, were spared the effort and expense of having to build from the ground up, so to speak, a favorable environment for their new laborers. Indeed, growers tapped the villages for food preparers, cooks, trouble shooters, English teachers, liaisons, and, of course, foremen.[72] The villages' highly organized cultural, political, and religious practices absorbed the new contingent, providing them with familiar and welcome experiences. This worked to the grower's advantage and obviously made life easier for the braceros. But the villages were now in a process of change that was to last to the present, as continual migrations undercut established internal structures. Villagers, braceros, and illegals at first integrated, but as the immigration continued through the next several decades, the villages became communities that were becoming urbanized, and in a constant state of flux. In time, as the second generation began to remove themselves to other neighborhoods villagers began to see strangers rather than familiar faces. Things would never be the same for them, as stable neighborhoods began to evolve, at increasing speed, into communities of temporary residents.

The second tension imposed upon the village came from the occupational reorganization taking place rooted in wartime and postwar industrialization. New factories and businesses mushroomed in the postwar era. Placentia was home to the Vultee Aircraft factory, employing one hundred workers, which manufactured aircraft components. At the close of the war the building that housed Vultee became the city's first factory, producing brooms on a mass scale and initially hiring twenty-five persons. Nearby Anaheim went through a similar change but on a larger scale. The granting of building permits reached unprecedented levels in the 1944–47 period, hitting its peak in 1946 when 554 building permits were granted. Building values underwent a parallel rise in 1946, with a total value of nearly $2 million. New industrial plants—General Electric plant, an Oranco Steel plant, a clothing factory, and a tool and machinery plant, among others—substantially altered this formerly agricultural city.[73] Similar changes were occurring throughout Orange County.

Between the wars, the occupational choices for Mexicans beyond picking or packing were few. World War II brought relief from the rigid occupational pattern. Hundreds of younger generation men were pulled into military service. A sizable portion of the picking force entered into construction, factory, and defense work. A large percentage of women entered packinghouses as packers, and into the defense industry and other industries.[74] The village, the base community, then assumed a novel occupational character, complemented by the returning veterans who deliberately sought employment outside of the citrus industry. In not a few cases they had learned skills in the service or took advantage of veterans' rights and privileges to enter college and formerly off-limits employment.

Many contemporary observers noted the declining role of the village labor force in agriculture and its increasing role in other industries. A 1947 study of the Anaheim Mexican village noted that before the war "many of the industries had not employed Mexican labor. . . . Today most of the large industries have Mexican American employees."[75] Villagers verify the opening of occupational variation during the war and in the postwar period. Lionel Magaña of La Jolla remarked that before the war "there was little going on in Placentia but picking" but that since then "there's so much more work—factory work, construction."[76] Waldo Ortega observed that at the end of the war "a demand for production and services . . . meant that jobs were open [and] they had to hire minorities and teach them . . . skills to do the job."[77] However, this occupational transition in many ways merely kept pace with occurring structural changes. The placement of the Mexican American work force in relation to the dominant society remained somewhat constant. As Mexican Americans moved into nonagricultural employment, they did so at the entry level, and in economies most affected by periodic unemployment.[78] Initially, for many Mexican Americans a bifurcated employment pattern existed, they sought work in industrial *and* agricultural economies as opportunities appeared. Nevertheless, for the native Mexican American work force agricultural employment became less and less attractive, and simultaneously bracero and other forms of Mexican immigrant labor assumed predominance in the groves and fields.[79] Both groups, however, served as pools of surplus labor, braceros in agriculture, and Mexican Americans in nonagricultural industries. Thirty years earlier the Mexican community served as the labor base for the impressive development of citrus. It is upon this same minority base that Orange County would begin its impressive postwar economic growth, a county later to be proclaimed a key financial center of the developed world.

The varied segments of the community would also have distinctive roles to play in the economy. It has been shown that in agriculture citizenship and gender are critical to the organization of labor. Certainly this was the case in the citrus region: women entered the packinghouse in greater numbers, and the braceros, the "noncitizens," filled the nonindustrial agricultural slots. The second generation, or citizens, as well as many legal immigrants moved into manufacturing and industrial employment. Some, especially the legal immigrants, continued employment in agriculture but were slowly squeezed out due to the preference of growers for noncitizens, or braceros, and illegal immigrant labor. Thus sectors of the Chicano community determined by gender, citizenship, and legal status were incorporated separately into the organization of labor, confirming, as Robert J. Thomas argued, that agribusiness firms "do not create the distinguishing statuses of citizenship, gender, or race, but rather seize upon them and transform those characteristics to the organization's advantage."[80] In the process, social sectors within the Mexican community were transformed into distinct sets of economic actors, consequently the socio-legal nature of the community reflected its economic character as well.

The labor market opportunism displayed by employers does not reflect the full process of limiting labor market opportunities. The schooling system contributed readily by producing undereducated children, supplying employers with cheap labor. Thus, the Mexican community faced a double jeopardy: internal qualities (gender, citizenship, legal status) made them vulnerable to heavy concentration in low paid occupations; external political institutions, the schools, which emphasized industrial education even after desegregating, helped reproduce the existing occupational character across generations.

The third change occurred in family life, upon which the war had a force-ful impact. The war itself pulled families in separate directions as sons and daughters entered military service, nonagricultural pursuits, or packing. As this process occurred, family labor and the labor of school-age children took a lesser place among the ways the family supported itself. Seasonal migra-tions, both for citrus picking and packing and vegetable and fruit labor, competed against bracero labor, bracero wages, and working conditions. Seasonal agricultural employment in northern counties, no longer the prov-ince of the villagers, took a back seat to a preference for local industrial work, even if at the lower rungs of the pay scale.

The use of young boys as *ratas* in picking, like family migrations, fell by the wayside. Moreover, the use of Mexican families in walnut picking decreased as trees were removed or picking was taken over by braceros. The combined effect stimulated extended participation in education as children could begin to enroll at the opening of each school year.

New occupational possibilities for women appeared—as clerks in stores, schoolteachers, waitresses, and factories, among other occupations. These women, in contrast to previous practice, began working to satisfy their individual needs and desires rather than to pass their pay check in its en-tirety on to the family.[81] The communal forms of family life of the past were altered by the increasing individuality within the still functioning extend-ed family structure. Employment for each member of the family ceased to be a matter relative to the head male's occupation, a condition fostered by a combination of circumstances within the process of the citrus industry.

Not only did women enter into new lines of work, they also participat-ed directly in the union movement. Although sources of information are few and impressionistic, we do know that cannery workers at the Fuller-ton Val Vita plant, "75 percent of whom were Mexican women," organized a United Cannery, Agricultural, Packing, and Allied Workers of America local. According to historian Vicki Ruiz, the Fullerton plant, "the largest cannery in California," was "unmatched for deplorable working condi-tions."[82] After a bitter union campaign, punctuated by management vio-lence, workers voted overwhelmingly (262 for, 68 against) in favor of join-ing the leftist-UCAPAWA. Later, the union movement spread to dehydration plants in the Santa Ana area. Thus, during the war, women, like the men before them, entered directly into the union movement and in so doing engaged in independent political action connecting them with the national union agenda.

The villages never experienced gangs or gang activity until the 1940s. Gangs made their appearance in the urban context challenging not only urban middle-class sensibilities but also those of rural areas. Some Ana-heim youths adopted the pachuco image in the 1940s, and as the move-ment emerged, it displayed an urban "hip" versus rural "hick" cleavage.

John Arce recalled that the trend-setting pachucos of Anaheim derided the unsophisticated youth of his Independencia village. This instance of urban-rural distinction in teenage male behavior has been identified in other areas of southern California as well.[83] The appearance of pachucos did not necessarily bring increased crime. One 1947 study of the Anaheim Mexican villages contended that juvenile arrests in the villages were the result of increased surveillance and more stringent applications of enforcement than to an increased incidence of antisocial behavior in the Mexican communities.[84] In Placentia, as in many of the villages, police routinely harassed Mexican residents, especially in the evening hours. Fred Aguirre, who would serve on the city council, recalls that in Placentia, Mexicans were commonly arrested for "drunk and disorderly" conduct regardless of the actual circumstances. Sentences for Mexicans generally involved physical labor, for example, janitorial work in city buildings, but judges did not apply such to the English-speaking community. In one incident, which was the direct cause of Aguirre's organizing of a chapter of LULAC, police entered into his family home, dragged his brother out, and arrested him for drunkenness. In those days, stated Aguirre, the police were above the law and enforced it as they pleased.[85] Excessive force and arbitrary beatings were not unusual, but through LULAC pressure, especially its voter registration drive, local improvement in police-community relations was achieved.[86]

Since 1950

Paralleling to some degree the social and economic changes in the *colonia,* physical improvements began to appear. Paved streets, sidewalks and sewer lines, rarities at one time in many of the villages, made them more hospitable and healthier. In previous years winter rains had made dirt streets impassable, often preventing children from attending school. In some cases, the political impact of LULAC locals resulted in *colonia* development projects providing them services that the dominant communities had taken for granted. But not all changes were requested by the villages nor were they all for the better. Logan *colonia* in Santa Ana was rezoned in the postwar era as an industrial area.[87] Atwood followed along a similar course several years later. Into the early 1950s the association-owned family housing in Campo Colorado and Campo Pomona would be torn down, residents moving into nearby *colonias.* (Much later the frenzy of freeway construction would slice La Jolla and Logan, creating another dislocation.)

Significant electoral successes, however, would not appear until the mid-1950s and through the 1970s. Mexican Americans were elected to the city councils or mayoralties of La Habra, Placentia, Orange, and Fullerton. Yet for all of the changes that occurred between 1940 and about 1950, the *colonia* remained an enclave of old and new Mexican immigrants, along with some of those of the second and subsequent generations.

Urbanization slowly enveloped the villages until they were no longer isolated or semi-isolated rural-like hamlets. Urban developers "offering high prices for land began to find the Southern California orange grower a ready seller."[88] Grove after grove disappeared, some 75,000 choice acres across the region between 1946–56. In Orange County, the decline was most dramatic. Valencia production reached a peak of 67,000 acres in 1947; ten years later acreage halved to 36,000, and by 1967 less than 20,000 acres produced Valencias, and much of it in new outlying growing areas. Disappearing citrus groves were replaced by mushrooming housing tracts that transformed Orange County into an emerging regional suburbia and as the county transformed so did the *colonias.* La Jolla, Atwood, Corona, Stanton, Manzanillo, Independencia, and El Modena were absorbed into growing cities. As the spatial distance between the Mexican communities and the dominant communities shortened, the urban barrio entered the social stage, assuming the welcoming role formerly played by the citrus worker village. By the time that the later successive waves of postwar immigration occurred, the outline of the future barrio had already taken shape. Between 1940 and 1950, the community increased in size by some 7,000 persons to approximately 21,000.[89]

The remaining two decades, however, witnessed spectacular growth in the Mexican population, reaching over 117,000 by 1970, and more than doubling by 1980 to 286,339. In three generations, the Mexican community grew from less than 4,000 to over 286,000. In this period of population growth, geographically spreading *colonias* welcomed the new arrivals, while new communities were formed to shelter the surplus. By the mid-1970s at least eleven new barrios had formed and the process continues without respite. Urbanization, however, did not substantially alter the decades' social relationship between the Mexican American community and the dominant society. Mexican immigrants continue to arrive, and their cheap labor is welcomed by employers. The communities remain residential centers largely for labor in manufacturing, service industries, and the receding patchwork of agricultural fields. Mexican labor remains a commodity valuable as it has been throughout the twentieth century in what is, and has been, one of the most productive and wealthiest counties in the United States. In this economic context Mexican community history continues.

Conclusion

The fate of the citrus village is part of a pattern of Chicano community development emerging in the twentieth century notable for a rising and falling of specific community forms. The preceding narrative has examined the rise of Mexican immigrant communities in the Orange County sector of the southern California citrus belt, with particular attention paid to the influence of the citrus industry in that community's development and life. The history of citrus labor villages is inextricably interwoven with citrus production. Thus, as the industry evolved and eventually declined, the community as it was followed suit.

The character of the southwestern economy has influenced the creation of a variety of Mexican community forms. For example, company towns, urban barrios, rural villages, and migrant settlements were established on the needs of railroad, mining, agriculture, stockraising, lumbering, and industry.[1] These widely varying forms indicate a heterogeneous community style in Chicano history and culture. Arizona mining towns, as an example, employing considerable Mexican labor possessed an identifiable character distinguishing them from Texas sharecropping communities, or cities with a large commercial/ industrial character like Los Angeles.

At the turn of the century, rural and semirural Mexican population concentrations dotted the Southwest desert landscape. By the early 1900s, commodity production in large-scale agriculture, mining, and transportation assumed predominance within the economy. Centers of a newly evolving system of production drew not only the Mexican population to them but other minority groups and the Anglo population as well. Minority and Anglo populations and community forms were largely distributed according to the emerging production pattern.

Since the principal economic thrust occurred in the countryside in the second half of the nineteenth century, it comes as no surprise that the Mexican population in the early twentieth century, like other nationalities, established their residence, family, and community in rural as well as urbanizing areas. Often communities appeared for only brief periods and disappeared as a mine was exhausted, a railroad track was completed, or the price of a commodity, such as cotton, dropped precipitously. The Mexican community, affected by the demand for its labor power, and dependent upon the local production pattern for its survival, settled according to that economic infrastructure, with rural to urban settlements equally critical in the immigrant experience.

This study of citrus labor villages originated in an interest in expanding the scope of Chicano historiography beyond the urban arena. Widening the research focus can only strengthen a field distinguished for many significant contributions to American West, Southwest, and ethnic history. Furthermore, a more comprehensive approach insures a stronger foundation on which to build a comparative nationwide ethnic history. Several observations relevant to that comparative and comprehensive interest have emerged in this study.

First, the substantial differentiation in lifestyle between urban and rural Chicanos is capable of comparison and deserves attention. A number of examples verify the contrasting experiences. In the regions where family labor is widespread, the independence of women as economic actor is sharply curtailed in comparison to her urban counterpart. Family labor is also absent in the citrus industry, therefore of little significance in maintaining production; however, women are widely employed in the packinghouses, paradoxically earning wages equal to those of their male counterparts, the pickers. This factor certainly distinguished female employment in citrus from that of migrant family labor, such as in cotton production. Women packers had a sense of self-worth based on their individual labor and talents that was all but impossible for women who worked as part of a family unit. In the family unit, the male head was the sole wage earner and wages were paid directly to him by his employer or the labor contractor, seldom to the individuals who composed the family. Thus, women in family picking labor rarely received individual compensation for their labor.

A measure of the wide distinction between the experience of women in cotton production and women in urban production appears when comparing the work of Ruth Allen to that of Vicki Ruiz. Allen's classic 1933 study of women in Texas cotton production noted that among Mexican women who did field work for hire, only a small percentage "received the income from their labor. In the case of the . . . married women the husbands received all the income."[2] Among 110 women who worked in a family unit, not one "reported that there was any arrangement to pay for her labor."[3] Allen further states, "But even when the woman is a hired laborer, she has no individual economic existence. Her husband, father, or brother handles the financial affairs. She does not collect her own money; she does not know how much is paid for her services; she seldom knows how much cotton she picks a day or how many acres she chops. The wage paid is a family wage, and the family is distinctly patriarchal in its organization."[4] Vicki Ruiz's 1987 study of California cannery and packing women of the 1930s and 1940s arrived at substantially different observations. In the Los Angeles area, Ruiz found that "many women had dreams of white collar careers" and although women workers sought work to augment family income, they labored as individual wage earners even if they generally received less than men for the same work.[5] At work women developed a "cannery culture," a consciousness of common interests that fueled the movement toward unionization where ethnic women affected "every facet of decision making."[6]

Citrus packers responded to their work in a similar fashion. Julia Aguirre felt that the packinghouse offered "a greater opportunity for women" and provided "a sense of importance and purpose. . . . I learned about my own rights."[7] Furthermore, she added, "it was better, a lot better than picking cotton. . . . [picking cotton] was miserable. . . . [in comparison] packing oranges was heaven. . . . it was a step ahead. . . . at least we had a stable life."[8]

In education received, there has also been substantial variation according to the economy. Educational opportunity in the urban setting is much more egalitarian than in the rural migrant settlements. Rural migrants were far less likely to attend school, or if attending at all, to attend only a portion of the school year. Statistics for Texas taken in 1945 indicate that only half of Mexican children were enrolled in school. In part, this was due to a deliberate policy by boards of education across the state to bar Mexican children, especially migrant children, from school enrollment. However, in citrus towns opportunities for schooling were greater due to the absence of family labor, but less so than in the urban context because of occasional migrations for agricultural work.

Dr. Ernesto Galarza recognized the political distinction between urban and rural Mexican communities—a distinction that divided some civil rights activists in the 1940s and as recently as the 1970s.[9] César Chávez, for example, left the Community Service Organization in the mid-1950s because the latter focused attention on urban issues. Chávez sought to deal with the problems of the rural Mexican community, a decision with far-reaching and well-known effects on the history of farmworker unions and California agriculture. That urban and rural areas contain distinguishable issues is further underscored by the differing emphases on school reform during the 1960s and 1970s. Rural activists generally demanded integration, while urban activists turned toward separatism, community control of neighborhood schools, and bilingual education. The observation in 1971 of Alan Exelbrod, staff attorney with the Mexican-American Legal Defense Fund, underscored a rural-urban political dichotomy:

While there is a tendency today to think that Chicanos, wherever located, share the same educational goals, this is not the case. In rural areas and small urban centers, integration is sought because segregated education invariably means inferior facilities for Chicano schools, as well as psychological feelings of second class citizenship. In large urban areas . . . there is little desire for integration. The leaders of these "barrios" resist education policies which undermine community control of schools and retard the enactment of bilingual/bicultural education.[10]

The variations manifest in other ways too. Villages entirely comprising Mexican residents and geographically separate from Anglo communities in rural areas are clearly evident in the citrus area. The high level intervention of the citrus industry in Mexican village affairs sought, among other things, to engineer cultural change and shape educational objectives. This kind of direct intervention by specific employers, and its success, is quite uncommon in the urban context.

Second, there exists a critical distinction in settlement patterns between the comparative experiences of European immigrants and those from Mexico. John Higham has underscored the urban quality of the ethnic experience of European immigrants. For Mexican immigrants during the first half of the century, the opposite is true, that their ethnic experience was significantly rural in quality. Unlike European immigrants settling along the eastern seaboard and the Northeast, Mexican immigrants entered desert and semidesert, punctuated by fertile agricultural valleys, rich mining sites, and commercial and manufacturing towns and cities. One searches in vain for smokestack urbanized industrial regions like those of the Northeast. Contrary to John Higham's description of the immigrant in American history, Mexican immigrants entered and settled into an economic region based largely on agriculture, stockraising, mining and smelting, railroads and railroad construction, and manufacturing. Fully 62 percent of foreign-born Europeans in the United States lived in urban places in 1890.[11] In contrast, fifty years later, only 50 percent of Mexicans in the United States lived in urban places. Even that figure is misleading, as a large sector of Mexican urban dwellers at that time labored a portion of each year in agriculture. Data for the 1920s and 1930s demonstrate that one-third of agricultural workers lived in urban areas, and probably worked in both settings. This bifurcated sector, as the UCLA Mexican-American Study Project pointed out in 1970 had "almost no twentieth century counterpart among European immigrant groups."[12]

Unfortunately, the growing number of histories on the Chicano people neither confront the significant rural experience nor the variation in settlement placement. An old misperception in that historiography, that Chicanos have been an urban group throughout the twentieth century, deserves correction. The suggestion has been made that even though the rural communities have in fact harbored a significant portion of the Chicano population, urban historical study nevertheless is sufficient to generalize to the entire population.[13] Is there but one Chicano historical community experience—the urban one? The conclusions reached through the study of citrus villages do not support such contentions. If we desire to describe *and* explain Mexican-Anglo contact, we must recognize the distinct contexts in which contact has occurred.

An all-encompassing urban history leans heavily toward overgeneralization, while the opposite approach—that Chicanos are so heterogeneous that generalization is difficult, if not impossible—is equally wide of the mark. This analysis proceeds from a view that both generalizations and particularities coexist within the historical experience and that it is the task of the historian to identify the constituent elements of any complex historical process. As a consequence of emphasis on urban life, the historian focuses on industrial blue-collar labor to the neglect (and exclusion) of rural and small-to-medium Chicano communities and their lifestyles and histories. An alternative perspective is suggested here based on the underlying economic development of the Southwest in the late nineteenth and, especially, the early twentieth centuries. This growth encouraged an abundant variety of community forms running the gamut from rural agricultural to urban industrial communities.

The above logically leads us to ask whether variation in community continues as a critical factor in the Chicano experience. The answer is clearly in the affirmative. Examples of squatter labor villages, one of the original forms taken by citrus worker villages in the 1910s and 1920s, are much in evidence today in southern California, especially in agricultural zones bordering suburban housing. Recent articles in southern California newspapers have called attention to the spread of squatter villages, an example, wrote one journalist, of "ingenuity . . . their creative use of whatever material may be available."[14] This description of a hamlet of two hundred squatters in rural San Diego county is striking: "Here, where wood is plentiful, most homes are framed with chopped willow stakes and bamboo, bound together with agricultural string and hosing. Many have also built small sleeping cubicles of scrap timber. For foundations they use crushed soda cans, placed below the posts." In the village an "entrepreneur has set up a barber shop, with a car seat as his stand" and a number of women sell meals over a makeshift counter. In another area of the community, the sports-minded set up a recreation area, with a volleyball net strung between trees. At the common shrine of La Virgen de Guadalupe, villagers pray for protection from the U.S. Border Patrol and roving bands of thieves.[15]

Estimates have placed the number of persons residing in makeshift housing in the thousands, perhaps as many as ten thousand. The housing constitutes the largest concentration of substandard "living conditions found" anywhere in California, although "scattered settlements . . . in fields, canyons, caves and beneath roadways and bridges" are found throughout California's farming sector.[16] Some housing has been used by unscrupulous employers to keep workers as virtual slaves—one case involving sixty workers was described as a "modern day serfdom."[17] This spreading residential pattern is part of a revival of immigrant rural settlement throughout the agricultural valleys of California. The recent northern California earthquake destroyed many houses in the agriculturally-based town of Watsonville, scene after scene shown on television displayed not Anglo faces but the faces of Mexican worker families, the majority of the population.

Between 1980 and 1990, the fastest growing Mexican immigrant communities in California have not been in the urban areas, but in rural areas. Over five hundred thousand residents inhabit hundreds of small population centers from the central valley to the border. In sixty communities Mexicans form the majority of the residents. In addition, rural Mexicans are much more culturally homogeneous and segregated than in urban barrios. Most of the residents are recent immigrants. Their annual earnings fall below the poverty level in most cases, and during harvests the population of the towns swells considerably. The rural Mexican community is usually a cluster of working poor living in isolation, invisible to, and ignored by, the vast majority of Californians.[18]

Research also documents the rise of coherent communities straddling the U.S.-Mexico border, that is, the appearance of an entirely new community form distinct from any found in the past. Josiah Heyman of the Michigan Technological Institute has carried out considerable research on the trend toward binational communities.[19] In these small- to medium-sized towns, work, family, and sometimes residence often blend the two sides of the borders into one.

Older residents of the Mexican side of the border point out the new consciousness sweeping the citizens of border towns. A former Tijuana resident recalled that, as a young man growing up in the 1940s, he and his cohorts considered themselves unambiguously Mexican.[20] Further, Tijuana at that time was distinctively a Mexican city, culturally, politically, and economically. However, this former resident points out that the firm identification with Mexico has weakened while a new consciousness, an international consciousness is on the upswing. A Tijuana business executive offered a similar assessment, describing today's Tijuana as a "binational city," and contending that "it's not a Mexican city."[21] Analysts discern a pattern of a growing integration of California with Mexico's Baja California. The latter's governor remarked that the trend will increase, creating a situation whereby the previous distinction created by the border "will matter less and less as the years go by."[22]

The second theme threading through the history of citrus villages and of Chicano history concerns the role of the Mexican consulate. While historians have usually examined the political impact of the Mexican American generation fairly comprehensively, the politics of the first generation is stereotyped. Usually the first wave of immigrants is presented as cheap labor; active in patriotic, self-help, and labor organizations; espousing Mexicanismo; segregated, but content to live among compatriots. Absent from the literature is an analysis of the political culture of those first settlers, and especially of the influence and the political objectives of the Mexican consulate. This void is especially significant in recent studies of Chicano political history, histories that begin with the second generation as if they are rising within a political vacuum.

The late Ralph Gúzman, political scientist at the University of California, Santa Cruz, pointed out in his seminal essays on Chicano politics the influence of the consulate on the culture of the Mexican community. His observation that "the direct influence of Mexico has been and continues to be significant" must be appreciated.[23]

Historians of the Chicano experience have either lauded the consulate for acting as a protector of Mexican interests, or they have relegated the consul to a minor player on the Chicano stage.[24] Neither of these interpretations portray the consul's role in its full complexity. The evidence argues that the consulate, within its sphere of influence, sought participation in the political affairs of the U.S. through providing a prominent bulwark against working class radicalism. In that regard, it is highly probable that the U.S. government nodded approvingly regarding the consular actions in Mexican labor unions.[25] In the final analysis, the Mexican consul played a major role in California's labor struggles of the 1930s through fomenting the spread of conservative unions and engaging in union busting, especially against unions led by the Communist party but also against those of the noncommunist leftists. A perusal of the *Western Worker,* newspaper of the Communist party in the west, during the 1933–36 period illustrates the pattern of sharp conflict between the party and the consul. This pattern was not confined to the two, however, and extended to Mexican citizens in Mexican unions. It is particularly important to recognize that the consular antiradicalism impacted against both Mexican citizens and Anglo-Americans. As such, the consular officials engaged a political struggle and arrayed itself on the right.

The UCLA Mexican-American Study noted this aspect of consulate intervention, one that stood out in the life of the citrus villagers: "Mexican diplomats played an extensive role in worker organizations, including conciliation and arbitration in labor disputes, sponsorship of unions, *and establishment of anti-communist associations* [emphasis mine]."[26]

Again, the question of continuity arises: Do such diplomatic endeavors permeate the political life of the Chicano community today? Again the answer is affirmative. For example, during the Chicano movement of the 1960s and 1970s, extensive contact occurred between a substantial number of Chicano activists and officials of the administration of Mexican president Echevarria. At the invitation of the Mexican government, contingents of Chicano activists were treated to special meetings with ranking officials, even the president.

More recently, Mexican president Carlos Salinas de Gortari has "pledged to improve contact between the Mexican government and Mexicans in the United States."[27] Mexican secretary of state Fernando Solana elaborated on that pledge in the keynote speech at the 1990 annual meeting of the Mexican-American Legal Defense and Educational Fund: "the Mexican government wishes to establish closer ties with the Mexican-American community. Because of our shared language, beliefs and values, we see the Mexican-American community as an ideal vehicle for better and more effective communications with the United States. Traditionally, there have been contacts between the Mexican government and the Mexican American community. However, we need to broaden their scope and make them more fruitful."[28] The speech was followed by the visit of the undersecretary of the Department of Foreign Affairs to "several University of California campuses," where he announced the Mexican government's plan "to reach out to Mexicans and people of Mexican descent living outside of Mexico" through a new directorate in foreign affairs.[29] His hosts at the University of California, including Chicano professors and students involved in a week-long conference on Chicano Society and Culture, embraced the proposal and suggested an enlarged and ongoing formal interaction. A sign of the growing interest of the Mexican government in Chicano affairs was the awarding of La Medalla Aguila Azteca in November 1990 to three well-known figures: César Chávez, union leader; Américo Paredes, author; and Julián Samora, scholar. For the first time, the prize "bestowed on non-Mexicans for meritorious contributions to the Mexican people" was awarded to a Chicano.[30]

On the other hand, Chicano leaders have suggested that Chicanos "use" Mexico as a leverage to gain greater clout in national policy making. Vilma Martínez, former head of the Mexican American Legal Defense and Education Fund, once claimed "that Washington will finally have to listen to us because of Mexico."[31] Presumably scholarships and other programs such as the Becas de Aztlán begun by the Echevarria Administration and offering over $10 million in scholarships between 1980–85 for Chicanos to study in Mexico, fulfill in some manner the principle goals of the Chicano people.[32]

There is a substantial interest and activity in Chicano to Mexican government relations. Chicanos have a considerable list of wide-ranging interests in pursuing international interaction. Businesses, civil rights activists, politicians, and unionists have parceled sections of the political dialogue. Mexico, on the other hand, writes Juan Gómez-Quiñónez, is willing to negotiate providing the agenda for discussion "coincide with Mexican foreign policy interests."[33] One needs add to the caveat that negotiation proceeds from Mexico's domestic policy interests as well and in the early 1990s it is the North American Free Trade Agreement that guides Mexico's activities in relation to the Chicano people.

The Mexican government, still under control of the Partido Revolucionario Institucional, designs its foreign policy based on its perceived national political interests. National concerns are as fundamental today to Mexico as they were fifty years ago when PRI was founded, and when the Mexican community allowed itself to become as loyal a partner to the Mexican government as one of that government's labor unions.[34] It remains a serious issue, one with a long history, a history that should be studied well and weighed carefully—but unfortunately current Chicano historiography offers little direction.

The third theme relates to the generational process, that is, the appearance of the second and subsequent generations. At least one historian has admonished his colleagues to get on with the study of postimmigrant Mexican society.[35] This suggestion is problematical because of the continual appearance of immigrants, their settlement, and the rise of the second generation—all are critical to the Chicano experience in the postwar period.

The politicocultural rite of passage did not end with the rise of the Mexican American generation of the 1940s, a generation imbued with a self-conscious ethnicity and an appreciation of civil rights. We must consider the institutionalization of the process of becoming a Mexican American—an enduring feature of the Chicano social fabric. Although the particular activism and political objectives of the 1940s Mexican American generation has passed into history, the process of becoming an ethnic minority—a Mexican American—is an essential part of the Mexican experience in the United States. What this also means is that the Chicano community contains a dynamic complex of generations—from new immigrants to later generations. Political action and organization cannot ignore the cultural as well as legal variations within communities composed of undocumented immigrants, temporary legal immigrants, permanent residents, and the second and subsequent generations of citizens with voting rights.

Indeed, the history of the immigrant generation did not end in the 1940s, nor did the Mexican American generation end in the 1950s. An amalgam of their experiences comprises postwar Chicano history. Immigration continually reproduces the generational dynamics of the 1920–40 period and thus an ongoing process of political acculturation. The layering of generations living in close proximity, often in the same barrio, suggests that ethnic consciousness is stratified, so to speak, rather than integrated presenting substantial obstacles to a unified political agenda and action.

Each new Mexican American generation has only a U.S. experience on which to base their politicocultural consciousness. The immigrant, or Mexican, generation, on the other hand, acquires or achieves a politicocultural character honed by a comparative perspective. The Mexican immigrants juxtapose, either deliberately or unconsciously, their Mexican experience with their U.S. experience. The relative improvement in their living standards as a result of the move from one nation to another, their adjustment to the new way of life in the United States, as well as their legal status as noncitizens, impede political participation and awareness.

The issue of generational process logically leads to the matter of immigration, the key to explaining the origins of the Chicano minority. Immigration, however, cannot be well understood apart from the economic ties binding the United Ststes and Mexico. It is not the conquest of 1848 but the incremental extension of United States economic power into the Mexican nation that has been, and continues to be, at the center of the Chicano historical experience in the twentieth century. Dr. Ernesto Galarza's analysis of the underlying factors producing migration in the late 1940s is applicable today, perhaps even more so. The migrant, wrote Galarza in 1949, "is forced to seek better conditions north of the border by the slow but relentless pressure of United States agricultural, financial, and oil corporate interests on the entire economic and social evolution of the Mexican nation."[36] The study of Chicano history cannot ignore the primacy of the international imperial dimension in the ongoing formation and evolution of the Chicano people. The Chicano minority is an immigrant people whose roots are to be found in the structured inequality between the United States and Mexico, one that in any other context (e.g., the old Soviet Union in relation to Eastern Europe) would be described as imperialism. Mexican dependence upon U.S. finance capital, trade, technology, tourism, export of raw materials, and agricultural products, the "safety valve" of immigration, and the extension of foreign-based *maquiladora* plants to employ surplus labor reflect neither an economic independence nor a status as the United States's equal trading partner. Instead, Mexico has evolved much as an extension of the North American economy, more so in the past two decades, as is amply illustrated by the recent debate over the North American Free Trade Agreement between Mexico, Canada, and the United States.

NAFTA specifies, among other things, that Mexican cheap labor will increasingly be tapped "at the source" rather than at the plant on the U.S.

side. Adolfo Aguilar Zinser, researcher at the National University of Mexico, described the then-pending agreement as the formalization of an existing international relation: "But in fact," states Aguilar, "the United States will maintain the higher-paid jobs and technology and Mexico will specialize only in cheap labor."[37] Already *maquiladora* plants employ five hundred thousand along the U.S.-Mexico border, a region producing a large sector of electronics sold in the United States. Critics point out that less than 2 percent of the materials consumed in production come from Mexican sources, and of the $3.5 billion in salaries annually poured into the Mexican economy, most of it is spent on the U.S. side. Thus, the principal benefit accruing to Mexico from U.S. economic intervention (and this is true whether NAFTA passed or not) is the employment of its surplus labor. Yet throughout the 1970s and 1980s, during an expansion of *maquiladora* plants, undocumented migration continued to grow and spill into the Southwest, especially Southern California. Not even the Immigration Act of 1986, intended to control illegal migration, had a measurable impact. Why? Jorge Castaneda, professor of political science at the National Autonomous University of Mexico in Mexico City, boils the issue down to wages. The differential in earning power between the United States and Mexico is the magnet drawing migrants from as far away as Oaxaca, Yucatan, and Mexico City.[38] Add the enormous number of unemployed in Mexico, a factor cheapening already rock-bottom wages, and it is the United States—not the *maquiladora* (which on average pays only one-third the U.S. minimum wage), which the Mexican laborer perceives as the ultimate solution to his or her fundamental needs.

Some economists argue that in the future the merging of the two economies is imminent. The work of Professor Raúl Fernández, of the University of California, Irvine, a specialist in border history and economy, concludes that the border region will be internationalized, economically, socially, and culturally by the year 2000. Professor Fernandez's observation is echoed by others. For example, Wesley Smith, Latin American policy analyst at the Washington, D.C.–based Heritage Foundation, a conservative public policy research institute, in support of the Free Trade Agreement writes: "The best way to ensure that Mexico prospers under a democratic, free market economy is to link its future inextricably with ours . . . our choice is clear: Integrate low-cost labor from countries like Mexico into our production . . . or . . . abandon our position as the world's economic leader."[39]

The question then arises: If economic integration occurs, who will be the primary beneficiary? Will it be the corporate enterprises long accustomed to cheap Mexican labor, or will Mexico move further along the path of industrialization and toward equal partnership with the United States? Recent Mexican federal legislation, in anticipation of NAFTA, unilaterally removed major obstacles to foreign capital and landownership, propelled privatization of the economy, and "upgraded" government labor unions. The legislative measures demonstrated the Mexican governments' intention to meet the conditions of foreign investment. With NAFTA securely in place, Mexico joined its future more securely to that of the northern superpower. In the past, these ties failed to remove Mexico from the roll-call of under-developed nations. New arrangements integrated into a historically conditioned structure augur little appreciable affect on Mexico's economic status. Within the parameters of existing international relations, migration to the border region and immigration to the United States will continue unabated, and settlements will expand, creating continual community and sociocultural change.

Notes

Introduction

1. Ernesto Galarza, *Merchants of Labor: The Mexican Bracero Story* (Charlotte, N.C.: McNally and Loftin, 1964), 32.

2. Elizabeth Broadbent, "The Distribution of the Mexican Population in the United States" (Ph.D. diss., University of Chicago, 1941), 61.

3. See David J. Weber, "The New Chicano Urban History," *History Teacher* 16, no. 2 (Feb. 1983): 224–30; see also Eugene E. Garcia, Francisco A. Lomeli, Isidro D. Ortiz, eds., *Chicano Studies: A Multi-Disciplinary Approach* (New York: Teachers College, Columbia University Press, 1984). The editors write: "Historically, Chicanos have been seen as a rural population. The fact that at least since 1930 the overwhelming majority of the Chicano population has been concentrated in the urban centers of the country has been neglected" (19). Such an argument has little evidence to support it; in fact, in 1930 one-half of the Mexican population in the U.S. was rural, and remained so until World War II.

4. Fortunately, the urban emphasis in Chicano historiography is waning. Some recent Chicano historiography takes a more complex approach. Sarah Deutsch's analysis of the *transition* from rural to urban life, Vicki Ruiz's examination of women's organizations in the agriculture-based food processing industry, Richard Griswold del Castillo's forthcoming biographical study of César Chávez, Robert Alvarez's study of Baja California migrating families, Arnoldo de Leon's several works and Denis Nodín Valdes's history of agricultural workers in the Upper Midwest all provide several variations of community studies significant for future research. They demonstrate that many communities do not fall into the urban pattern described in the earlier literature. Finally, Poyo and Hinojosa's *Journal of American History* article illustrates, through the concrete study of early Texas settlements, the complexity and enduring significance of those specific communities. Sarah Deutsch, *No Separate Refuge: Culture, Class, and Gender on an Anglo-Hispanic Frontier in the American Southwest, 1880–1940* (New York: Oxford University Press, 1987); Robert Alvarez, *Familia: Migration and Adaptation in Baja and Alta California, 1800–1975* (Berkeley: University of California Press, 1987); Gerald E. Poyo and Gilberto M. Hinojosa, "Spanish Texas and Borderlands Historiography in Transition: Implications for U.S. History," *Journal of Ameri-*

can History 75 (Sept. 1988): 393–416; Vicki Ruiz, *Cannery Women, Cannery Lives* (Albuquerque: University of New Mexico Press, 1987); Dennis Nodín Valdes, *Al Norte: Agricultural Workers in the Great Lakes Region, 1917–1970* (Austin: University of Texas Press, 1991).

5. See, for example, David Montejano, *Anglos and Mexicans in the Making of Texas, 1836–1986* (Austin: The University of Texas Press, 1987); Robert J. Thomas, *Citizenship, Gender, and Work: Social Organization of Industrial Agriculture* (Berkeley: The University of California Press, 1985); Vicki Ruiz, *Cannery Women, Cannery Lives;* Rosalinda M. González, "Distinctions in Western Women's Experience: Ethnicity, Class, and Social Change," in *The Women's West,* ed. Susan Armitage (Norman: University of Oklahoma Press, 1987).

6. A full exposition of this approach applied to Chicano historiography can be found in Gilbert G. González and Raúl A. Fernández, "Chicano History: Transcending Cultural Models," *Pacific Historical Review* (1994).

7. Lizabeth Cohen, *Making a New Deal: Industrial Workers in Chicago, 1919–1939* (Cambridge, Mass.: Cambridge University Press, 1990); Gary Gerstle, *Working-class Americanism: The Politics of Labor in a Textile City, 1914–1960* (Cambridge, Mass.: Cambridge University Press, 1989); Dennis Nodín Valdes, *Al Norte;* David Montejano, *Anglos and Mexicans in the Making of Texas;* Cletus E. Daniel, *Bitter Harvest: A History of California Farmworkers, 1870–1941* (Berkeley: University of California Press, 1981)

8. W. R. Wellman and E. W. Brown, *Oranges.* University of California, College of Agriculture, Agricultural Experiment Station. Series on California Crops and Prices, Bulletin 457, Aug. 1928. (Berkeley: University of California, 1928), 7.

9. U.S. Congress Senate Committee on Education and Labor, *Violations of Free Speech and the Rights of Labor.* Report of the Committee on Education and Labor, Part 1 (Washington, D.C.: Government Printing Office, 1942), 538.

10. "Cooperation at a Profit," *Fortune* 14 (July 1936): 47.

11. Two examples of the tremendous growth of citrus are illustrated by statistics on acreage expansion. Between 1916 and 1921, the years of increasing Mexican immigration, citrus acreage expanded by 51 percent. In Orange County, adjacent to Los Angeles County, acreage expanded from 40 acres in 1870, to 5,000 in 1900, to 40,500 in 1928, finally reaching 78,000 in 1945.

Based on five-year averages for the periods 1919–20 to 1923–24 and 1939–40 to 1943–44 we find that orange acreage expanded from 166,229 acres to 234,858. Similarly, production grew significantly between 1899 and 1940, from 1,245,000 boxes of packed citrus to 45,340,000 boxes. (For general statistics, see Herbert John Webber and Leon Dexter Batchelor, eds., *The Citrus Industry,* vol. 1 [Berkeley: The University of California Press, 1943].)

12. Mark Reisler, *By the Sweat of Their Brow: Mexican Immigrant Labor in the United States, 1900–1940* (Westport, Conn.: Greenwood Press, 1976), 1–23; see also Carey McWilliams, *North From Mexico: The Spanish Speaking People of the United States* (Philadelphia: J. B. Lippincott Co., 1949); Paul S. Taylor, *Mexican Labor in the United States,* vol. 1 (Berkeley: University of California Press, 1930); vol. 2 (Berkeley: University of California Press, 1932).

13. Lloyd H. Fisher, *The Harvest Labor Market in California* (Cambridge, Mass.: Harvard University Press, 1953), 31. See also Juan L. Gonzáles, Jr. *Mexican and Mexican American Farm Workers* (New York: Praeger Publishers, 1985); Linda C. Majka and Theo J. Majka, *Farm Workers, Agribusiness, and the State* (Philadelphia, Pa.: Temple University Press, 1982); Dennis Nodin Valdes, *Al Norte.*

14. Mexican communities had several identifying terms. The residents called them *colonias,* sometimes *campos,* and the terms "camps" sometimes "Little Mexicos" or "Jim-towns" were used by the dominant community.

15. Carey McWilliams, *Southern California Country: An Island on the Land* (New York: Duell, Sloan and Pearce, 1946), 218.

16. Paul Garland Williamson, "Labor in the California Citrus Industry" (Master's thesis, University of California, Berkeley, 1946), 44. This number represented one-quarter of all agricultural workers in the state.

17. M. R. Benedict, "The Economic and Social Structure of California Agriculture," in *California Agriculture,* ed. Claude B. Hutchison (Berkeley: University of California Press, 1946), 406.

18. Harry W. Lawton and Lewis G. Weathers, "The Origin of Citrus Research in California and the Founding of the Citrus Research Center and Agricultural Experiment Station." Xerox copy in hands of author. n.p., 1987, 7.

19. See, for example, Carey McWilliams's *Southern California Country* (218) or Richard Mines and R. Anzaldua's "New Migrants vs. Old Migrants: Alternative Labor Market Structures in the California Citrus Industry." Monograph in U.S.-Mexican Studies, 9. Program in United States–Mexican Studies (University of California, San Diego, 1982).

20. Paul Garland Williamson, "Labor in the California Citrus Industry."

21. See James B. Allen, *The Company Town in the American West* (Norman: University of Oklahoma Press, 1967).

22. See Richard A. García, *Rise of the Mexican American Middle Class: San Antonio, 1929–1941* (College Station: Texas A & M University Press, 1991), 29–30. Professor García points out that the large Mexican *colonia* in San Antonio found employment in the garment industry, pecan shelling, "bakeries, foundaries, machine shops, printing plants, publishing concerns, ice molding plants, Mexican food producers and processors, confectionary and beverage producers, slaughtering plants, and meat packing plants" and many more.

23. Nancy Hewitt presents a powerful argument for the importance of examining women in the particular social and material circumstances of their communities in "Beyond the Search for Sisterhood: American Women's History in the 1980s," *Social History* 10 (Oct. 1985): 299–321.

24. Richard García identifies a parallel process in San Antonio; John Higham and William L. Yancey et al. point out the same cultural transformation affecting European immigrants. See Richard A. Garcia, *Rise of the Mexican American Middle Class;* John Higham, "Integrating America: The Problem of Assimilation in the Nineteenth Century," *Journal of American Ethnic History* 1, no. 1 (Fall 1981): 8–9; William L. Yancey, Eugene P. Ericksen, and Richard Juliani, "Emergent Ethnicity: A Review and Reformulation," *American Sociological Review* 41 (June 1976): 391–403.

25. U.S. Congress. Senate Committee on Education and Labor. *Violations of Free Speech and Rights of Labor.* Report of the Committee on Education and Labor (Washington, D.C.: Government Printing Office, 1942), 541.

26. Paul Garland Williamson, "Labor in the California Citrus," 95.

27. Carey McWilliams, *Southern California Country,* 218. "Jim Town" applied to any rural Mexican community. Not surprising, a Mexican *colonia* near Whittier, Calif. came to be known as "Jim Town" and remains so-named today even though split in two by a eight lane freeway. See "Plight of Two Jim Towns," *The [Whittier] Daily News,* Jan. 19, 1973.

28. "Living Standards of Orange County Mexicans," Santa Ana, Calif.: Orange County Department of Social Welfare, 1940, 15.

29. Jessie Hayden, "The La Habra Experiment in Mexican Social Education" (Master's thesis, Claremont Colleges, Claremont, California, 1934), 63 and passim.

30. See, for example, Juan Gómez-Quiñónez, *Sembradores: Ricardo Flores Magon y el Partido Liberal Mexicano: A Eulogy and Critique* (Los Angeles: Aztlan Publications, University of California, Los Angeles, 1973); see also Jose Limón, "El Primer Congreso Mexicanista de 1911: A Precursor to Contemporary Chicanismo," *Aztlan* 5, nos. 1, 2 (Spring and Fall 1974): 85–117.

31. See Francisco Balderrama, *In Defense of La Raza: The Los Angeles Mexican Consulate and the Mexican Community, 1929–1936* (Tucson: University of Arizona Press, 1982); Mario T. García, *Mexican Americans: Leadership, Ideology, and Identity, 1930–1960* (New Haven: Yale University Press, 1989); Juan Gómez-Quiñónez, *Chicano Politics: Reality and Promise, 1940–1990* (Albuquerque: University of New Mexico Press, 1990); Carlos Munóz, Jr., *Youth, Identity, Power: The Chicano Movement* (New York: Verso, 1989); Christine Sierra, "Chicano Political Development: Historical Considerations" in *Chicano Studies. A Multidisciplinary Approach,* eds. Eugene E. García, Francisco Lomeli, and Isidro D. Ortiz (New York: Teachers College Press, 1984), 79–98.

1. History, Labor, and Social Relations in the Citrus Industry

1. Evidence suggests that as early as 4000 B.C. the citron (a variety of citrus fruit) was known to the Mesopotamians. Ancient European civilizations were also familiar with the citron; it was mentioned in 300 B.C. in the writings of the Greek Theophrastus. The Chinese also had the opportunity, over several centuries, to develop a citrus science—references to citrus are found in writings "antedating the Christian era by three centuries." In one 1178 A.D Chinese treatise the author discusses "grafting, transplanting, fertilization, irrigation, fungus diseases, and boring insects" (still major concerns of modern citrus culture). The author wrote on issues familiar to the modern rancher and with a knowledge comparable with that of the twentieth century, continued: "Use a small scissors for removing the fruit from the branches, cutting them off even

with the surface of the skin and carefully placing them in a basket. To protect them from injury one must be very careful for fear that the skins be cut, causing the volatile oils to escape, when the fruit will easily spoil" (Rahno Mabel MacCurdy, *The History of the California Fruit Growers Exchange* [Los Angeles: The California Fruit Growers Exchange, 1925], 1).

2. Herbert John Webber, "History and Development of the Citrus Industry," in *The Citrus Industry,* vol. 1, eds. Herbert John Webber and Leon Dexter Batchelor (Berkeley: University of California Press, 1946), 1.

3. Nephtune Fogelberg and A. W. McKay, *The Citrus Industry and the California Fruit Growers Exchange* (Washington, D.C.: U.S. Department of Agriculture Circular C-121, June 1940), 2.

4. Frank Adams, "The Historical Background of California Agriculture," in *California Agriculture,* ed. Claude B. Hutchison (Berkeley: University of California Press, 1946), 12–13.

5. MacCurdy, *The History of the California Fruit Growers Exchange,* 2.

6. Ibid., 4.

7. Harry Lawton and Lewis G. Weathers, "The Origins of Citrus Research in California and the Founding of the Citrus Research Center and Agricultural Experiment Station." Xerox copy, n.d., n.p., 5.

8. Lawton and Weathers, "The Origins of Citrus Research," 12.

9. MacCurdy, *The History of the California Fruit Growers Exchange,* 11.

10. Charles C. Teague, *Fifty Years a Rancher* (Los Angeles: Ward Ritchie Press, 1944), 85.

11. Carey McWilliams, *Southern California Country,* 210.

12. Herbert John Webber, "The Commercial Citrus Regions of the World: Their Physiographic, Climactic, and Economic Characters," in *The Citrus Industry,* vol. 1, eds. Herbert John Webber and Leon Dexter Batchelor, (Berkeley: University of California Press, 1943), 71; and Paul Garland Williamson, "Labor in the California Citrus Industry," 9.

13. H. R. Wellman, *Oranges.* University of California, College of Agriculture, Agricultural Experiment Station. Series on California Crops and Prices, Bulletin 457, Aug. 1928 (Berkeley, Calif.: University of California Printing Office, 1928), 1.

14. Paul Garland Williamson, "Labor in the California Citrus Industry," 9.

15. W. A. Spalding, "Colorful Early Days of California Citrus Industry," *The California Citrograph* 27 (July 1932): 353.

16. Paul Garland Williamson, "Labor in the California Citrus Industry," 3.

17. Charles C. Teague, *Fifty Years a Rancher,* 74.

18. The historian for the California Fruit Growers Exchange, Rahno MacCurdy, observed that when the growers furnished the capital and the distributor assumed no risk and had his profits practically guaranteed, the incentive for careful marketing lessened. Shipments went forward recklessly, demoralizing markets and returning in many cases a loss to the producer (Rahno Mabel MacCurdy, *The History of California Fruit Growers Exchange,* 15).

19. Ibid.

20. Carey McWilliams, *Southern California Country,* 211.

21. Ibid.

22. Quoted in Paul Garland Williamson, "Labor in the California Citrus Industry," 8.

23. Paul Garland Williamson reported, "From 1907 to 1937 the Exchange spent $24,453,028.00 on advertising," Paul Garland Williamson, "Labor in the California Citrus Industry," 26.

24. Ibid., 212.

25. U.S. Senate Committee on Education and Labor, *Violations of Free Speech and Rights of Labor.* Report of the Committee on Education and Labor (Washington, D.C.: Government Printing Office, 1942), 538.

26. Charles C. Teague, *Fifty Years a Rancher,* 88–89.

27. Ibid., 89.

28. U.S. Committee on Education and Labor, *Violations,* 539.

29. Paul Garland Williamson, "Labor in the California Citrus Industry," 14.

30. Some of the larger enterprises included:

Limoneira Ranch	1,850 acres
Mills Orchard	1,760 acres
Chapman Orchards	1,750 acres
Murphy Ranch	1,200 acres
Rancho Sespe	1,000 acres
Bastanchury Ranch	4,000 acres
San Joaquin Ranch	3,000 acres

[Paul Garland Williamson, "Labor in the California Citrus Industry," 19–20.]

31. Ibid., 25.

32. Carey McWilliams, *Southern California Country,* 212.

33. J. D. Culbertson, "Housing of Ranch Labor." First Annual Report of the California Citrus Institute, June 1, 1920, 97.

34. Ibid., 98.

35. Paul Garland Williamson, "Labor in the California Citrus Industry," 31.

36. Ibid., 32.

37. Charles C. Teague, *Fifty Years a Rancher,* 143.

38. Ibid.

39. Lloyd H. Fisher, *The Harvest Labor Market in California,* 25, 26. Lloyd Fisher wrote, "In nearly every little town constituting the center of a specialized agricultural community, one or more Japanese bosses can be found. These bosses, labor contractors, or employment agents are the leaders of the groups of Japanese laborers whom they associated with them. Usually the smaller contractors conduct lodging houses and stores, where the men live on a cooperative plan. The boss secures work for his men from the ranchers, and carries on all dealings with the employer as to the wages or contract price for the work, collects the wages of the gang, and pays the men their individual earnings."

40. Ibid., 29. Also, Cletus E. Daniel, *Bitter Harvest,* 75.

41. Ibid., 30.

42. Mark Reisler, *By the Sweat of Their Brow,* 3–19.

43. Lloyd Fisher, *The Harvest Labor Market,* 31.

44. *The California Citrograph,* the publication of the California Fruit Grow-

ers Exchange, praised the liberal immigration policy, which it strongly supported. An editorial read: "The government has at last recognized the farmers' needs in suspending the literacy test and the contract labor law against Mexican agricultural workers. This means that large numbers of Mexicans can be brought into the country under contract and will have the most beneficial effect in the border states. This is certainly a wise move on the part of the government." *The California Citrograph* 2, no. 8 (June 1917): 1.

45. Charles C. Teague, *Fifty Years a Rancher,* 141.

46. The picking force probably accounted for 7 million dollars to eight million dollars of the value of the Exchange's fruit in 1938–39 (U.S. Senate Committee on Education and Labor, *Violations,* 542).

47. "How to Pick Fruit to Avoid Injuries," *The California Citrograph* 27, no. 1 (Jan. 1942): 68.

48. Ibid.

49. Ibid.

50. In an address before the Lemon Men's Club in 1924, the manager of the Leffingwell Ranch, Harry A. Schuyler, stated, "We use experienced Americans as foremen of crews and when the crews are large, often a Mexican is used as a subforeman, to help with the handling of the crew" (Harry S. Schuyler, "The Picking and Hauling of Lemons," *The California Citrograph* 9, no. 7 [July 1924]: 332).

51. Paul Garland Williamson, "Labor in the California Citrus Industry," 95.

52. U.S. Senate Committee on Education and Labor, *Violations,* 542.

53. Ibid.

54. Interview with John Arce, Sept. 5, 1991, Irvine, Calif.

55. Interview with Enrique Zúniga and Francisco Zúniga, Fullerton, Calif., Dec. 10, 1987; interview with Celso Medina and Henry Medina, San Juan Capistrano, Calif., Oct. 23, 1990.

56. U.S. Senate Committee on Education and Labor, *Violations,* 542.

57. Ibid.

58. A 1921 *Citrograph* article reported that several associations paid a base wage of $2.70 per day (or 30 cents per nine hours) combined with a bonus on all boxes picked over the forty-per-day minimum ("What System of Paying Pickers Results in the Least Fruit Injury," *The California Citrograph* 6, no. 7 [July 1921]: 310).

59. Ibid.

60. California State Department of Industrial Relations. *Mexicans in California.* Report of Governor C. C. Young's Mexican Fact Finding Committee (San Francisco: State Building, 1930), 101.

61. Cletus E. Daniel, *Bitter Harvest,* 103.

62. Lizabeth Cohen, *Making a New Deal.*

63. "Picking, Washing, Storage, Grading, Packing of Lemons," *The California Citrograph* 27, no. 5 (May 1942): 264.

64. "The Picking and Hauling of Lemons," *The California Citrograph* 10, no. 7 (July 1924): 332.

65. Interview with Francisco Chico, Anaheim, Calif., Dec. 8, 1988; interview with Clemente Hernández, Placentia, Calif., Sept. 6, 1988; interview with

Celso Medina, San Juan Capistrano, Calif., Dec. 4, 1990; interview with Lionel Magaña, Placentia, Calif., Aug. 25, 1989.

66. U.S. Department of Labor Wage and Hour Division. *Report on the Citrus Fruit Packing Industry Under the Fair Labor Standards Act.* Research and Statistics Branch. Wage and Hour Division (Washington, D.C.: Mimeographed, Apr. 29, 1940), 5.

67. Ibid., 9–13.

68. Interview with Julia Aguirre, Placentia, Calif., Aug. 8, 1989.

69. Interview with Lionel Magaña.

70. Interview with Erma Magaña and Margarita Martínez, Placentia, Calif., Aug. 3, 1989; interview with Julia Aguirre.

71. Ibid.

72. Interview with Angelina Cruz, Escondido, Calif., Sept. 12, 1991.

73. Interview with Julia Aguirre.

74. Interview with Erma Magaña and Margarita Martínez; interview with Julia Aguirre.

75. Interview with Erma Magaña and Margarita Martínez.

76. Interview with Erma Magaña and Margarita Martínez; interview with Angelina Cruz.

77. Interview with Angelina Cruz.

78. Interview with Julia Aguirre.

79. Ibid.

80. J. D. Culbertson, "Housing of Ranch Labor," 99.

81. Ibid.

82. Ibid.

83. Paul Garland Williamson, "Labor in the California Citrus Industry," 99.

84. During the transition period in which both Japanese and Mexicans were employed on some ranches, their living quarters reflected the changing social composition in the work force. For example, at the Leffingwell Ranch in Whittier, two housing camps were maintained for pickers, one for the Japanese, another for the Mexicans, and a third for white skilled workers ("Those Who Have Achieved in the Citrus Industry," *The California Citrograph* [May 1918]). The Limoniera Ranch in Ventura County employed only Japanese up to 1913. Thereafter, Mexicans not only became the main picking labor at the ranch but also throughout the citrus belt. A paper presented at the Annual Citrus Institute held in Redlands reflected on this transition. The manager of the San Fernando Citrus Association stated that, "At present [1920] our picking crews are drawn from the general Mexican population of the town, except that our own association recently converted an old Japanese camp into quarters for eleven Mexican families" ("Co-Operative Handling of Labor," *The California Citrograph* 5, no. 8 [Aug. 1920]: 315).

85. Ibid.

86. Ibid.

87. A. D. Shamel, "Housing the Employees of California Citrus Ranches," *The California Citrograph* 3, no. 3 (Mar. 1918): 96.

88. Ibid.

89. Ibid.

90. Ibid.

91. J. D. Culbertson, "Housing of Ranch Labor," 97.

92. "Mexican Labor," *The California Citrograph* 3, no. 3 (Mar. 1918): 97.

93. A. D. Shamel, "Housing the Employees," 308.

94. Ibid., 204.

95. Ibid.

96. At the October 1919 meeting of the Lemon Men's Club the topic for discussion was "Housing of Labor." Speakers included C. C. Teague, owner of the Limoniera Ranch and President of the California Fruit Growers Exchange and L. R. Bradley, manager of the Upland Lemon Growers Exchange. At the annual Citrus Institute meeting in 1920, J. D. Culbertson addressed the assembly on the problem of "Housing Ranch Labor" ("How to House and Treat Citrus Ranch Employees," *The California Citrograph* 4, no. 4 [Mar. 1919]: 12).

97. "Good Housing Pays," *The California Citrograph* 6, no. 4 (Mar. 1921): 147.

98. Ibid.

99. George B. Hodgkin, "Making the Labor Camp Pay," *The California Citrograph* 6, no. 8 (Aug. 1921): 354.

100. "The Well Housed Employee," *The California Citrograph* 3, no. 9 (Sept. 1918): 253. The article states that "the Mexican laborer, who has a comfortable little cottage in which he may maintain his family, is the contented man, and is less likely to be attracted by the blandishments of another 25 cents a day."

101. A separate bunkhouse for Filipino pickers survived well into the 1940s in Placentia and at Villa Park in Orange County. Interview with George Key, Placentia, Calif., Aug. 20, 1987.

102. A. D. Shamel, "Housing the Employees," 177.

103. Ibid.

104. Ibid.

105. "How to House and Treat Citrus Ranch Employees," *The California Citrograph* 4, no. 11 (Nov. 1919): 12.

106. George B. Hodgkin, "Attractive Houses for Employees," *The California Citrograph* 6, no. 5 (May 1921): 249.

107. "San Dimas Lemon Ass'n Improves Grounds and House," *The California Citrograph* 14, no. 12 (Dec. 1929): 60–2.

108. A. D. Shamel, "Housing the Employees," 70–71.

109. Ibid., 96–97.

110. Ibid.

111. Ibid.

112. Ibid.

113. George B. Hodgkin, "Some Essential Features of Housing Employees," *The California Citrograph* 5, no. 9 (Sept. 1920): 346.

114. "Those Who Have Achieved in the Citrus Industry," *The California Citrograph* 5, no. 5 (May 1918): 161.

115. Harry A. Schuyler, "The Picking and Hauling of Lemons," 332.

2. The Economy, Migration, and Community
Formation in Orange County

1. Mary Lisbeth Haas, "The Barrios of Santa Ana: Community, Class, and Urbanization, 1850–1947" (Ph.D. diss., University of California, 1985), 19.

2. Richard Dale Batman, "Anaheim Was an Oasis in a Wilderness," *Journal of the West* 4, no. 1 (Jan. 1965): 16.

3. Carey McWilliams, *Southern California Country*, 217.

4. Ibid., 214.

5. J. A. Prizer, *Early History of the Placentia Orange Growers Association* (Placentia, Calif.: Placentia Orange Growers Association, 1945), 6.

6. Raymond M. Holt, "The Fruits of Viticulture in Orange County," *Historical Society of Southern California Quarterly* 28 (Mar. 1946): 16–7.

7. Leo S. Friis, *Orange County through Four Centuries* (Santa Ana, Calif.: Pioneer Press, 1965), 105.

8. Samuel Armor, *History of Orange County California, with Biographical Sketches* (Los Angeles: Historic Record Company, 1921), 151–59.

9. Delbert G. Higgins and J. Sherman Denney, "Holly Sugar Co. Building Is Razed," *Huntington Beach News*, June 27, 1975.

10. Jim Sleeper, Jr., "Raps from a Gavel to Signal End of Another Historic County Era," Newspaper clipping on file, Bowers Museum, Santa Ana, Calif.

11. Leo S. Friis, *Orange County through Four Centuries*, 81.

12. Jim Sleeper, "Raps from a Gavel."

13. See Lloyd H. Fisher, *The Harvest Labor Market*, chs. 1, 2.

14. See Kathleen Hunter, "The Gold Is Gone," *The Los Angeles Times* (Orange County Edition), Mar. 31, 1991.

15. R. L. Adams, "Farm Labor," *Journal of Farm Economics* 19, no. 4 (Nov. 1937): 913. Adams wrote: "In the course of . . . various periods California turned successively to Chinese, Japanese, East Indian, Mexicans, and Filipino labor. Still more recently the migrant white laborer from the Southern Great Plains"; see also Carey McWilliams, *Factories in the Fields: The Story of Migratory Farm Labor in California* (1935; reprint, Santa Barbara, Calif.: Peregrine, 1978).

16. Raymond M. Holt, "The Fruits of Viticulture," 11–12. ". . . help was easy to secure for the Indians and Mexicans for miles around were willing to come and help at Campo Aleman (German Camp). . . . During the early years of the colony, the chief hired help laborers were the indians." For a discussion of the transition years, 1850–1900, see Albert Camarillo, *Chicanos in a Changing Society: From Mexican Pueblos to American Barrios in Santa Barbara and Southern California, 1848–1930* (Cambridge, Mass.: Harvard University Press, 1979); also Robert Glass Cleland, *The Cattle on a Thousand Hills: Southern California, 1810–1850* (San Marino, Calif.: Huntington Library, 1952) and Leonard Pitt, *The Decline of the Californios: A Social History of the Spanish-Speaking Californians, 1846–1890* (Berkeley: University of California Press, 1971).

17. Leonard Pitt, *The Decline of the Californios*, 12. The author writes,

"The few Mexicans holding land in the area during the great drought . . . were forced to sell out. . . . In order to exist, some of these people became day laborers and established a nucleus for subsequent Mexican immigrants. Settling in colonies near the source of labor, replacing the Indian and imported Chinese, these people eventually became the chief supply of field labor."

18. Stephan Gould, "The Chinese in Tustin," *Orange Countian* 1 (1973): 27.

19. Ibid., 23.

20. Ibid., 29.

21. *Orange County, California: Pioneer Tales, 1769–1936,* Works Project Administration Project #3105, Works Project Administration (1936), 172.

22. Ibid., 265.

23. Fern Hill Colman, "History of the Celery Industry," *Orange County History Series* 3 (Apr. 1939): 102–3.

24. Edmund de S. Brunner, *Orange County, California: Church and Community Survey. A Preliminary Abstract* (New York: Committee on Social and Religious Surveys, 1922), 5. See also Charles C. Teague, *Fifty Years a Rancher,* Passim.

25. Interview with George C. Key, Placentia, Calif., Aug. 27, 1987.

26. *Fullerton Tribune,* May 22, 1907. For a general treatment of Asian Americans, see Ron Takaki, *Strangers from a Different Shore: A History of Asian Americans* (Boston, Mass.: Little Brown and Co., 1989), Chapter Nine; also Sucheng Chan, *This Bittersweet Soil: The Chinese in California Agriculture, 1860–1910* (Berkeley: The University of California Press, 1986), Chapter Eight.

27. *Santa Ana Register,* Feb. 6, 1915.

28. Ibid., Feb. 11, 1910.

29. Ibid., June 22, 1910.

30. *La Habra Star,* Aug. 4, 1920.

31. Ibid., Nov. 12, 1920.

32. Ibid., Oct. 31, 1919.

33. Edmund de S. Brunner, *Irrigation and Religion: A Study of Religion and Social Conditions in Two California Counties* (New York: George H. Doran, 1922), 86. The resolution read: "the Japanese [are] an unassimilable element in the population. . . . the cancellation of the gentleman's agreement, exclusion of picture brides, rigorous exclusion of Japanese immigrants and the amendment to the Federal Constitution to provide that no child born in the United States of foreign parentage shall be considered an American citizen unless both parents are of a race that is eligible to citizenship."

34. Lloyd Fisher, *The Harvest Labor Market,* 25–30; see Carey McWilliams, *Factories in the Fields,* 103–33; Levi Varden Fuller, "The Supply of Agricultural Labor as a Factor in the Evolution of Farm Organization in California" (Ph.D. diss., Berkeley, University of California, 1934).

35. *Anaheim Gazette,* July 31, 1913.

36. *La Habra Star,* Sept. 21, 1918.

37. St. Boniface Church, *The Story of a Parish* (Anaheim, Calif.: St. Boniface Parish, 1961), 149.

38. E. C. Eckman et al., *Soil Survey of the Anaheim Area, California.* U.S. Department of Agriculture, Bureau of Soils (Washington: Government Printing Office, 1919), 18.

39. *Anaheim Gazette,* Aug. 23, 1917. The Orange County pattern in this regard did not differ from other beet growing areas. See, for example, Dennis Nodín Valdes, *Al Norte,* 9–29; also Carey McWilliams, *Ill Fares the Land: Migrants and Migratory Labor in California* (1942; reprint, New York: Arno, 1967), 109–29.

40. *Anaheim Gazette,* Nov. 15, 1917.

41. Works Project Administration Project #3105, 227. A pioneer resident noted that: "During the windy days Mexicans drove past the hotel in wagons drawn by broncos. They had come from the sheep shearing on the San Joaquin Ranch. Most of them lived in the direction of Wilmington. The shearers were accompanied by their women."

42. Jack Klein, "California's Oldest Valencia Orchard," *California Cultivator* (Sept. 26, 1936): 683, 711.

43. J. A. Prizer, "Early History of the Placentia Orange Growers Association" (Placentia, Calif.: Placentia Orange Growers Exchange, 1945), n.p.

44. Harold E. Wahlbert, "Progress of County Traced Through Agriculture," *Santa Ana Daily Register,* Nov. 22, 1939.

45. Jim Sleeper, Jr., "The Story of Orange County's Golden Harvest," *The Santa Ana Register,* Nov. 17, 1968.

46. Harold E. Wahlbert, "Progress of County."

47. Paul Garland Williamson, "Labor in the California Citrus Industry," 15; see Nephtune Fogelbert and A. W. McKay, *The Citrus Industry and the California Fruit Growers Exchange.* (Washington, D.C.: U.S. Department of Agriculture, 1940), 13–15.

48. Ibid.

49. Paul S. Taylor, *Mexican Labor in the United States. Migration Statistics IV,* vol. 12, no. 3(Berkeley: University of California Press, 1933), 37–41.

50. Jessie Hayden, "The La Habra Experiment," 149.

51. Warren O. Mendenhall, "A Comparative Study of Achievement and Ability of the Children of Two Segregated Mexican Schools" (Master's thesis, University of Southern California, 1937), 83.

52. Interview with Fred Aguirre, Placentia, Calif., Sept. 17, 1987; interview with Celso Medina and Henry Medina, San Juan Capistrano, Calif., Oct. 9, 1990.

53. Interview with Clemente Hernández, Placentia, Calif., Sept. 20, 1988.

54. Hernández Interview; interview with Eduardo Negrete, Anaheim, Calif., February 1, 1989. The account of Robert Alvarez, Jr. parallels in many ways the life histories of the interviews made by this author. See Robert Alvarez, Jr., *Familia.*

55. Interview with Francisco Chico, Anaheim, Calif., Dec. 7, 1988.

56. Interview with Julia Aguirre, Placentia, Calif., Aug. 8, 1989.

57. Jessie Hayden, "The La Habra Experiment," 44.

58. Interview with Celso de Casas, Placentia, Calif., Oct. 1, 1987.

59. Mary Lisbeth Haas, "The Barrios of Santa Ana," 48.

60. Elizabeth Broadbent, "The Distribution of the Mexican Population in the United States," 3, 27, 74.

61. Rob Kling, Spencer Olin, and Mark Poster, *Post-Suburban California: The Transformation of Orange County Since World War II* (Berkeley: The University of California Press, 1991), 3.

62. Warren O. Mendenhall, "A Comparative Study of Achievement," 16.

63. *La Habra Star,* Oct. 24, 1923.

64. Interview with Celso de Casas, Placentia, Calif., Sept. 21, 1987.

65. Interview with Lionel Magaña and Erma Magaña, Placentia, Calif., Aug. 25, 1989; also St. Boniface Church, *The Story of a Parish,* 147–48.

66. *Anaheim Gazette,* Oct. 8, 1925.

67. Ibid.

68. Ibid., Oct. 1, 1925.

69. Ibid., Oct. 8, 1925.

70. Interview with Fred Aguirre.

71. Interview with Celso and Henry Medina, San Juan Capistrano, Calif., Oct. 23, 1990.

72. Orman Day, "Family Members Prosper after Humble Beginning in the County," *Orange County Register,* July 11, 1981.

73. Placentia Orange Growers Association, Board of Directors *Minutes,* Fullerton, Calif., July 26, 1920.

74. Ibid., Aug. 2, 1920.

75. Placentia (California) Orange Growers Association, *Manager's Annual Report,* 1925.

76. Druzilla Mackey, [Untitled Memoirs] in Louis E. Plummer, "A History of the Fullerton Union High School and Fullerton Junior College, 1893–1943" (Fullerton, California, 1949), 86.

77. Interview with Arletta Kelly by B. E. Schmidt, May 22, 1968, Tape No. 48, Oral History Program, California State University, Fullerton.

78. Ibid.

79. Mexicans in other contexts experienced similar tugs from the countryside. See, for example, William J. Knox, "The Economic Status of the Mexican Immigrant in San Antonio, Texas" (Master's thesis, University of Texas, Austin, 1927). More recently Dennis Nodin Valdes found a similar pattern existing in the Midwest during the 1920s and 1930s. See Dennis Nodín Valdes, *Al Norte,* 11, 27.

80. Druzilla Mackey, [Untitled Memoirs], 85.

81. *La Habra Star,* Aug. 26, 1921.

82. *Placentia Courier,* Feb. 15, 1935.

83. Interview with Santiago Canales, Anaheim, Calif., Oct. 21, 1988; interview with Chaoi Vásquez by Ronald Bandera, 1970, Tape No. 609, Oral History Program, California State University, Fullerton.

84. Department of Social Welfare, Orange County, California. "Living Standards of Orange County Mexican Families," Orange County, Calif., Departmental Mimeo, Mar. 9, 1940, 5.

85. Druzilla Mackey, [Untitled Memoirs], 87.

86. Jessie Hayden, "The La Habra Experiment," 54.

87. Warren O. Mendenhall, "A Comparative Study of Achievement," 78.

88. Department of Social Welfare, Orange County, California, "Living Standards," 5.

89. *Placentia Courier,* Jan. 27, 1931.

90. Ibid., Oct. 30, 1931.

91. Interview with Lionel Magaña, Placentia, Calif., Aug. 25, 1987.

92. Jessie Hayden, "The La Habra Experiment," 55.

93. Ibid., 54.

94. Department of Social Welfare, Orange County, California, "Living Standards," 4.

95. Ibid., 5; Mexican women were certainly not alone in carrying large household responsibilities. Susan Ware documented the creative adjustment of women to the Depression and much of what she describes is similar to the activities of Mexican women in the citrus villages. See Susan Ware, *Holding Their Own: American Women in the 1930s* (Boston: Twyane Publishers, 1982), Chapter One; see also Robert A. Slayton, *Back of the Yards: The Making of a Local Democracy* (Chicago: University of Chicago Press, 1986), 70–75.

96. Ibid.

97. Interview with Angelina Cruz, Escondido, Calif., Sept. 12, 1991.

98. Department of Social Welfare, Orange County, California, "Living Standards," 10.

99. Interview with Elpidio Arce, Sept. 13, 1991, Corona, Calif.

100. Interview with Lionel Magaña and Erma Magaña, Placentia, Calif., Oct. 25, 1989.

101. Interview with Teresa Vásquez, Placentia, Calif., Aug. 26, 1988.

102. Jessie Hayden, "The La Habra Experiment," 18.

103. Interview with Erma Magaña and Margarita Martínez, Aug. 23, 1989.

104. Interview with Erma Magaña and Margarita Martínez, Placentia, Calif., Aug. 3, 1989.

105. Interview with Erma Magaña and Margarita Martínez; interview with Julia Aguirre.

106. Department of Social Welfare, Orange County, California, "Living Standards," 7; see also Jessie Hayden, "The La Habra Experiment," 17.

107. Interview with Tony González, Jess Mejía, and Johnny Luna, La Habra, Calif., Jan. 12, 1988; interview with Pascual Rivas, Tustin, Calif., Feb. 10, 1989.

108. Department of Social Welfare, Orange County, California, "Living Standards," 8.

109. Ibid., 12.

110. Interview with Fred Aguirre; also Department of Social Welfare, Orange County, California, "Living Standards," 4.

111. *La Habra Star,* Mar. 29, 1935

112. Interview with John Arce, Irvine, Calif., Sept. 5, 1991; interview with Elpidio Arce, Corona, Calif., Sept. 12, 1991.

113. Jessie Hayden, "The La Habra Experiment," 35; also interview with John Arce.

114. Interview with Pascual Rivas and Guadalupe Rivas, Tustin, Calif., Feb. 17, 1989.

115. Emilio Martínez, "Corrido de Esteban Muñiz," Stanton, California, 1940.

116. Interview with John Arce.

117. Jessie Hayden, "The La Habra Experiment," 106.

118. Interview with John Arce.

119. Interview with Arletta Kelly by B. E. Schmidt. Arletta Kelly, who taught Americanization in the North Orange County area, recalled: "Most of them [Mexicans] had old jalopies of some sort and they would all get together and go in their old Model T Fords or something comparable to that."

120. Interviews with Lionel Magaña and Erma Magaña, Placentia, Calif., Aug. 25, 1987.

121. Interview with Chester Whitten, Placentia, Calif.

122. Interview with Emilio Martínez, Feb. 3, 1989, Stanton, Calif.; *Anaheim Gazette*, Apr. 30, 1931.

123. Interview with Fred Aguirre.

124. Department of Social Welfare, Orange County, California, "Living Standards," 1; Warren O. Mendenhall, "A Comparative Study of Achievement," 79. For a general description of conditions among Mexicans during the Depression, see Francisco Balderrama, *In Defense of La Raza* (Tucson: University of Arizona Press, 1982), chap. 1.

125. Interview with Fred Aguirre.

126. Written by Emilio Martínez, Anaheim, Calif., May 1935.

127. Interview with Pascual Rivas, Feb. 17, 1989.

128. See Abraham Hoffman, *Unwanted Mexican Americans in the Great Depression: Repatriation Pressures, 1929–1939* (Tucson: University of Arizona Press, 1974).

129. Interview with Francisco Chico; interview with Emilio Martínez, Stanton, Calif., Feb. 6, 1989.

130. Interview with Teresa Vásquez; interview with Francisco Chico, Anaheim, Calif., Dec. 8, 1988; interview with Eduardo Negrete.

131. Interview with Hector Tarango, Santa Ana, Calif., Apr. 15, 1989; interview with Santiago Canales, Anaheim, Calif., Sept. 7, 1988.

132. Interview with Cecil Rospow, Placentia, Calif., July 18, 1988; interview with George Key, Placentia, Calif., Aug. 7, 1987; interview with Fred Aguirre.

133. Junius Meriam, *Learning English Incidentally. A Study of Bilingual Children* (Washington, D.C.: Government Printing Office, 1938), 2.

134. Interview with Teresa Vásquez, Placentia, Calif., July 13, 1987.

135. Ibid.

136. Interview with Erma Magaña, Placentia, Calif., Aug. 3, 1989; interview with Francisco Chico, Anaheim, Calif., Feb. 7, 1988.

3. Village Culture, Lifestyle, and Organization

1. Mexican communities were not alone among immigrants in the United States in the creation of a nationalist spirit with ties to the home country. See

Robert A. Slayton, *Back of the Yards,* 113–27; Ronald Takaki, *Strangers from a Different Shore,* 117–31; Felix Padilla, *Puerto Rican Chicago* (Notre Dame, Ind.: University of Notre Dame Press, 1987), 222.

2. *La Opinion,* July 20, 1927. The newspaper reported: "The (general meeting attended by forty-eight men) took place in the residence of Señor Lucio Martínez, and elected by majority vote to the Junta Patriótica were the following men: president, Baltazar González; vice president, Alejo Diáz; secretary, Feliciano Vargas; treasurer, Lucio Martínez; sergeant-at-arms, José Vargas, Francisco Gutierrez, Emilio Magaña, José Aguirre, and Emilio Vargas."

3. *Placentia Courier,* Sept. 12, 1930.

4. Interview with Fred Aguirre, Placentia, Calif., Sept. 17, 1987.

5. Ibid.

6. Ibid.

7. Interview with Fred Aguirre.

8. *Placentia Courier,* Sept. 19, 1930.

9. Ibid., Sept. 30, 1935.

10. Interview with Lionel Magaña, Placentia, Calif., Aug. 25, 1987.

11. *Placentia Courier,* Sept. 13, 1939.

12. Ibid.

13. *Placentia Courier,* Sept. 22, 1933.

14. Jessie Hayden, "The La Habra Experiment," 42; also *The La Habra Star,* Sept. 12, 1921.

15. Interview with Johnny Luna and Tony González, La Habra, Calif., Jan. 12, 1988; interview with Lionel Magaña and Erma Magaña, Placentia, Calif., Aug. 3, 1989.

16. Interview with Lionel Magaña and Erma Magaña, Placentia, Calif., Aug. 25, 1987.

17. For example, *The Placentia Courier* for Sept. 20, 1935 announced that "police officers reported few disturbances and only one case of getting into the courts as a result of the event [Dieciséis de Septiembre]."

18. Interview with Eduardo Negrete, Fullerton, Calif., Jan. 25, 1989.

19. See Francisco Balderrama, *In Defense of La Raza;* also, Ruth Tuck, *Not with a Fist: Mexican Americans in a Southwest City* (New York: Harcourt, Brace and Company, 1946), Passim.

20. Interview with Celso Medina, San Juan Capistrano, Calif., Oct. 23, 1990.

21. *La Opinion,* May 13, 1927.

22. Francisco Balderrama, *In Defense of La Raza,* 9–10.

23. *La Opinion,* Oct. 3, 1926.

24. Ibid. Consulates also utilized the patriotic committees to advance their own plans for repatriating immigrants. During the 1920s and Depression 1930s, the consulates voiced plans for the distribution of lands to repatriates, and in many cases, the offer was taken. Thus, for example, the strong nationalism broadcast in the Dieciséis festivities certainly benefited political stability in Mexico upon immigrants' return. However, the promises, when kept, granted land of little value in Baja California. Those few who accepted the offer barely eked out a living (Interview with Francisco Chico, Anaheim, Calif., Dec. 8, 1988).

25. Interview with Emilio Martínez, Stanton, Calif., Feb. 3, 1989; interview with Pascual Rivas, Tustin, Calif., Feb. 17, 1989.

26. *Anaheim Gazette,* Sept. 19, 1940.

27. Interview with Pascual Rivas.

28. *Placentia Courier,* Sept. 19, 1947.

29. *La Habra Star,* Dec. 27, 1922.

30. Ibid.

31. *La Habra Star,* Jan. 2, 1924.

32. Interview with Fred Aguirre.

33. Ibid.

34. Jessie Hayden, "The La Habra Experiment," 37.

35. Interview with Lionel Magaña.

36. Interview with Fred Aguirre.

37. *La Habra Star,* Dec. 14, 1923.

38. Jessie Hayden, "The La Habra Experiment," 76.

39. Interview with Lionel Magaña.

40. Ibid.

41. Interview with Lionel Magaña; interview with Celso de Casas, Oct. 1, 1989.

42. Jessie Hayden, "The La Habra Experiment," 65–67.

43. Ibid., 68.

44. Ibid., 69.

45. Interview with Lionel Magaña; interview with Francisco Chico.

46. Edmund S. Brunner, *Orange County, California,* 18, 19. See also Vernon Monroe McCombs, *From over the Border: A Study of the Mexicans in the United States* (New York: Council of Women for Home Missions, 1925).

47. Ibid.

48. Jessie Hayden, "The La Habra Experiment," 82–90.

49. *Placentia Courier,* Feb. 17, 1939.

50. Interview with Clemente Hernández, Placentia, Calif., Sept. 6, 1988; interview with Hector Tarango, Santa Ana, Calif., Apr. 15, 1989.

51. Interview with Franciso Zúniga and Alfred Zúniga, Fullerton, Calif., Dec. 10, 1987.

52. Interview with Erma Magaña and Margarita Martínez, Placentia, Calif., Aug. 3, 1989.

53. Interview with Lionel Magaña, Placentia, Calif., Aug. 25, 1989.

54. Jessie Hayden, "The La Habra Experiment," 31.

55. *La Habra Star,* Mar. 27, 1931.

56. *Orange County Plain Dealer,* Apr. 30, 1923.

57. Ibid., Sept. 21, 1923.

58. Ibid., Sept. 24, 1933.

59. Ibid., Sept. 17, 1933.

60. *The Orange County Register,* Dec. 18, 1991.

61. *Placentia Courier,* Jan. 24, 1930.

62. Interview with Pascual Rivas.

63. Interview with Lionel Magaña.

64. Interview with John Arce, Irvine, Calif., Sept. 5, 1991.

65. Ibid.

66. *The Orange County Register,* Apr. 4, 1982.

67. Mario Garcia, *Desert Immigrants* (New Haven: Yale University Press, 1981), 202.

4. Schooling Village Children

1. An extensive literature exists reflecting on the development of mass compulsory public schooling. See, for example, Paula S. Fass, *Outside In* (New York: Oxford University Press, 1989); Raymond E. Callahan, *Education and the Cult of Efficiency* (Chicago: University of Chicago Press, 1962); David Nasaw, *Schooled to Order: A Social History of Public Schooling in America* (New York: Oxford University Press, 1979); Joel H. Spring, *Education and the Rise of the Corporate State* (Boston: Beacon Press, 1972).

2. *La Habra Star,* June 28, 1919.

3. Ibid., Dec. 22, 1920.

4. Ibid.

5. Simon L. Treff, "The Education of Mexican Children in Orange County" (Master's thesis, University of Southern California, 1934), 23.

6. Ibid., 15.

7. Junius Meriam, *Learning English Incidentally: A Study of Bilingual Children* (Washington, D. C.: Government Printing Office, 1938), 2.

8. Ibid., 14.

9. Ibid., 94.

10. Interview with Fred Aguirre, Placentia, Calif., Sept. 17, 1987.

11. *Placentia Courier,* Dec. 21, 1932.

12. Ibid., Feb. 14, 1936.

13. Ibid., Oct. 27, 1939. The quote continued, "together with art, music, shop, homemaking and physical education make up the school program."

14. *Placentia Courier,* May 23, 1930.

15. Ibid., Jan. 23, 1931.

16. Ibid., May 15, 1931.

17. John Scott Cornelius, "The Effects of Certain Changes of Curriculum and Methods on the School Achievement of Mexican Children in a Segregated School" (Master's thesis, University of California, 1941), 10.

18. Ibid.

19. *Placentia Courier,* May 27, 1938.

20. Ibid.

21. Ibid., Sept. 2, 1938.

22. Warren O. Mendenhall, "A Comparative Study of Achievement," 99.

23. *Placentia Courier,* May 27, 1938.

24. Ibid.

25. Interview with Bert Valadez, Yorba Linda, Calif., Aug. 18, 1987.

26. Simon L. Treff, "The Educating of Mexican Children," 64–65. Treff wrote of Mexican schools in the county: "American children are consistently better housed." See also Gilbert G. González, *Chicano Education in the Era of Segregation* (Philadelphia: Balch Institute, 1990), Chapter Seven, passim.

27. La Habra, California, Board of Education *Minutes,* Aug. 31, 1924.

28. Interview with Bert Valadez.

29. Interview with Chester Whitten by Robin Rodarte and Richard Gutier-rez, in *Harvest: A Compilation of Taped Interviews on the Minority Peoples of Orange County* (Fullerton, Calif.: California State University, Fullerton, 1974).

30. Ibid.

31. Simon L. Treff, "The Education of Mexican Children," Passim; and John Scott Cornelius, "The Effects of Certain Changes."

32. La Habra Board of Education *Minutes,* May 26, 1924.

33. Interview with Chester Whitten, Placentia, Calif., Aug. 13, 1987.

34. La Habra Board of Education *Minutes,* Jan. 6, 1933; also the *Placentia Courier,* Dec. 21, 1932.

35. *La Habra Star,* Oct. 28, 1932.

36. Ibid.

37. Ibid.

38. Simon L. Treff, "The Education of Mexican Children," 1.

39. *Placentia Courier,* Dec. 17, 1939.

40. Letter from Cecil Rospow to the author, Aug. 11, 1988, Placentia, Calif.

41. Simon L. Treff, "The Education of Mexican Children," 55.

42. Interview with Bert Valadez.

43. La Habra Board of Education *Minutes,* Oct. 12, 1936.

44. *Placentia Courier,* Dec. 3, 1939.

45. Interview with Chester Whitten.

46. Interview with Bert Valadez.

47. *Placentia Courier,* Feb. 2, 1940.

48. See *La Habra Star,* Jan. 11, 1935; Jan. 25, 1935; Feb. 1, 1935.

49. *Placentia Courier,* Apr. 12, 1935.

50. Ibid., May 17, 1935; June 7, 1935.

51. *Anaheim Gazette,* Mar. 4, 1926.

52. *Placentia Courier,* May 23, 1930.

53. Ibid., May 22, 1931; May 6, 1932.

54. *La Habra Star,* Apr. 30, 1924.

55. Ibid., Feb. 20, 1925.

56. *Placentia Courier,* Sept. 22, 1927. The *Courier* article stated: "Due to ["the pupils harvesting walnuts"] and in efforts to cooperate with the walnut growers and permit the children to earn the walnut money while they may, the three schools in these sections started this morning on half-day sessions. This will permit the children to gather walnuts in the afternoons and it is hoped will bring them in for their classes in the forenoons."

57. *La Habra Star,* Oct. 11, 1929.

58. Interview with Teresa Vásquez, Placentia, Calif., Aug. 26, 1988.

59. *La Habra Star,* Mar. 12, 1930.

60. Ibid., May 27, 1932.

61. Simon L. Treff, "The Education of Mexican Children," 32.

62. Jessie Hayden, "The La Habra Experiment," 140.

63. *Placentia Courier,* Feb. 21, 1936.

64. Interview with Chester Whitten by Robin Rodarte and Richard Guti-errez.

65. *Placentia Courier,* June 12, 1931. Ms. Martínez enrolled in junior college, majored in journalism and was chosen by the *Placentia Courier* paper to be a role model through writing a weekly column, "Americanization News." For two years she reported on the activities in the Placentia villages, emphasizing the positive and noting in particular the work in the schools and the Americanization centers. Several years later school children wrote weekly briefings on the activities of each grade in the three Placentia schools. Naturally these articles were inspired (and probably written) by the teachers. However, as in the case of the weekly articles in the *La Habra Star,* the objective was to inform the townspeople of the positive changes occurring within the Mexican community through education. The reporting always framed within the dominant community's expectations and objectives of education for the Mexican community.

66. See *Placentia Courier,* June 1, 1934; June 5, 1936.

67. *La Habra Star,* Apr. 29, 1932.

68. Ibid.

69. Interview with Santiago Canales, Anaheim, Calif., Oct. 21, 1988.

70. Warren O. Mendenhall, "A Comparative Study of Achievement," 98.

71. *La Habra Star,* Apr. 12, 1935; interview with Francisco Zúniga and Alfredo Zúniga, Fullerton, Calif., Dec. 10, 1987.

72. Interview with Henry Medina, San Juan Capistrano, Oct. 9, 1990; interview with Fred Aguirre; interview with Eduardo Negrete, Jan. 25, 1989.

73. Quoted in Maria Newman, "A Person Gets Tired of Being Pushed Around," *Los Angeles Times Celebrate,* vol. 3, May 21, 1989, 73.

5. Americanizing Village Adults

1. See Joseph Hraba, *American Ethnicity* (Ithaca: F. E. Peacock Publishers, Inc., 1979); also Fred Wacker, *Ethnicity, Pluralism, and Race* (Westport, Conn.: Greenwood Press, 1983).

2. See Richard O. Boyer and Herbert M. Morais, *Labor's Untold Story* (New York: United Electrical Radio and Machine Workers of America, 1972); Jeremy Brecher, *Strike!* (San Francisco: Straight Arrow Books, 1972); Sidney Lens, *The Labor Wars* (Garden City, N.Y.: Anchor Doubleday, 1974); John Higham, *Send These to Me* (Baltimore, Md.: The Johns Hopkins Press, 1984).

3. David Ward, *Cities and Immigrants: A Geography of Change in Nineteenth Century America* (New York: Oxford University Press, 1971), 51.

4. For a discussion of the Wheatland Riot, see Cletus E. Daniel, *Bitter Harvest,* 88–98.

5. The California State Commission of Immigration and Housing. *Ninth Annual Report,* Jan. 9, 1923 (Sacramento, Calif.: California State Printing Office, 1923), 13. The Commission is thoroughly discussed in Cletus E. Daniel, *Bitter Harvest,* 91–104.

6. California State Commission of Immigration and Housing. *Ninth Annual Report,* 25.

7. *California Citrograph,* Nov. 1919, 31. The league also directly inter-

vened in labor disputes whenever possible. According to the organizations' head the 1918 strike in Pomona was stopped by the league " when a Russian agitator tried to stir them [pickers] up," Nov. 1919, 12, 13; also Mar. 1919, 130.

8. Ibid., 64.

9. Interview with Henry Medina and Celso Medina, San Juan Capistrano, Calif., Oct. 23, 1990; interview with Chester Whitten by Robin Rodarte and Richard Gutierrez in *Harvest. A Compilation of Taped Interviews on the Minority Peoples of Orange County* (Fullerton, Calif.: California State University, Fullerton, 1974).

10. The California State Commission of Immigration and Housing, *Ninth Annual Report,* 64.

11. Ibid., 89. See also George Sanchez, "Go After the Women: Americanization and the Mexican Immigrant Woman, 1915–1929," Chicano Studies Program, Working Paper Series, No. 6 (Palo Alto: Stanford University) and Gilbert G. González, *Chicano Education in the Era of Segregation,* chap. 3.

12. Ibid., 98. For an account of Americanization in the eastern states, see Maxine Seller, "The Education of Immigrant Women, 1900–1935," *Journal of Urban History* 6, no. 3 (1978): 307–30; see also Gary Gerstle, *Working-Class Americanism.*

13. Ibid.

14. Ibid., 99

15. Ibid., 100.

16. Ibid.

17. The California State Commission of Immigration and Housing. *The Annual Report,* Jan. 1925 (Sacramento, Calif.: California State Printing Office, 1925), 14.

18. George B. Hodgkin, "Making the Labor Camp Pay," *California Citrograph* 7, no. 8 (Aug. 1921): 354.

19. Ibid.

20. Ethel Richardson, "Doing the Things That Couldn't Be Done," *The Survey Graphic* 56 (June 1926): 298.

21. Merton E. Hill, *The Development of an Americanization Program* (Ontario, Calif.: Board of Trustees of the Chaffey Union High School and the Chaffey Junior College, 1928), 12; see also Gilbert G. González, *Chicano Education in the Era of Segregation,* 46.

22. Druzilla Mackey, [Untitled Memoirs], 81.

23. Ibid., 84; see also Ethel Richardson, "Doing the Things that Couldn't Be Done."

24. *La Habra Star,* June 5, 1931.

25. La Habra Board of Education *Minutes,* La Habra, Calif., Apr. 24, 1922.

26. Interview with Arletta Kelly by B. E. Schmidt, 1968, Tape No. 48, Oral History Program, California State University, Fullerton.

27. The Placentia (California) Orange Growers Association, Board of Directors *Minutes,* Oct. 3, 1927.

28. *La Habra Star,* Oct. 26, 1921.

29. Ibid., Apr. 21, 1922.

30. *Anaheim Gazette,* Oct. 8, 1925.

31. *La Habra Star,* Oct. 21, 1925.

32. *Anaheim Gazette,* Dec. 24, 1925.

33. *La Habra Star,* Oct. 21, 1925.

34. On February 11, 1931, the *La Habra Star* headlined: "Much Wanted Mex Stages Jail Break"; and a week later the same paper headlined "Local Mexican Given Jail Term." In such a manner the image of the Mexican was popularized.

35. Ibid., Nov. 8, 1929

36. *La Habra Star,* Jan. 25, 1928.

37. This assessment is based on a thorough reading of several local newspapers, *Anaheim Gazette, Orange Daily News, La Habra Star, Placentia Courier, Santa Ana Register,* and the *Fullerton Daily News Tribune.*

38. Helen Walker, "The Conflict of Cultures in First Generation Mexicans in Santa Ana, California" (Master's thesis, University of Southern California, 1928), 38.

39. Louis E. Plummer, *A History of the Fullerton Union High School and Fullerton Junior College, 1893–1943* (Fullerton, Calif.: Fullerton Union High School District, 1943), 81; Druzilla Mackey, [Untitled Memoirs], 82.

40. Druzilla Mackey, [Untitled Memoirs], 87.

41. Interview with Chester Whitten by Robin Rodarte and Richard Gutierrez.

42. *Placentia Courier,* Sept. 11, 1931.

43. Druzilla Mackey, [Untitled Memoirs], 84. In her words: "One brought me a quart of milk, every day, others fresh corn and one good friend brought me two fresh eggs each morning during the whole of my stay in the camp. I was invited to eat one good hot meal every day in some one or other of the houses . . . I found them delicious."

44. Ibid., 86.

45. Ibid., 87.

46. Placentia (California) Mutual Orange Growers Association, Board of Directors *Minutes,* Mar. 13, 1923.

47. *The (Fullerton [Calif.] Junior College) Weekly Torch,* Mar. 9, 1923.

48. Ibid.

49. Mackey [Untitled Memoirs], 87.

50. Ibid.

51. *The Weekly Torch,* Jan. 12, 1923.

52. Ibid., June 8, 1923.

53. Mackey, [Untitled Memoirs], 85.

54. *The Weekly Torch,* Mar. 2, 1923.

55. Ibid., Feb. 12, 1926.

56. Ibid., Jan. 2, 1924.

57. *La Habra Star,* May 22, 1925.

58. Ibid., May 9, 1928.

59. Over the years, from 1920 to 1947, articles on town functions appearing in the *Anaheim Gazette, La Habra Star, Placentia Courier,* and *Santa Ana Register* testify to this social separation.

60. *La Habra Star,* Nov. 12, 1924.

61. Interview with Fred Aguirre, Placentia, Calif., Sept. 17, 1987.

62. *La Habra Star,* Sept. 30, 1925.

63. *Placentia Courier,* Apr. 15, 1932.

64. Ibid., July 12, 1928.

65. Ibid., Apr. 12, 1929.

66. Ibid., Sept. 6, 1929.

67. Ibid., Jan. 17, 1930.

68. *La Habra Star,* Apr. 29, 1932.

69. George B. Hodgkin, "Making the Labor Camp Pay," 354.

70. *Placentia Courier,* May 10, 1929; also *La Habra Star,* Feb. 26, 1932.

71. *La Habra Star,* Dec. 20, 1929.

72. Ibid., July 17, 1931

73. Ibid., Apr. 29, 1932.

74. Richard Romo, *East Los Angeles: A History of Barrio* (Austin: University of Texas Press, 1983), 65.

75. Ibid., 71.

76. Lizabeth Cohen, *Making a New Deal.*

77. Mary S. Gibson, "Schools For the Whole Family," *Survey Graphic* 56 (June 1926), 301.

78. Romo, *East Los Angeles,* 115–16; see also Douglas Guy Monroy, "Mexicanos in Los Angeles, 1930–1941: An Ethnic Group in Relation to Class Forces" (Ph.D. diss., University of California, Los Angeles, 1978). Passim.

79. Mary S. Gibson, "Schools for the Whole Family," 300.

80. Druzilla Mackey, [Untitled Memoirs], 87.

81. *The Placentia Courier* reported "the Bastanchury Ranch . . . to ship 100 Mexicans back to their native land, having dismissed them as employees" (Mar. 31, 1933). A month earlier the *Courier* announced, "Orange County's welfare burden was lightened last week with the exodus of 437 Mexican men, women, and children, on their way back to Mexico." (Apr. 7, 1933).

82. Interview with Eduardo Negrete, Fullerton, Calif., Feb. 1, 1989; interview with Francisco Chico, Anaheim, Calif., Dec. 7, 1989.

83. Druzilla Mackey, [Untitled Memoirs], 88.

84. Ibid.

6. Unionization and the 1936 Strike

1. *Fortune* magazine ran a feature-length article on the citrus industry written before the strike and published in July 1936, while the strike was in progress. The author noted the absence of strikes in the citrus industry, stating "you will find nothing about labor trouble among the . . . men and women who pick and pack the citrus crop," and citrus "labor is contented." The author must have felt very foolish when one of the more violent strikes broke just as the journal hit the store shelves ("Cooperation at a Profit," *Fortune* 14 [July 1936]: 54).

2. A perusal of the literature demonstrates little attention to the Orange

Country Strike. See, for examples, Rodolfo Acuña, *Occupied America: A History of Chicanos,* 2d edition (New York: Harper and Row, 1981); Carey McWilliams, *North From Mexico.*

3. Stuart Jameison, *Labor Unionism in American Agriculture.* United States Department of Labor. Bureau of Labor Statistics. Bulletin No. 836 (1945; reprint, New York: Arno Press, 1976), 126–27.

4. The organization of pickers into unions was inevitable and several minor and major union drives and strikes over the years caused to varying degrees, problems for the growers. In the teens and twenties numerous demands for higher wages (which included) threats of walkouts or strikes, were generally settled without collective bargaining, although sometimes the settlement involved violence between pickers and growers. Only once before the 1930s, was there any serious clash involving a union and a strike. This occurred in the foothill area of Los Angeles County, comprising Covina, Azusa, Glendora, Charter Oaks, La Verne, Claremont, Pomona, and nearby towns. In March 1919, two hundred pickers in the Claremont area stopped work, demanding $4.00 per eight-hour day. Growers and their allies charged the trouble to IWW "bolsheviks." The number of strikers expanded to over eight hundred pickers before some four hundred vigilantes swooped down on the strike headquarters and loaded thirty-one strikers, including the leadership, onto a truck and dumped them in the Boyle Heights area of Los Angeles. No labor problems existed in the area for the next ten years. In February 1920, a lesser strike of pickers in Corona, demanding an increase to $3.69 from $3.00 per day, ended shortly after it was launched when strikebreakers from El Paso were brought in. Most attempts to gain higher wages were localized, and were often the result of spontaneous actions rather than deliberate organizational efforts (Paul Garland Williamson, "Labor in the California Citrus Industry," 122–23).

5. U.S. Congress. Senate Committee on Education and Labor. *Violations of Free Speech and Rights of Labor.* Report of the Committee on Education and Labor, part 1 (Washington, D. C.: Government Printing Office, 1942), 546–48.

6. U.S. Congress. Senate Committee on Education and Labor, *Violations,* 549–50.

7. Ibid., 549–51.

8. Ibid.

9. See Cletus E. Daniel, *Bitter Harvest;* Lloyd H. Fisher, *The Harvest Labor Market;* Linda C. Majka and Theo J. Majka, *Farmworkers, Agribusiness and the State;* Carey McWilliams, *Factories in the Fields.*

10. Gregg Andrews, *Shoulder to Shoulder? The American Federation of Labor, the United States, and the Mexican Revolution* (Berkeley: University of California Press, 1991), 198.

11. Linda C. Majka and Theo J. Majka, *Farm Workers, Agribusinesses, and the State,* 11; also, Cletus E. Daniel, *Bitter Harvest,* ch. 7.

12. California State Department of Industrial Relations. *Mexicans in California.* (San Francisco: State Building, 1930), 126–27.

13. See James D. Cockcroft, *Mexico Class Formation, Capital Accumulation and the State* (New York: Monthly Review Press, 1983), 115–45. The

manifesto and therefore CUOM has been interpreted to be the direct ideological descendant of the anarchistic Partido Liberal Mexicano led by Ricardo Flores Magon and based in Los Angeles in the advent of the Mexican Revolution (see, for example, Douglas Guy Monroy "Anarquismo y Comunismo: Mexican Radicalism and the Communist Party in Los Angeles During the 1930s," *Labor History* 24, no. 1 [1983]). It is extremely doubtful that the Mexican government would have joined with an anarchist organization to form a labor union, or that the pro-government CROM, led by the corrupt opportunist Luis Morones, would have been willing to sponsor anarchism among Mexican workers. A plausible explanation for this misinterpretation is that the language of anarchism cloaked a fundamentally conservative effort to control labor. One must view CUOM within the longer-term trends of the postrevolutionary government policies of Mexico.

14. California State Department of Industrial Relations, *Mexicans in California,* 127.

15. Ibid.

16. Ibid., 128–29.

17. See *The Western Worker* (Western Organ of the Communist Party USA) 1932–1934.

18. Stuart Jameison, *Labor Unionism in American Agriculture,* 108–9.

19. Ibid., 122.

20. Ibid., 123.

21. Ibid.

22. See Douglas Guy Monroy, "Anarquismo y Comunismo,"

23. See *La Opinion,* May 27, 1936; May 28, 1936; May 29, 1936.

24. Under the contractor system, an independent contractor enters into an agreement with a grower for assembling work crews at a set price. Upon completion of the work, the contractor receives a bulk payment and is then responsible to pay the laborers at an agreed rate. There is no direct contract between grower and worker.

25. Interview with Clemente Hernández, Placentia, Calif., Sept. 6, 1988.

26. Interview with Henry Medina and Celso Medina, San Juan Capistrano, Calif., Oct. 9, 1990; interview with Emilio Martínez, Stanton, Calif., Feb. 3, 1989; interview with Pablo Alcántar, Yorba Linda, Calif., Mar. 7, 1989; interview with Clemente Hernández.

27. California State Department of Industrial Relations, *Mexicans in California,* 131; also interview with Pablo Alcántar, Yorba Linda, Calif., Feb. 21, 1989.

28. Interview with Clemente Hernández; interview with Henry Medina and Celso Medina.

29. Interview with Henry Medina and Celso Medina; see also *La Opinion,* June 15, 1936.

30. Department of Social Welfare, Orange County, California "Living Standards of Orange County Mexican Families." Orange County, Calif., Mar. 9, 1940; *La Opinion,* June 15, 1936. Americanization supervisor Druzilla Mackey assisted the pickers' union in compiling statistics relating to their yearly income.

31. Louis Reccow, "The Orange County Citrus Strike of 1935–1936: The 'Forgotten People' in Revolt" (Ph.D. diss., University of Southern California, 1971), 66.

32. Interview with Emilio Martínez.

33. Interview with Pablo Alcántar.

34. *Santa Ana Register,* Oct. 30, 1935.

35. California State Department of Industrial Relations, *Mexicans in California,* 132.

36. *Santa Ana Register,* Nov. 5, 1935.

37. Louis Reccow, "The Orange County Citrus Strike," 97.

38. *Santa Ana Register,* Oct. 31, 1935.

39. Ibid., May 7, 1936; *La Opinion,* June 21, 1936.

40. Louis Reccow, "The Orange County Citrus Strike," 109.

41. Ibid., 110.

42. The continual consular presence in the affairs of Mexican labor prompted the Santa Ana Workers' Club (an organization of unemployed) representative Frank Delgado to label the pickers union a "company union." The club of unemployed tolerated, if not espoused, those same ideological views that Lucio found counterproductive. Club meetings discussed the viability of alternatives to the capitalist system, class exploitation, oppression of the masses and the like. One such speaker declared at a club forum that the "worker's time has come and will only continue—through worker's . . . militant organization" (*Santa Ana Register,* June 21, 1935). Evidently a current of militancy challenged the consul from within and without the ranks of organized labor.

43. *Santa Ana Register,* June 9, 1936.

44. Ibid., June 10, 1936.

45. Ibid.

46. Ibid.

47. *Santa Ana Register,* June 13, 1936.

48. Interview with Henry Medina and Celso Medina.

49. Interview with Joe Raya, Placentia, Calif., Oct. 1, 1987.

50. Placentia (California) Orange Growers Association, Board of Directors *Minutes,* June 15, 1936.

51. Interview with Erma Magaña and Margarita Martínez, Placentia, Calif., Aug. 3, 1989.

52. *Santa Ana Register,* June 11, 1936.

53. Interview with Pablo Alcantar

54. Interview with Henry Medina and Celso Medina.

55. *Western Worker,* July 20, 1936.

56. *La Opinion,* June 17, 1936.

57. *Fullerton Daily Tribune,* July 12, 1936.

58. Interview with Henry Medina and Celso Medina.

59. *Santa Ana Register,* June 12, 1936; also *Los Angeles Times,* June 12, 1936.

60. *Santa Ana Register,* June 12, 1936.

61. Ibid., June 13, 1936.

62. *Los Angeles Times,* June 13, 1936.

63. *Orange Daily News,* June 15, 1936.

64. Ibid. The Board of Directors *Minutes* of the Placentia Orange Growers, July 2, 1936, in part revealed this cooperative spirit: "Moved by Lang, seconded by Hemphell, that we give the sheriff and state authorities all possible support in protection of the orange pickers against any violence, and that we recommend to the Placentia Orange County Exchange that it take similar action."

65. *Santa Ana Register,* June 13, 1936.

66. Interview with Henry Medina and Celso Medina.

67. *Orange Daily News,* June 15, 1936.

68. *Fullerton Daily Tribune,* June 15, 1936.

69. *Santa Ana Register,* June 18, 1936.

70. Ibid., June 12, 1936.

71. Ibid., July 7, 1936.

72. Ibid., June 24, 1936.

73. *La Opinion,* July 12, 1936; June 27, 1936; *Fullerton Daily Tribune,* July 12, 1936 and June 27, 1936; also *Santa Ana Register,* June 27, 1936.

74. *Daily Worker,* July 23, 1936.

75. *La Opinion,* June 22, 1936.

76. *Fullerton Daily Tribune,* July 10, 1936.

77. Lyrics supplied by Emilio Martínez, during an interview at Stanton, Calif., Feb. 9, 1989.

78. *Santa Ana Register,* July 3, 1936.

79. Ibid., June 27, 1936.

80. Ibid.

81. Ibid.

82. Ibid., June 19, 1936.

83. Ibid., June 27, 1936.

84. *La Opinion,* July 15, 1936.

85. Interview with Lionel Magaña, Placentia, Calif., Aug. 25, 1987.

86. *Santa Ana Register,* June 16, 1936.

87. Interview with Clemente Hernández.

88. *Santa Ana Register,* June 18, 1936.

89. Ibid.

90. Ibid., June 20, 1936.

91. Ibid.

92. Ibid., June 13, 1936.

93. Ibid., June 17, 1936.

94. Ibid., June 24, 1936.

95. Ibid., July 3, 1936.

96. *Placentia Courier,* July 10, 1936.

97. *Los Angeles Times,* July 7, 1936.

98. *Placentia Courier,* July 10, 1936.

99. Ibid.

100. *Los Angeles Times,* July 3, 1936.

101. Ibid., July 14, 1936. Growers associations did not shy away from violence as a general strategy to thwart strikes. Several years before the strike the Placentia Mutual Orange Growers authorized the packinghouse night

watchmen to carry a sawed-off shotgun in the event labor troubles, including a "radical element" brewing in "various parts of the state," spilled into the county "at the start of the Valencia season" (Board of Directors *Minutes,* Placentia Mutual Orange Growers Association, Jan. 30, 1934).

102. *Los Angeles Times,* July 13, 1936.

103. *Santa Ana Register,* July 10, 1936.

104. *Los Angeles Times,* July 11, 1936.

105. *Placentia Courier,* July 10, 1936.

106. *Santa Ana Register,* July 6, 1936.

107. Ibid., July 13, 1936. The Register's article states: "An interesting report came from an unimpeachable source today that the vigilante raiders who stormed a meeting at Placentia last week were 'apprehended and arrested' shortly after their disappearance from the downtown scene where they wielded clubs and tear gas bombs." The report added that "the men were immediately released from custody and allowed to go free."

108. *Los Angeles Times,* July 15, 1936.

109. According to one union journal, Harry Chandler, publisher of the *Los Angeles Times,* large landowner in Mexico, and a friend of several large Orange County citrus ranchers (who also owned large tracts in Mexico), had a hand in arranging the meetings between the consulate and the growers. Chandler's secretary John Dolan serving in the unexpected capacity of legal advisor to the consulate represented Chandler in the negotiations. Dolan proposed the consulate offer concessions to the growers. There is also some discussion of an alleged $7,000 fee for Dolan's services paid by the consulate. Whether the above is true or not cannot be verified. If it is, it indicates the manner in which small local union issues can become entangled and submerged by large scale economic and political power [David Price, "Orange County Strike," *Pacific Weekly,* Aug. 24, 1936, 117].

110. *Placentia Courier,* July 17, 1936.

111. *Santa Ana Register,* July 17, 1936.

112. Ibid.

113. *Los Angeles Times,* July 19, 1936.

114. *Placentia Courier,* July 24, 1936; also *Orange Daily News,* July 15, 1936.

115. *Santa Ana Register,* July 20, 1936.

116. Ibid., July 25, 1936.

117. Ibid., July 23, 1936.

118. *La Opinion,* July 27, 1936.

119. *Orange Daily News,* July 25, 1936.

120. *La Opinion,* July 22, 1936.

121. *La Habra Star,* Aug. 14, 1936.

122. Interview with Henry Medina and Celso Medina.

123. Interview with Chester Whitten, Placentia, Calif., Aug. 13, 1987.

124. Druzilla Mackey, [Untitled Memoirs], 88.

125. Placentia Mutual Orange Growers, Board of Directors *Minutes,* Sept. 6, 1938.

126. *La Habra Star,* Dec. 25, 1936.

127. Louis Reccow, "The Orange County Citrus Strike," 230.

128. U.S. Congress, Senate Committee on Education and Labor, *Violations,* 549.

129. Stuart Jameison, *Labor Unionism in American Agriculture,* 166.

130. *Placentia Courier,* July 3, 1936.

131. Charles C. Teague, *Fifty Years a Rancher,* 141.

7. World War II

1. Ernesto Galarza, *Merchants of Labor,* 42.

2. Anaheim Cooperative Orange Association *Minutes,* Nov. 12, 1941; Roy J. Smith, Professor of Agricultural Economics at UCLA wrote in 1942: "managers are finding it difficult to keep pickers" ["Methods of Paying Citrus Pickers," *California Citrograph* 28, no. 8 (Aug. 1942): 267].

3. *Orange County Farm Bureau News* 24, no. 9 (Sept. 1942), 4.

4. "Agriculture's Labor Needs," *California Citrograph* 29, no. 1 (Jan. 1943): 67.

5. *Placentia Courier,* July 10, 1942; also *Placentia Courier,* July 24, 1942.

6. Anaheim Orange Growers Association *Minutes,* May 9, 1944.

7. *Placentia Courier,* June 19, 1942.

8. Ibid., July 10, 1942.

9. Interview with George A. Graham by Donna Barasch, 1972, Tape 69-7, Oral History Program, California State University, Fullerton,

10. "The Farm Labor Situation," *California Citrograph* 30, no. 12 (Dec. 1944): 35.

11. Interview with George A. Graham by Donna C. Barasch.

12. Charles C. Teague, "California's Farm Labor Problem and What is Being Done to Solve It," *California Citrograph* 29, no. 5 (May 1943): 172.

13. Ibid.

14. *California Citrograph* 30, no. 4 (Apr. 1944): 166.

15. Ibid.

16. *Placentia Courier,* Apr. 23, 1943; Apr. 16, 1943.

17. Ibid., Mar. 12, 1943.

18. Ibid., July 25, 1943.

19. The journal *Agricultural Life* emphasized the bracero in different contexts, always underscoring the contentment and satisfaction experienced by braceros.

20. *Placentia Courier,* June 11, 1943; Sept. 15, 1944, headlines read: "Rotary Club Eats Tortilla Dinner as Served Nationals; Learn of Program."

21. George A. Graham, "History of Citrus Growers, Inc., Formation and Development." Mimeo, 1958. Bowers Museum Archives, Santa Ana, Calif.

22. Interview with Eduardo Negrete, Anaheim, Calif., Jan. 25, 1989.

23. Placentia Orange Growers Association, *Manager's Annual Report,* 1945. The manager wrote: "Jamaican Negroes proved quite troublesome, very poor pickers and disinclined to turn out the work."

24. The *California Citrograph* reported that in 1944, "experience in the use of prisoners of war for farm work is mixed. In some cases they have been sat-

isfactory, and in other cases unsatisfactory," *California Citrograph* 29, no. 12 (Dec. 1944): 35. George A. Graham, head of the Citrus Growers, Inc. reported that 225 POWs could not pick as much fruit as 130 braceros (*Placentia Courier,* Apr. 20, 1945).

25. Villa Park Orchards Association *Annual Report* (Villa Park, Calif., 1946).

26. *California Citrograph* 30, no. 10 (Oct. 1945): 379.

27. Interview with Henry Medina and Celso Medina, San Juan Capistrano, Calif., Dec. 4, 1990.

28. Paul Garland Williamson, "Labor in the California Citrus Industry," 55.

29. Ibid., 56–58.

30. Placentia Mutual Orange Association *Minutes,* Oct. 10, 1944.

31. Ibid., Oct. 9, 1945.

32. Ibid., Jan. 8, 1946.

33. Anaheim Cooperative Orange Association *Minutes,* July 11, 1944.

34. Placentia Orange Growers Association, *Report of the Manager* (Placentia, California, 1944), 7.

35. Paul Garland Williamson, "Labor in the California Citrus Industry," 60.

36. Ibid.

37. Interview with Erma Magaña and Margarita Martínez, Placentia, Calif., Aug. 3, 1989; interview with Julia Aguirre, Placentia, Calif., Aug. 8, 1989.

38. Packinghouses bemoaned the competition from the defense industry, as illustrated in the January 17, 1942, Yorba Linda Citrus Association *Minutes,* which states: "The present war with its defense activities was stated to be creating labor shortage in the citrus industry because of higher wages paid in defense work." The 1942 Annual Report for the Villa Park Orchards Association offered a similar assessment: "The labor problem was a trying one with so many of our experienced workers in military service or in defense plants, making it necessary to 'break in' many new workers throughout the season."

Several aircraft feeder plants were operating in the county by 1943, hiring men and women according to news releases. The Placentia plant alone hired approximately one hundred employees—naturally it siphoned workers from existing industries and opened the doors for those previously out of the labor force (*Placentia Courier,* Sept. 20, 1943).

39. *Placentia Courier,* Mar. 12, 1943.

40. Interview with Fred Aguirre, Placentia, Calif., Sept. 17, 1987.

41. Interview with Erma Magaña, Placentia, Calif., Aug. 3, 1989; interview with Lionel Magaña, Placentia, Calif., Aug. 25, 1989. See also Mary Lisbeth Haas, "The Barrios of Santa Ana," 161.

42. Lizabeth Cohen, *Making a New Deal,* 365. Professor Cohen writes:

> An important reason why workers of diverse ethnicities and races succeeded in asserting themselves collectively as Democrats and as unionists by the 1930s was that they had more in common culturally from which to forge alliances. More of them were second generation Americans. . . .

During the 1930s American industrial workers sought to overcome the miseries and frustrations that had long plagued their lives neither through anticapitalist and extragovernmental revolutionary uprisings nor through the perpetuation of the status quo of welfare capitalism but rather through this growing investment in two institutions ... an activist welfare state concerned with equalizing wealth and privilege and a national union movement of factory workers. ...

43. Mexican American Movement. *Its Scope, Origin and Personnel,* 1944, n.p.

44. Ibid.

45. Mexican American Movement, *Handbook.* The Supreme Council of the Mexican American Movement, N.D., 5.

46. Ibid., 3.

47. Ibid.

48. *Placentia Courier,* Oct. 27, 1944.

49. Ibid., Dec. 24, 1944.

50. Ibid., June 21, 1946.

51. Ibid., June 6, 1947.

52. *Anaheim Gazette,* Feb. 7, 1946.

53. James Maurice Jensen, "The Mexican American in an Orange County Community" (Master's thesis, Claremont Graduate School, 1947), 97.

54. *Placentia Courier,* June 1, 1945.

55. Interview with Fred Aguirre; interview with Lionel Magaña; interview with Gualberto Valadez, Yorba Linda, Calif., Aug. 18, 1987.

56. Interview with Virginia Vargas by George Mirsch, 1971, Tape No. 588, Oral History Program, California State University, Fullerton.

57. The political actions of the local community was of a piece with the actions occurring across Mexican American communities of the Southwest. What has not been studied is that the minority's civil rights campaign occurred during a national effort to promote voluntary integration. The state department's office of the inter-American affairs, directed by Nelson Rockefeller, focused on social reform as a means to encourage Latin American solidarity with the war, and later cold war effort. Policy makers understood that the treatment of U.S. minorities at the hands of the majority would affect the United States' ability to realize foreign policy objectives—especially in strategically critical regions of the world populated by peoples of color. The OIAA then directed a campaign in the Southwest to ameliorate Mexican and Anglo relations through stimulating voluntary school desegregation efforts at the local levels. That campaign undoubtedly affected the thinking of the judiciary; it had a significant impact on many educators, and it provided a positive environment for those opposing segregation. Unfortunately the OIAA effected little significant desegregation action. It is probably true that the Mendez case was filed at a propitious time due to international factors (see Gilbert G. González, *Chicano Education in the Era of Segregation,* chap. 6).

58. Interview with Gualberto Valadez. Valadez was a founding member of MAM, the first Placentia council president, later served as national president.

59. Beatrice Griffith, *American Me* (Cambridge, Mass.: Houghton Mifflin Company, 1948), 292.

60. Letter from Associated Farmers of Orange County, Inc. to Mr. Isadore González, May 5, 1947.

61. Interview with Hector Tarango, Santa Ana, Calif., Apr. 15, 1989.

62. Interview with Hector Tarango; interview with Tony Luna, Santa Ana, Calif., Mar. 27, 1991.

63. American Council on Race Relations, *Report* 2, no. 2 (June, 1947): 3.

64. Quoted in Mary M. Peters, "The Segregation of Mexican-American Children in the Elementary Schools of California: Its Legal and Administrative Aspects" (Master's thesis, University of California, Los Angeles, 1948), 84.

65. Lester H. Phillips, "Segregation in Education: A California Case Study," *Phylon* 10 (1949): 407.

66. *The Latin American,* May 31, 1949.

67. *Novedad* 1, no. 1 (Aug. 1951): 4.

68. Ibid.

69. Interview with Hector Tarango.

70. "Foreword" by Ignacio L. Lopez in Ruth Tuck, *Not with the Fist* (New York: Harcourt, Brace, and Co., 1946), 9.

71. Nearly all persons interviewed recall a smooth process of integrating the old immigrant, their children with the new immigrants.

72. Interview with Eduardo Negrete, Fullerton, Calif., Feb. 1, 1989.

73. James Maurice Jensen, "The Mexican American," 17–18.

74. Interview with Julia Aguirre.

75. James Maurice Jensen, "The Mexican American," 52.

76. Quoted to Mary Lisbeth Haas, "The Bracero in Orange County, California: A Work Force for Economic Transition" (Program in United States–Mexican Studies, Q-060, University of California, San Diego, 1981), 31.

77. Ibid.

78. Ibid., 37.

79. Ibid., 33–34.

80. See the work of Robert J. Thomas, *Citizenship, Gender, and Work,* 27.

81. Interview with Angelina Cruz, Sept. 12, 1991, Escondido, Calif.

82. Vicki Ruiz, *Cannery Women, Cannery Lives,* 81–83.

83. Mauricio Mazon, *The Zoot-Suit Riots* (Austin: University of Texas Press, 1984), 5. Professor Mazon quoted sociologist Joan Moore's illuminating analysis of gangs in San Fernando Valley area of Los Angeles: "But the real model for the Polviados were the pachucos of Los Angeles. The gang started in the early 1940s and made a point of keeping up with the latest clothing fads, going to Murray's and Young's in downtown Los Angeles for their drapes and fingertip coats, and to Price's for their double-soled shoes. The Polviados consciously set themselves apart from the rural Chicanos of Pacoima, Canoga Park, Van Nuys and other Valley barrios, whom they considered backward, square, "farmers" (as quoted in Mauricio Mazon, *The Zoot-Suit Riots,* 5.

84. James Maurice Jensen, "The Mexican American," 105.

85. Interview with Fred Aguirre.

86. Ibid.

87. *Los Angeles Times,* June 26, 1977.

88. Richard Mines and Ricardo Anzaldua, *New Migrants and Old Migrants: Alternative Labor Market Structures in the California Citrus Industry* (San Diego: Program in U.S.-Mexican Studies, University of California, San Diego, 1982), 6–7.

89. This is based on an estimate of 1950 census data, which did not count the Mexican-born and native-born. The estimate was tabulated by demographer William Gayk. See William Gayk, "The Changing Demography of Orange County," *Journal of Orange County Studies* 1, no. 3-4 (Fall/Spring 1990): 18.

Conclusion

1. The variety of Mexican communities is illustrated in the substantial number of publications focusing on community life. The following comprises a small sampling: Shirley Achor, *Mexican Americans in a Dallas Barrio* (Tucson: University of Arizona Press, 1978); Margaret Clark, *Health in the Mexican American Culture: A Community Study* (Berkeley: University of California Press, 1959); Deutsch, *No Separate Refuge;* Richard A. García, *Rise of the Mexican American Middle Class;* James B. Lane and Edward J. Escobar, *Forging a Community: The Latino Experience in Northwest Indiana, 1919–1925* (Chicago: Cattails Press, 1987); Ricardo Romo, *East Los Angeles;* Paul S. Taylor, *Mexican Labor in the United States: Chicago and the Calumet Region,* vol. 7, no. 2 (Berkeley: University of California Publication in Economics, 1932).

2. Ruth Alice Allen, *Labor of Women in the Production of Cotton* (1933; reprint, New York: Arno Press, 1975), 231.

3. Ibid.

4. Ibid., 234.

5. Vicki Ruiz, *Cannery Women, Cannery Lives.*

6. Ibid., 39.

7. Interview with Julia Aguirre, Placentia, Calif.

8. Ibid.

9. Ernesto Galarza, "Program for Action," *Common Ground* 10, no. 4 (Summer 1949): 33. Galarza noted "the separation of the urban from the rural groups, so that the full force of the Mexican community has never been brought to bear on the problems they have in common. The urban Mexican has never reached, as has the urban Negro, toward the rural Mexican so that both could improve their status."

10. Alan Exelbrod, "Chicano Education: In Swann's Way?" *Integrated Education* 9 (Aug. 3, 1971): 28.

11. John Higham, *Send These to Me,* 22.

12. Leo Grebler, Joan W. Moore, Ralph C. Guzman, *The Mexican American People* (New York: Free Press, 1970), 89.

13. Albert Camarillo, "Chicanos in the American City," in *Chicano Studies: A Multidisciplinary Approach,* eds. Eugene H. Garcia, Francisco Lomeli and Isidro D. Ortiz (New York: Teachers College Press, 1984), 23–24.

14. *Los Angeles Times,* Apr. 25, 1991.

15. Ibid.

16. Ibid., Mar. 20, 1991.

17. Ibid., Apr. 15, 1990. The enslavement of Mexican labor is not new—it occurs from time to time. Employers, especially commercial ranchers, find Mexican immigrants from rural agricultural Mexico a docile supply. In the case of the "modern day serfdom" cited above the employer imported labor directly from Oaxaca, Mexico because according to one worker "they were the most passive." However, ranch managers employed psychological control and selective physical punishment to further control workers who were never allowed to leave the ranch nor the compound where they slept and ate. They earned approximately $100 every two weeks for 200 hours of work.

18. *Latinos in a Changing Society,* Report of the SCR43 Task Force (Riverside, Calif.: University of California, 1990), 155–57.

19. Josiah McC. Heyman, *Life and Labor on the Border* (Tucson: University of Arizona Press, 1991).

20. Discussion with Dr. Juan Davila, Irvine, Calif., June 22, 1990.

21. Daniel Akst, "What the Baja Boom Means for Our State," *Los Angeles Times,* Feb. 18, 1992.

22. Ibid.

23. Ralph Guzman, "Politics and Policies of the Mexican-American Community," in *California Politics and Policies,* eds. Eugene P. Dvorin and Arthur J. Misner (Reading, Mass.: Addison-Wesley Publishing Co., 1966), 363.

24. Those authors who have either analyzed or commented upon the Mexican consulate in the southern California area during the 1930s include: Francisco Balderrama, *In Defense of La Raza;* Rodolfo Acuña, *Occupied America;* Ricardo Romo, *East Los Angeles;* Vicki Ruiz, *Cannery Women, Cannery Lives.*

25. See Abraham Hoffman, "The El Monte Berry Picker's Strike, 1933: International Involvement in a Local Labor Dispute," *Journal of the West* 12, no. 1 (Jan. 1973).

26. Leo Grebler, Joan W. Moore, Ralph C. Guzman, *The Mexican American People,* 93.

27. *UC MEXUS News* (Fall, 1990): 8.

28. Ibid.

29. Ibid.

30. Ibid., 9.

31. Quoted in Rodolfo O. de la Garza, "Chicanos and U.S. Foreign Policy," in *Mexican-U.S. Relations, Conflict and Convergence,* eds. Carlos Vásquez and Manuel García y Griego (Los Angeles: UCLA Chicano Studies Research Center Publications, 1983), 408.

32. Ibid.

33. Ibid.

34. See, for example, "Mexico's 'Don Fidel': The Indispensable Power Broker," *Los Angeles Times,* Apr. 23, 1991.

35. Mario García, *Mexican Americans,* 16.

36. Ernesto Galarza, "Program for Action," 31.

37. "Mexico Faces Free Trade With High Hopes and Skepticism," *Los Angeles Times,* May 25, 1991.

38. Ibid.

39. *The Orange County Register,* Apr. 3, 1991.

Bibliography

Books

Achor, Shirley. *Mexican Americans in a Dallas Barrio.* Tucson: University of Arizona Press, 1978.

Acuña, Rodolfo A. *Occupied America: A History of Chicanos,* 2d ed. New York: Harper and Row, 1981.

————. *A Community under Siege: A Chronicle of Chicanos East of the Los Angeles River, 1945–1975.* Los Angeles: Chicano Studies Resource Center Publications, University of California, Los Angeles, Monograph no. 11, 1984.

Adams, R. L. *Seasonal Labor Requirements for California Crops.* Berkeley: University of California, 1938.

Allen, Ruth Alice. *The Labor of Women in the Production of Cotton.* 1933. Reprint. New York: Arno Press, 1975.

Alvarez, Robert. *Familia: Migration and Adaptation in Baja and Alta California, 1880–1975.* Berkeley: University of California Press, 1987.

Andrews, Gregg. *Shoulder to Shoulder? The American Federation of Labor, the United States, and the Mexican Revolution.* Berkeley: University of California Press, 1991.

Armitage, Susan, ed. *The Women's West.* Norman: University of Oklahoma Press, 1987.

Armor, Samuel. *History of Orange County, California, with Biographical Sketches.* Los Angeles: Historic Record Co., 1921.

Arrington, Leonard J. *The Changing Structure of the Mountain West, 1850–1950.* Logan: Utah State University Press, 1963.

Bain, Beatrice, and Samuel Sidney Hoos. *California Orange Industry.* Berkeley: University of California Agricultural Experiment Station, Giannini Foundation of Agricultural Economics, 1966.

Balderrama, Francisco E. *In Defense of La Raza.* Tucson: University of Arizona Press, 1982.

Batchelor, Leon Dexter and Herbert John Webber, eds. *The Citrus Industry.* Vol. 2. Berkeley: University of California Press, 1948.

Bock, Phillip K., ed. *Peasants in the Modern World.* Albuquerque: University of New Mexico Press, 1969.

Bogardus, Emory S. "The Mexican in the United States." Los Angeles: University of Southern California School of Research Studies, no. 5, 1934.

Boyer, Richard O., and Herbert M. Morais. *Labor's Untold Story.* New York: United Electrical Radio and Machine Workers of America, 1972.

Braun, E. W., and H. R. Wellman. *Oranges.* Berkeley: University of California Printing Office, 1928.

Brecher, Jeremy. *Strike!* San Francisco: Straight Arrow Books, 1972.

Brunner, Edmund de S. *Irrigation and Religion: A Study of Religion and Social Conditions in Two California Counties.* New York: George H. Doran, 1922.

————. *Orange County, California. Church and Community Survey. A Preliminary Abstract.* New York: Committee on Social and Religious Surveys, 1922.

Callahan, Raymond E. *Education and the Cult of Efficiency.* Chicago: University of Chicago Press, 1962.

Camarillo, Albert. *Chicanos in California: A History of Mexican-Americans in California.* San Francisco: Boyd and Fraser Publishing Co., 1984.

————. *Chicanos in a Changing Society: From Mexican Pueblos to American Barrios in Santa Barbara and Southern California, 1848–1930.* Cambridge, Mass.: Cambridge University Press, 1979.

Campa, Arthur Leon. *Spanish Religious Folk Theatre in the Spanish Southwest.* Albuquerque: University of New Mexico Press, 1934.

Chambers, Clarke A. *California Farm Organization: A Historical Study of the Orange, the Farm Bureau and the Associated Farmers, 1929–1941.* Berkeley: University of California Press, 1952.

Chan, Sucheng, ed. *This Bittersweet Soil: The Chinese in California Agriculture.* Berkeley: University of California Press, 1986.

Clark, Margaret. *Health in the Mexican-American Culture. A Community Study.* Berkeley: University of California Press, 1959.

Cleland, Robert Glass. *Cattle on a Thousand Hills.* San Marino, Calif.: Huntington Library, 1951.

————. *Dodge, 1834–1950.* New York: Alfred A. Knopf, 1952.

Cockcroft, James D. *Mexico: Class Formation, Capital Accumulation and the State.* New York: Monthly Review Press, 1983.

Cohen, Lizabeth. *Making a New Deal: Industrial Workers in Chicago, 1919–1939.* Cambridge, Mass.: Cambridge University Press, 1990.

Daniel, Cletus E. *Bitter Harvest: A History of California Farmworkers, 1870–1941.* Berkeley: University of California Press, 1981.

de la Garza, Rodolfo O. et al. *The Mexican American Experience: An Interdisciplinary Anthology.* Austin: University of Texas Press, 1985.

Deutsch, Sarah. *No Separate Refuge: Culture, Class, and Gender on an Anglo-Hispanic Frontier in the American Southwest.* New York: Oxford University Press, 1987.

Dvorin, Eugene P., and Arthur J. Misner. *California Politics and Policies.* Reading, Mass.: Addison-Wesley Publishing Co., 1966.

Fass, Paula S. *Outside In: Minorities and the Transformation of American Education.* New York: Oxford University Press, 1989.

Fisher, Lloyd H. *The Harvest Labor Market in California.* Cambridge, Mass.: Harvard University Press, 1953.

Foley, Douglas et al. *From Peones to Politicos: Class and Ethnicity in a South Texas Town, 1900–1987.* Rev. ed. Austin: University of Texas Press, 1988.

Friis, Leo S. *Orange County through Four Centuries.* Santa Ana, Calif.: Pioneer Press, 1965.

Frost, Elsa C., ed. *El Trabajo y los Trabajadores en la Historia de Mexico.* Tucson: University of Arizona Press, 1979.

Galarza, Ernesto. *Merchants of Labor: The Mexican Bracero Story.* Santa Barbara, Calif.: McNally and Loftin Publishers, 1964.

García, Eugene, Francisco Lomeli, and Isidro Ortiz, eds. *Chicano Studies: A Multidiscplinary Approach.* New York: Teachers College Press, 1984.

García, Mario. *Desert Immigrants: The Mexicans of El Paso, 1880–1920.* New Haven: Yale University Press, 1981.

———. *Mexican Americans. Leadership, Ideology, and Identity, 1930–1960.* New Haven: Yale University Press, 1989.

García, Richard A. *Rise of the Mexican American Middle Class. San Antonio, 1929–1941.* College Station, Tex.: Texas A & M University Press, 1991.

Gerstle, Gary. *Working-class Americanism: The Politics of Labor in a Textile City, 1914–1960.* Cambridge, Mass.: Cambridge University Press, 1989.

Goldschmidt, Walter. *As You Sow. Three Studies in the Social Consequences of Agribusiness.* New York: Harcourt, Brace and World, 1974.

Goméz-Quiñónez, Juan. *Sembradores: Ricardo Flores Magon y el Partido Liberal Mexicano: A Eulogy and Critique.* Los Angeles: University of California, Aztlan Publications, 1973.

———. *Chicano Politics: Reality and Promise, 1940–1990.* Albuquerque: University of New Mexico Press, 1990.

Gonzáles, Juan L., Jr. *Mexican and Mexican American Farmworkers.* New York: Praeger Publishers, 1985.

González, Gilbert G. *Chicano Education in the Era of Segregation.* Philadelphia: Balch Institute Press, 1990.

Grebler, Leo, Joan W. Moore, and Ralph Guzman. *The Mexican American People.* New York: Free Press, 1970.

Griffith, Beatrice. *American Me.* Cambridge, Mass.: Houghton Mifflin Company, 1948.

Griswold del Castillo, Richard. *The Los Angeles Barrio, 1850–1890. A Social History.* Berkeley: University of California Press, 1979.

———. *La Familia: Chicano Families in the Urban Southwest, 1848 to the Present.* Notre Dame: University of Notre Dame Press, 1984.

Haas, Lisbeth. *The Bracero in Orange County, California: A Work Force for Economic Transition.* Program in U.S.-Mexico Studies. Working Papers in U.S.-Mexican Studies, Nov. 29, 1981.

Henry, Mary B. *Santa Ana's Problem in Americanization.* Santa Ana, Calif.: Santa Ana Board of Education, 1920.

Heyman, Josiah McC. *Life and Labor on the Border.* Tucson: University of Arizona Press, 1991.

Higham, John. *Send These to Me. Immigrants in Urban America.* Rev. ed. Baltimore: The Johns Hopkins University Press, 1984.

Hill, Merton. *The Development of an Americanization Program.* Ontario: The Board of Trustees of the Chaffey Union High School and Chaffey Junior College, 1928.

Hinojosa, Gilbert M. *A Borderlands Town in Transition, Laredo, 1755–1870.* College Station: Texas A & M University Press, 1983.

Hoffman, Abraham. *Unwanted Mexican Americans in the Great Depression: Repatriation Pressures, 1929–1939.* Tucson: University of Arizona Press, 1974.

Hutchison, Claude B., ed. *California Agriculture.* Berkeley: University of California Press, 1946.

Jervey, Edward Drewry. *The History of Methodism in Southern California and Arizona.* Nashville, Tenn.: Parthenon Press, 1960.

Johnston, John Clark. *Citrus Growing in California.* Circular Division of Agricultural Sciences, University of California, Berkeley, 1953.

Kling, Rob, Spencer Olin, and Mark Poster. *Post-Suburban California: The Transformation of Orange County Since World War II.* Berkeley: University of California Press, 1991.

Lane, James B., and Edward J. Escobar, eds. *Forging a Community: The Latino Experiences in Northwest Indiana, 1919–1975.* Chicago: Cattails Press, 1987.

Lens, Sidney. *The Labor Wars.* Garden City, N.Y.: Anchor Doubleday, 1974.

Leubke, Frederich C. *Ethnicity on the Great Plains.* Lincoln: University of Nebraska Press, 1980.

Lyle, Shannon, and Madaline Shannon. *Minority Migrants in the Urban Community.* Beverly Hills: Sage Press, 1973.

MacCurdy, Rahno M. *The History of the California Fruit Growers Exchange.* Los Angeles: George Rice and Sons, 1925.

Madsen, William. *Mexican Americans of South Texas.* New York: Holt, Rinehart and Winston, 1964.

Majka, Linda C., and Theo J. Majka. *Farmworkers, Agribusiness and the State.* Philadelphia: Temple University Press, 1982.

Mazon, Mauricio. *The Zoot-Suit Riots, The Psychology of Symbolic Annihilation.* Austin: University of Texas Press, 1984.

McCombs, Vernon Monroe. *From Over the Border: A Study of the Mexicans in the United States.* New York: Council of Women for Home Missions, 1925.

McWilliams, Carey. *Ill Fares the Land: Migrants and Migratory Labor in California.* 1942. Reprint. New York: Arno Press, 1967.

———. *North from Mexico. The Spanish Speaking People of the United States.* 1949. Reprint. New York: Greenwood Press, 1968.

———. *Factories in the Field: The Story of Migratory Farm Labor in California.* 1935. Reprint. Santa Barbara, Calif.: Peregrine Press, 1971.

Melzer, Richard. *Madrid Revisited: Life and Labor in a New Mexican Mining Camp in the Years of the Great Depression.* Santa Fe, N.M.: Lightning Tree, 1976.

Mines, Richard, and R. Anzaldua. *New Migrants vs. Old Migrants: Alternative Labor Market Structures in the Southern California Citrus Industry.* San Diego: University of California Program in U.S.-Mexico Studies, 1982.

Montejano, David. *Anglos and Mexicans in the Making of Texas, 1836–1986.* Austin: University of Texas Press, 1987.

Muñoz, Carlos, Jr. *Youth, Identity, Power: The Chicano Movement.* New York: Verso Press, 1989.

Mutual Orange Distributors. *A Manual for Citrus Growers.* Redlands, Calif.: Mutual Orange Distributors, 1937.

Nash, Gerald D. *The American West in the Twentieth Century: A Short History of an Urban Oases.* Englewood Cliffs, N.J.: Prentice-Hall, 1973.

Nasaw, David. *Schooled to Order: A Social History of Public Schooling in America.* New York: Oxford University Press, 1979.

Orleans, Peter and William Russell Ellis, Jr., eds. *Urban Affairs Annual Review.* Vol. 5. Beverly Hills, Calif.: Sage Publications, 1971.

Pflueger, Donald H., ed. *Charles C. Chapman: The Career of a Creative Californian, 1853–1944.* Los Angeles: Anderson, Ritchie, and Sernon, 1976.

Pitt, Leonard. *The Decline of the Californios: A Social History of the Spanish-Speaking Californians, 1846–1890.* Berkeley: University of California Press, 1971.

Plummer, Louis E. *A History of Fullerton Union High School and Fullerton Junior College, 1893–1943.* Fullerton, Calif.: Fullerton Unified High School District, 1949.

Prizer, J. A. *Early History of the Placentia Orange Growers Association.* Placentia, Calif.: Placentia Orange Growers Association, 1945.

Reisler, Mark. *By the Sweat of Their Brow: Mexican Immigrant Labor in the United States, 1900–1940.* Westport, Conn.: Greenwood Press, 1976.

Romo, Ricardo. *East Los Angeles: A History of a Barrio.* Austin: University of Texas Press, 1983.

Romo, Ricardo, and Raymundo Paredes, eds. *New Directions in Chicano Scholarship.* La Jolla: University of California, San Diego, 1978.

Rubel, Arthur J. *Across the Tracks: Mexican-Americans in a Texas City.* Austin: University of Texas Press, 1966.

Ruiz, Vicki. *Cannery Women, Cannery Lives: Mexican Women, Unionization, and the California Food Processing Industry, 1930–1950.* Albuquerque: University of New Mexico Press, 1987.

Schwartz, Harry. *Seasonal Farm Labor in the United States with Special Reference to Hired Workers in Fruit and Vegetable and Sugar-Beet Production.* New York: Columbia University Press, 1945.

Sheridan, Thomas E. *Los Tucsonenses: The Mexican Community in Tucson, 1845–1941.* Tucson: University of Arizona Press, 1986.

Shockley, John Staples. *Chicano Revolt in a Texas Town.* Notre Dame: University of Notre Dame Press, 1974.

Slayton, Robert. *Back of the Yards: The Making of Local Democracy.* Chicago: University of Chicago Press, 1986.

Southern California Conference of the Methodist Episcopal Church. Los Angeles: Commercial Printing House, 1911.

Spalding, William Andrew. *The Orange and Its Culture in California.* N.P., 1885.
Spring, Joel. *Education and the Rise of the Corporate State.* Boston, Mass.: Beacon Press, 1972.
The Story of a Parish. Anaheim, Calif.: St. Boniface Parish, 1961.
Takaki, Ron. *Strangers from a Different Shore: A History of Asian-Americans.* Boston: Little Brown and Co., 1989.
Talbert, T. A. *My Sixty Years in California.* Huntington Beach, Calif.: Huntington Beach News Press, 1952.
Taylor, Paul S. *Mexican Labor in the United States: Chicago and the Calumet Region.* Vol. 7, No. 2. Berkeley: University of California Publications in Economics, 1932.
Taylor, Paul S. *Mexican Labor in the United States. Migration Statistics.* Vol. 12. Berkeley: University of California Press, 1933.
Taylor, Paul S. *An American-Mexican Frontier.* Chapel Hill: University of North Carolina Press, 1934.
Teague, Charles C. *Fifty Years a Rancher.* Los Angeles: Ward Ritchie Press, 1944.
Thernstrom, Stephan. *Harvard Encyclopedia of American Ethnic Groups.* Cambridge, Mass.: Belknap Press, 1980.
Thomas, Robert J. *Citizenship, Gender, and Work. Social Organization of Industrial Agriculture.* Berkeley: University of California Press, 1985.
Tuck, Ruth. *Not with a Fist. Mexican-Americans in a Southwest City.* New York: Harcourt, Brace, and Company, 1946.
Ware, Susan. *Holding Their Own: American Women in the 1930s.* Boston: Twayne Publishers, 1982.
Wellman, H. R., and E. W. Braun. *Oranges.* Berkeley: University of California Printing Office, 1928.
Valdes, Dennis Nodín. *Al Norte: Agricultural Workers in the Great Lakes Region, 1917–1970.* Austin: University of Texas Press, 1991.
Vásquez, Carlos, and Manuel García y Griego, eds. *Mexican-U.S. Relations: Conflict and Convergence.* Los Angeles: University of California, Chicano Studies Center Publications, 1983.

Articles and Chapters

Adams, Frank. "The Historical Background of California Agriculture." In Hutchison, *California Agriculture,* 1–50.
Adams, R. L. "Farm Labor." *Journal of Farm Economics* 19.4 (1937): 913–25.
Almaguer, Tomas. "Racial Domination and Class Conflict in Capitalist Agriculture: The Oxnard Sugar Beet Workers' Strike of 1903." *Labor History* 25.3 (1984): 325–50.
Almazan, Marco A. "The Mexicans Keep 'Em Rolling." *Inter-American* 4 (Oct. 1945): 20–3, 36.
Anzaldua, Ricardo and Richard Mines. "New Migrants vs. Old Migrants: Alternative Labor Market Structures in the California Citrus Industry." La

Jolla, Calif.: Program in U.S. Mexican Studies, University of California, San Diego, Vol. 7 (1982).

Armour, Samuel. "Beet Sugar Industry." *History of Orange County* 11 (1921): 151–59.

Barbosa-Dasilva, J. F. "Participation of Mexican-Americans in Voluntary Associations." *Research Reports in the Social Sciences* 2.1 (1968): 33–43.

Barrera, Mario. "The Historical Evolution of Chicano Ethnic Goals." *Sage Race Relations Abstracts* 10 (Feb. 1985): 1–48.

Batman, Richard Dale. "Anaheim was an Oasis in a Wilderness." *Journal of the West* 4.1 (Jan. 1965): 1–20.

Batten, Neil, and Raymond A. Mohl. "From Discrimination to Repatriation: Mexican Life in Gary, Indiana, during the Great Depression." *Pacific Historical Review* 42.3 (Aug. 1973): 370–88.

Benedict, M. R. "The Economic and Social Structure of California Agriculture." In Hutchison, *California Agriculture* 395–436.

Bliven, Bruce. "Hey Rube." *The New Republic* (Feb. 18, 1939): 10–2.

Briggs, Vernon M., Jr. "Chicanos and Rural Poverty: A Continuing Issue for the 1970s." *Poverty and Human Resources* 7.1 (Mar. 1972): 3–23.

Bustamante, Antonio Rios. "New Mexico in the Eighteenth Century: Life, Labor, and Trade in the Villa de San Felipe de Albuquerque, 1706–1790." *Aztlan* 7.3 (Fall 1976): 357–417.

Camarillo, Albert. "Chicano Urban History: A Study of Compton's Barrio, 1936–1970." *Aztlan* 2.2 (Fall 1971): 76–106.

Camarillo, Albert. "Chicanos in the American City." In García, Lomeli, and Ortiz, *Chicano Studies,* 23–39.

Camarillo, Albert. "Observations on the 'New' Chicano History: Historiography of the 1970s." Stanford University: Stanford Center for Chicano Research, 1984.

Carlson, Alvar W. "The Settling Processes of Mexican Americans in Northwestern Ohio." *Journal of Mexican American History* 5 (1975): 24–42.

"The Chicano Experience in the United States." *Social Science Quarterly* 53 (1973): 727–37.

Colman, Fern Hill. "History of the Celery Industry." *Orange County History Series* 3 (Apr. 1939): 98–106.

"Cooperation at a Profit." *Fortune* 14 (July 1936): 47–55, 90, 92, 95.

Cortes, Carlos. "Mexicans." In Thernstrom, *Harvard Encyclopedia* 697–719.

Culbertson, J. D. "Housing of Ranch Labor." In California Citrus Institute, *First Annual Report,* 97–105.

Day, Orman. "Family Members Prosper after Humble Beginning in the County." *Orange County Register,* July 11, 1981.

de la Garza, Rodolfo. "Chicanos and U.S. Foreign Policy." In Vásquez and García y Griego, *Mexican-U.S. Relations,* 399–415.

De Leon, Arnoldo. "Los Tasinques and the Sheep Shearers Union of North America: A Strike in West Texas, 1934." West Texas Historical Association *Yearbook* (1979): 3–16.

Dickson, Lucile E. "The Founding and Early History of Anaheim, California." *Historical Society of Southern California* 11 (1919): 26–37.

Dobie, J. Frank. "Ranch Mexicans." *Survey* 66 (May 1932): 167–70.

Dozier, Edward P. "Peasant Culture and Urbanization: Mexican Americans in the Southwest." In Bock, *Peasants in the Modern World,* 140–59.

Elwes, Hugh C. "Points about Mexican Labor." *Engineering and Mining Journal* 90 (Oct. 1, 1910): 662.

Exelbrod, Alan. "Chicano Education: In Swann's Way?" *Integrated Education* 9 (Aug. 1971): 28–32.

Fewkes, J. Walter. "The Pueblo Settlements Near El Paso." *American Anthropologist* 4.1 (1902): 57–75.

Fraser, Campbell Evan. "Management of Mexican Labor." *The Engineering and Mining Journal* 91 (June 3, 1911): 1104.

Galarza, Ernesto. "Program for Action." *Common Ground* 10.4 (Summer 1949): 27–38.

Gamboa, Erasmo. "Mexican Migration into Washington State: A History, 1940–1950." *Pacific Historical Quarterly* 72.3 (July 1981): 121–31.

García, Richard A. "Class, Consciousness, and Ideology: The Mexican Community of San Antonio, Texas, 1930–1940." *Aztlan* 9 (1978): 23–69.

Gayk, William. "The Changing Demography of Orange County." *Journal of Orange County Studies* 1.3/4 (Fall/Spring 1990): 13–8.

Gibson, Mary S. "Schools for the Whole Family. *Survey Graphic* 56 (June 1926): 301.

González, Gilbert G. *Racism, Education, and the Mexican Community in Los Angeles,* 1920–1930." *Societas* 4.4 (Sept. 1974): 287–301.

———. "Segregation of Mexican Children in a Southern California City: The Legacy of Expansionism and the American Southwest." *The Western Historical Quarterly* 16.1 (Jan. 1985): 55–76.

———. Gilbert G. "'The Mexican Played the Role of . . . Atlas': Mexican Communities in Orange County, 1850–1950." *Journal of Orange County Studies* 1.3/4 (Jan. 1990): 19–27.

González, Rosalinda M. "Distinctions in Western Women's Experience: Ethnicity, Class, and Social Change." In Armitage, *The Women's West.*

Gould, Stephen. "The Chinese in Tustin." *Orange Countiana* 1 (1973): 23–7.

Griswold del Castillo, Richard. "Quantitative History in the American Southwest: A Survey and Critique." *Western Historical Quarterly* 15 (1984): 407–26.

"Grove and Packinghouse Labor Exempt Under NRA Codes." *Citrus Leaves* 13 (Sept. 1933): 3–18.

Guzman, Ralph. "Politics and Policies from the Mexican-American Community." In Dvorin and Misner, *California Politics,* 350–381.

Haas, Lisbeth. "The Bracero in Orange County, California: A Work Force for Economic Transition." San Diego: University of California Program in U.S.-Mexico Studies, 1981.

Handman, Max S. "San Antonio." *Survey* 66 (May 1, 1931): 163–66.

Hewitt, Nancy. "Beyond the Search for Sisterhood: American Women's History in the 1980s." *Social History* 10 (Oct. 1985): 299–321.

Higgins, Delbert G., and J. Sherman Denny, "Holly Sugar Co. Building is Razed," *Huntington Beach News,* June 27, 1975.

Higham, John. "Integrating America: The Problem of Assimilation in the Nineteenth Century." *Journal of American Ethnic History* 1.1 (1981): 7–25.

———. "Current Trends in the Study of Ethnicity in the United States." *Journal of American Ethnic History* 2.2 (Fall 1982): 5–15.

Hoffman, Abraham. "The El Monte Berry Strike: International Involvement in a Local Labor Dispute." *Journal of the West* 12.1 (Jan. 1973): 71–84.

Holt, Raymond M. "The Fruits of Viticulture in Orange County." *Historical Society of Southern California Quarterly* 28 (Mar. 1946): 7–33.

Humphrey, Norman D. "Migration and Settlement of Detroit Mexicans" *Economic Geography* 19.4 (Oct. 1943): 358–61.

———. "The Changing Structure of the Detroit Mexican Family: An Index of Acculturation." *American Sociological Review* 9.6 (1944): 622–26.

———. "The Integration of the Detroit 'Mexican Colony'." *American Journal of Economics and Sociology* 3.2 (Jan. 1944): 155–66.

———. "Mexican Middletown." *Common Ground* 6.3 (Spring 1946): 20–8.

———. "The Cultural Background of the Mexican Immigrant." *Rural Sociology* 13.3 (1948): 239–56.

Hunter, Kathleen. "The Gold is Gone." *Los Angeles Times* (Orange County Edition), Mar. 31, 1991.

Jones, Lamar B. "Labor and Management in California Agriculture, 1864–1964." *Labor History* 11.4 (Winter 1970): 23–40.

Limon, José. "El Primer Congreso Mexicanista de 1911: A Precursor to Contemporary Chicanismo." *Aztlan* 5.1/2 (Spring/Fall 1974): 85–117.

Loomis, Charles P. "El Cerrito, New Mexico: A Changing Village." *New Mexico Historical Review* 33 (Jan. 1958): 53–75.

Luckingham, Bradford. "The American Southwest: An Urban View." *Western Historical Quarterly* 15.3 (July 1984): 261–80.

Mackey, Druzilla. "[Untitled Memoirs]." In Plummer, *A History of the Fullerton Union High School,* 82–88.

Magnuson, Thorsten A. "History of the Beet Sugar Industry in California." *Historical Society of Southern California* 2 (1918–20): 68–79.

Martin, Philip L., and Richard Mines. "Immigrant Workers and the California Citrus Industry." *Industrial Relations* 23.1 (Winter 1984): 139–49.

McWilliams, Carey. "They Saved the Crops." *The Inter-American* 11.2 (Aug. 1943): 10–4.

———. "California and the Wetback." *Common Ground* 9.4 (Summer 1949): 15–9.

Meany, George. "Peonage in California." *American Federationist* 48 (May 1941): 3–5, 31.

"Mexican Labor Pact." *Business Week* (Sept. 5, 1942): 50.

Monroy, Douglas. "Anarquismo y Comunismo: Mexican Radicalism and the Communist Party in Los Angeles During the 1930s." *Labor History* 24.1 (1983).

———. "Like Swallows at the Old Mission: Mexicans and the Racial Politics of Growth in Los Angeles in the Interwar Period." *Western Historical Quarterly* 14.4 (Oct. 1983).

Neuberger, Richard L. "Who Are the Associated Farmers?" *Survey Graphic* 28.9 (Sept. 1939): 517–21, 555–57.

Nostrand, Richard. "El Cerrito Revisited." *New Mexico Historical Review* 57.2 (1982): 109–22.

Orleans, Peter, and William Russell Ellis, Jr., eds. "Race, Change, and Urban Society." In Orleans and Ellis, *Urban Affairs Annual Review.*

Ostermen, Joseph D. "Venture, Gain, Loss and Change in Old El Toro's Orange County." *Californians* (July/Aug. 1983): 6–12.

Park, Joseph F. "The 1903 'Mexican Affair' at Clifton." *Journal of Arizona History* 18 (1977): 148–99.

Parker, Edwin R. "Selection of Orchard State." *Citrus Industry* 2 (1948): 223–54.

Phillips, Lester H. "Segregation in Education: A California Case Study." *Phylon* 10 (1949): 407–13.

"Placentia Mutual Teaches Mexicans." *Orange County Review* 2 (Oct. 1922): 30.

Poyo, Gerald E., and Gilberto M. Hinojosa. "Spanish Texas and Borderlands Historiography in Transition: Implications for U.S. History." *Journal of American History* 75.2 (Sept. 1988): 393–416.

Price, D. O. "Rural to Urban Migration of Mexican Americans, Negroes, and Anglos." *International Migration Review* 5 (1971): 281–308.

Price, David. "Orange County Strike." *Pacific Weekly* 5 (Aug. 24, 1936): 116–17.

Pritchard, Robert L. "Orange County during the Depressed Thirties: A Study in Twentieth-Century California Local History." *Historical Society of Southern California* 50 (1968): 191–207.

Richardson, Ethel. "Doing the Thing That Couldn't Be Done." *Survey Graphic* 56 (June 1926): 297–99, 333–36.

Romo, Ricardo. "The Urbanization of Southwestern Chicanos in the Early 20th Century." *New Scholar* 6 (1977): 183–207.

Rosaldo, Renato. "Chicano Studies, 1970–1984." *Annual Review of Anthopology* 14 (1985): 405–27.

Rubenstein, Harry R. "The Great Gallup Coal Strike of 1933." *New Mexico Historical Review* 52 (Apr. 1977): 173–92.

Sanchez, George. "Go After the Women: Americanization and the Mexican Immigrant Women, 1915–1929." Palo Alto, Calif.: Stanford University Center for Chicano Research, 1985.

Sandoval, David A. "An Economic Analysis of New Mexico History." *New Mexico Business* 20.2 (Feb. 1967): 1–34.

Schwartz, Harry. "Organizational Problems of Agricultural Labor Unions." *Journal of Farm Economics* 8.2 (May 1941): 456–66.

———. "Recent Development Among Farm Labor Unions." *Journal of Farm Economics* 8.4 (Nov. 1941): 833–42.

Seller, Maxine. "The Education of Immigrant Women, 1900–1935." *Journal of Urban History* 6.3 (1978): 307–30.

Sierra, Christine. "Chicano Political Development: Historical Considerations." In Garcia, Lomeli, and Ortiz., *Chicano Studies,* 79–98.

Sleeper, Jim. "Raps from the Gavel to Signal End of Another Historic County Era." Newspaper clipping. Santa Ana, Calif.: Bowers Museum Archives.

Sleeper, Jim. "The Story of Orange County's Golden Harvest." *Santa Ana Register,* Nov. 17, 1968.

Smith, Roy J. "Labor Stabilization in the Citrus Industry." *Los Angeles County Farm Bureau Monthly* 15 (Dec. 1941): 16, 30.

Stilwell, Hart. "The Wetback Tide." *Common Ground* 9.4 (Summer 1949): 3–15.

Stokes, Frank. "Let the Mexicans Organize." *The Nation* (Dec. 19, 1936): 731–32.

Stone, George C. "Financing the Orange Industry in California" *Pomona Valley Historian* 2 (1966): 159–174. Part 2: 3.1 (Jan. 1967): 31–47.

Stromquist, J. A. "California Oranges." *Industrial Pioneer* 1 (Mar. 1921): 23–6.

Taylor, Paul S. "Foundations of California Rural Society" *California Historical Quarterly* 24.3 (1945): 193–228.

Tennayuca, Emma, and Homer Brooks. "The Mexican Question in the Southwest" *The Communist* 18 (Mar. 1939): 257–68.

Tipton, Ellis M. "What We Want Is Action: Relations of Americans and Mexicans in San Dimas, California." *Common Ground* 7 (1946): 74–81.

Trager, William T. "Agricultural Workers in a California Town: Economics, Social Networks and Organizing for Change." *Human Organization* 34.1 (Spring 1975): 105–07.

Van Halen, Nelson. "The Bolsheviki and the Orange Growers" *Pacific Historical Review* 22 (Feb. 1953): 39–50.

Wahlbert, Harold E. "Progress of County Traced through Agriculture." *Santa Ana Register,* Nov. 22, 1939.

Walker, Helen W. "Mexican Journeys to Bethlehem." *Literary Digest* 77 (June 2, 1923): 103–4.

Walter, Paul Jr. "The Spanish Speaking Community." *Sociology and Social Research* 24.2 (Nov.-Dec. 1939): 150–57.

Waters, Lawrence Leslie. "Transient Mexican Agricultural Labor," *Southwest Social and Political Science Quarterly* 22 (June 1941): 49–66.

Weber, David. "The New Chicano Urban History." *The History Teacher* 16.2 (Feb. 1983): 224–30.

Webber, Herbert John. "History and Development of the Citrus Industry." In Webber and Batchelor, *Citrus Industry,* 1–40.

Webber, Herbert John. "The Commercial Regions of the World: Their Physiographic, Climactic, and Economic Characters." In Webber and Batchelor, *Citrus Industry* 71–128.

Whitaker, Percy Walton. "Fruit Tramps." *Century Magazine* 117 (Mar. 1929): 599–606.

Woirol, Gregory R. "'Rustling' Oranges in Lindsay." *California History* 62.2 (Summer 1983): 82–97.

Wollenberg, Charles. "Huelga, 1928 Style: The Imperial Valley Cantaloupe Worker's Strike." *Pacific Historical Review* 28 (Feb. 1969): 45–58.

———. "Race and Class in Rural California: The El Monte Berry Strike of 1933" *California Historical Quarterly* 51 (Summer 1972): 155–64.

Woodbridge, Dwight E. "La Cananea Mining Camp." *Engineering and Mining Journal* 82 (Oct. 6, 1906): 623.
Yancey, William L., Eugene P. Ericksen, and Richard Juliani. "Emergent Ethnicity: A Review and Reformulation." *American Sociological Review* 41 (June 1976): 391–403.
Zamora, Emilio, Jr. "Chicano Socialist Labor Activity in Texas, 1900–1920." *Aztlan:* 6.2 (Summer 1975): 221–38.

Theses and Dissertations

Broadbent, Elizabeth. "The Distribution of Mexican Population in the United States." Ph.D. diss., University of Chicago, 1941.
Cornelius, John Scott. "The Effects of Certain Changes of Curriculum and Methods on the School Achievement of Mexican Children in a Segregated School." Master's thesis, University of Southern California, 1941.
Dawson, Ray. "A History of Tustin, California with Special Emphasis upon Its Citrus Development." Master's thesis, University of Southern California, 1938.
Dennis, Margaret. "The History of the Beet-Sugar Industry in California." Master's thesis, University of Southern California, 1937.
Engle, Clara. "Orange County Citrus Strike. 1936: Historical Analyses and Social Conflict." Master's thesis, California State University, Fullerton, 1975.
Fuller, Levi Varden. "The Supply of Agricultural Labor as a Factor in the Evolution of Farm Organization in California." Ph.D. diss., University of California, Berkeley, 1939.
Haas, Lisbeth. "The Barrios of Santa Ana: Community, Class, and Organization." Ph.D. diss., University of California, Irvine, 1985
Hayden, Jessie. "The La Habra Experiment in Mexican Social Education." Master's thesis, Claremont College, 1934.
Herbert, John H. "A History of the Placentia Unified School District." Master's thesis, Chapman College, 1968.
Jensen, James Maurice. "The Mexican-American in an Orange County Community." Master's thesis, Claremont Graduate School, 1947.
Mendenhall, Warren, O. "A Comparative Study of Achievement and Ability of the Children in Two Segregated Schools." Master's thesis, University of Southern California, 1937.
Monroy, Douglas Guy. "Mexicanos in Los Angeles, 1930–1941: An Ethnic Group in Relation to Class Forces." Ph.D. diss., University of California, Los Angeles, 1978.
Parsons, Theodore W., Jr. "Ethnic Cleavage in a California School." Ph.D. diss., Stanford University, 1965.
Peters, Mary M. "The Segregation of Mexican American Children in the Elementary Schools of California: Its Legal and Administrative Aspects." Master's thesis, University of California, Los Angeles, 1948.
Reccow, Louis. "The Orange County Citrus Strikes of 1935–1936: The 'For-

gotten People' in Revolt." Ph.D. diss., University of Southern California, 1972.

Rinehart, Charles Herbert. "A Study of the Anaheim Community with Special Reference to Its Development." Master's thesis, University of Southern California, 1933.

Treff, Simon. "The Education of Mexican Children in Orange County." Master's thesis, University of Southern California, 1934.

Walker, Helen. "The Conflict of Cultures in First Generation Mexicans in Santa Ana, California." Master's thesis, University of Southern California, 1928.

Watt, Roberta. "History of Morenci, Arizona." Master's thesis, University of Arizona, 1956.

Williamson, Paul Garland. "Labor in the California Citrus Industry." Master's thesis, University of California, 1947.

Wood, Samuel E. "California State Commission of Immigration and Housing. A Study of Administrative Organization and Growth of Function." Ph.D. diss., University of California, 1942.

Interviews Conducted by Author

Aguirre, Fred. Sept. 17, 1987; Oct. 7, 1987. Placentia, Calif.
Aguirre, Julia. Aug. 8, 1989. Placentia, Calif.
Aguirre, Martina. Sept. 25, 1987. Placentia, Calif.
Alcántar, Pablo. Feb. 7, 1989; Feb. 21, 1989; Mar. 7, 1989. Yorba Linda, Calif.
Arce, Elpidio. Sept. 13, 1991. Corona, Calif.
Arce, John. Sept. 5, 1991. Irvine, Calif.
Brewer, Harold. Aug. 20, 1987. Villa Park, Calif.
Canales, James B. Sept. 7, 1988. Anaheim, Calif.
Canales, Santiago. Sept. 1, 1988; Sept. 7, 1988; Oct. 21, 1988. Anaheim, Calif.
Chico, Francisco. Dec. 7, 1988; Dec. 8, 1988. Anaheim, Calif.
Cruz, Angelina. Sept. 12, 1991. Escondido, Calif.
de Casas Sr., Celso. Sept. 21, 1987; Oct. 1, 1987. Placentia, Calif.
Gomez, Dan. Sept. 18, 1988. Orange, Calif.
González, Tony. Jan. 12, 1988. La Habra, Calif.
Hernández, Clemente. Sept. 6, 1988; Sept. 8, 1988; Sept. 20, 1988. Placentia, Calif.
Key, George. Aug. 7, 1987. Placentia, Calif.
Luna, Johnnie. Jan. 12, 1988. La Habra, Calif.
Luna, Tony. Mar. 27, 1991. Santa Ana, Calif.
Magaña, Erma. Aug. 3, 1989. Placentia, Calif.
Magaña, Lionel. Aug. 25, 1989. Placentia, Calif.
Marks, C. J. Nov. 17, 1986. Orange, Calif.
Martínez, Emilio. Feb. 3, 1989; Feb. 6, 1989; Feb. 9, 1989. Stanton, Calif.
Martínez, Guadalupe. Feb. 6, 1989. Stanton, Calif.
Martínez, Margarita. Aug. 3, 1989. Placentia, Calif.
Medina, Celso. Oct. 9, 1990; Oct. 16, 1990; Oct. 23, 1990, Dec. 4, 1990. San Juan Capistrano, Calif.

Medina, Henry. Oct. 9, 1990; Oct. 16, 1990; Oct. 23, 1990. San Juan Capist-
     rano, Calif.
Mejía, Jess. Jan. 12, 1988. La Habra, Calif.
Montaña, Raul. Apr. 12, 1990. Placentia, Calif.
Moreno, Enedina. Feb. 8, 1989. Fullerton, Calif.
Negrete, Eduardo. Jan. 25, 1989; Feb. 1, 1989. Fullerton, Calif.
Raya, Joe. Oct. 1, 1987. Placentia, Calif.
Raya, Rommie. Oct. 1, 1987. Placentia, Calif.
Rivas, Cuca. Feb. 17, 1989. Tustin, Calif.
Rivas, Pascual. Feb. 10, 1989; Feb. 17, 1989. Tustin, Calif.
Rospaw, Cecil. July 18, 1988. Placentia, Calif.
Tarango, Hector. Apr. 15, 1989. Santa Ana, Calif.
Torres, Roberto L. Sept. 18, 1988. Orange, Calif.
Valadez, Bert. Aug. 18, 1987. Yorba Linda, Calif.
Vásquez, Teresa. Aug. 26, 1988. Placentia, Calif.
Whitten, Chester. Aug. 13, 1987; Aug. 20, 1987. Placentia, Calif.
Zúniga, Alfredo. Dec. 10, 1987. Fullerton, Calif.
Zúniga, Enrique. Dec. 10, 1987. Fullerton, Calif.

Interviews Conducted by Others

Esqueda, Alfredo by Ronald Bandera. 1970, Tape no. 612. Oral History Col-
     lection. California State University, Fullerton.
Godiñez, Hector by Amalia González in *Harvest: A Compilation of Taped In-
     terviews on the Minority Peoples of Orange County.* Fullerton: Oral His-
     tory Program, California State University, Fullerton, 1974, 241–44.
Graham, George C. by Donna Barasch. 1972, Tape no. 69-7. Oral History Pro-
     gram. California State University, Fullerton.
Hunter, Rev. Allan H. by Christine Valenciana. 1971, Tape no. 744. Oral His-
     tory Collection. California State University, Fullerton.
Jara, Maggie by Pam Phillips. 1971, Tape no. 628. Oral History Collection.
     California State University, Fullerton.
Kelly, Arletta with B. E. Schmidt. 1968, Tape no. 48. Oral History Collection.
     California State University, Fullerton.
Kelly, Arletta by Alfredo Zúniga. 1971, Tape no. 486. Oral History Collection.
     California State University, Fullerton.
Lopez, Gloria by George Mirsh. 1971, Tape no. 589. Oral History Collection.
     California State University, Fullerton.
McClain, George and Connie by Ronald Bandera. 1970, Tape no. 476. Oral
     History Collection. California State University, Fullerton.
Vargas, Virginia by George Mirsh. 1971, Tape no. 588. Oral History Collec-
     tion. California State University, Fullerton.
Vásquez, Chaoi by Ronald Bandera. 1970, Tape no. 601. Oral History Collec-
     tion. California State University, Fullerton.
Whitten, Chester by Richard Gutierrez and Robin Rodarte in *Harvest: A Com-*

pilation of Taped Interviews on the Minority Peoples of Orange County.
Fullerton: California State University, Fullerton, 1974, 229–40.

Newspapers, Newsletters, and Professional Journals

Agricultural Life, 1957–58
American Council on Race Relations *Reports,* 1947
Anaheim Gazette, 1912–47
Associated Farmer, 1941–47
The California Citrograph, 1917–47
California Cultivator, 1912–31
California Fruit Grower
Citrus Leaves
El Quetzal, 1976–77
Fullerton Daily Tribune, 1936
Fullerton Junior College *The Weekly Torch* (Pleiedes), 1923–27
La Habra Star, 1910–38
La Opinion, 1926–27; 1936
Los Angeles Times, 1936; 1990–92
Novedad (Anaheim), 1951
Orange County Farm Bureau News, 1924–46
Orange County Plain Dealer (Anaheim), 1923–33
Orange County Tribune, 1894–1920
Orange Daily News, 1936
Pacific Rural Press, 1936
Placentia Courier, 1910–46
Rural Worker, 1936
Santa Ana Register, 1936
Orange County Register
Santa Paula Chronicle, 1941
UC MEXUS News, 1990
Western Worker, 1934–38

Government Publications

Black, Rexford S. *California State Labor Camps.* Sacramento: California State
    Unemployment Commission, 1932.
California Department of Industry Relations. Division of Housing and Immi-
    gration. Report of Fresno Conference in Agricultural Labor in California,
    May 26–27, 1939.
California. State Relief Administration. Discussion of Special Surveys and
    Studies. *Migratory Labor in California,* 1936.
California State Commission on Immigration and Housing. *Annual Reports.*
    1914–27. Sacramento: State Commission of Immigration and Housing.

California State Commission of Immigration and Housing. *Americanization: California's Answer.* Sacramento: California State Printing Office, 1920.

California State Commission of Immigration and Housing. *A Community Survey Made in Los Angeles City.* Sacramento: California State Printing Office, 1918.

California State Department of Industrial Relations. *Mexicans in California: Report of C. C. Young's Mexican Fact-Finding Committee.* San Francisco, Oct. 1930.

Chaffee, Porter. *Organization Effort of Mexican Agricultural Workers.* WPA Federal Writers Project. Oakland, Calif., 1938.

"Citrus Fruit Growing in the Southwest." U.S. Department of Agriculture Farmers' Bulletin No. 1447, 1925.

Eckmann, E. C. et al. *Soil Survey of the Anaheim Area, California.* U.S. Department of Agriculture. Bureau of Soils. Washington, D.C.: Government Printing Office, 1919.

Fogelberg, Nephtune, and A. W. McKay. "The Citrus Industry and the California Fruit Growers Exchange System." Farm Credit Administration. U.S. Department of Agriculture. Circular No. C-121. Washington, D.C.: Government Printing Office, 1940.

Jameison, Stuart. *Labor Unionism in American Agriculture.* United States Department of Labor. Bureau of Labor Statistics. Bulletin No. 836. 1945. Reprint. New York: Arno Press, 1976.

Latinos in a Changing California. Riverside: UC MEXUS Project, University of California, Riverside, 1990.

Los Angeles City Schools. Department of Immigration Education and Elementary Evening School. *First Annual Report: Elementary Adult Education.* Los Angeles: City School District, 1919.

Meriam, Junius Lathrop. *Learning English Incidentally: A Study of Bilingual Children.* Washington, D.C.: U.S. Government Printing Office, 1938.

Meriam, Junius L., and Gertrude Pastoret. "Bilingual Children Acquire English Accidentally." Washington, D.C.: Office of Education. Federal Workers Project 128. University of California, Los Angeles, 1937.

Orange County Department of Social Welfare. *Living Standards of Orange County Mexican Families.* Santa Ana, Calif.: Orange County Department of Social Welfare, Mar. 1940.

United States Congress. Senate Committee on Education and Labor. *Violations of Free Speech and Rights of Labor.* Report of the Committee on Education and Labor. Part 1. Washington, D.C.: Government Printing Office, 1942.

United States Department of Agriculture. *Yearbook of Agriculture.* Washington, D.C.: Government Printing Office, 1934.

United States Department of Agriculture. Bureau of Agricultural Economics. *Wages and Wage Rates of Farm Workers in the Citrus Harvest. Los Angeles Area, California. April/June, 1945.* Surveys of Wages and Wage Rates in Agricultural. Report No. 5. Washington, D.C., Dec. 1945.

United States Department of Agriculture War Food Administration. *The Annual Report of the Farm Security Administration. 1942–1943,* May 12, 1943.

United States Department of Labor, Women's Bureau. *Employment Conditions in Citrus Fruit Packing.* Report (mimeographed), 1940.

United States Department of Labor. "Wages and Hours of Citrus Fruit Packers," *Monthly Labor Review* 50 (June 1940): 1483–86.

United States Department of Labor, Wage and Hour Division. *Report of the Citrus Fruit Packing Industry under the Fair Labor Standards Act.* Washington, D.C.: U.S. Department of Labor, Apr. 29, 1940.

Works Progress Administration. *Cities and Towns: Orange County, California; Pioneer Tales, 1769–1869.* Orange County, California. Project No. 3105. Works Progress Administration, 1936.

Reports, Minutes, Pamphlets

Anaheim Cooperative Orange Association *Minutes,* 1929–46.

Brewer, H. ed. *The History of the Villa Park Orchards Association, Incorporated.* Villa Park, Calif.: Villa Park Orchards Association, ND.

California Citrus Institute. *First Annual Report.* San Bernardino, Calif., June 1, 1920.

Covina Orange Growers Association. *Annual Report: Season 1948–1949 for the Year Ended November 30, 1949.* Covina, Calif.: Covina Orange Growers Association, 1949.

Covina Orange Growers Association. *Fifty Years of Achievement: From 1899 to 1949.* Covina, Calif.: Covina Orange Growers Association, 1949.

Fullerton (Calif) Unified High School District. *Minutes,* 1900–1950.

Graham, George A. "History of Citrus Growers, Incorporated, Formation and Development." Mimeograph. Santa Ana, Calif.: Bowers Museum Archives, 1958.

Graham, Malbone W. Jr., and Joel Quinones. *Report of the Seventh Annual Conference of the Mexicans.* Claremont, Calif.: Claremont Colleges, 1927.

La Habra (Calif) Board of Education. *Minutes,* 1920–48.

League of United Latin American Citizens (Santa Ana, Calif.). *Minutes,* May 8, 1946.

Mexican American Movement. *Handbook.* The Supreme Council of the Mexican American Movement, N.D.

Mexican American Movement. *Its Scope, Origin, and Personnel,* July 12, 1944.

Orange County Board of Supervisors. *Minutes,* 1936.

Placentia Mutual Orange Growers Association. *Minutes,* 1915–50.

Placentia Orange Growers Association. *Manager's Annual Reports,* 1924–51.

Placentia Orange Growers Association. *Minutes,* 1912–46.

Santiago Orange Growers Association. *Minutes,* 1900–1950.

Villa Park Orchards Association. *Annual Reports,* 1942–52, 1986.

Yearbook of the Southern California Annual Conference of the Methodist Episcopal Church. Thirty-Fifth Session. Fresno, Calif., 1910; Los Angeles: Commercial Printing House, 1910.

Yorba Linda Citrus Association. *Minutes,* 1900–1950.

Yorba Linda Citrus Association. *Annual Reports,* 1918–19.

Miscellaneous Unpublished Manuscripts

Associated Farmers of Orange County, Inc.—Letter to Isadore A. Gonzáles. May 5, 1947.

Hamot, Esse in collaboration with Druzilla Mackey. "Eden. A Mexican Comedy of Manners." Huntington Library, 1930.

Lawton, Harry W., and Lewis G. Weathers. "The Origins of Citrus Research in California and the Founding of the Citrus Research Center and Agricultural Experiment Station." Unpublished manuscript (xerox copy). Riverside, Calif., 1987.

Lubin, Simon J. "Can the Radicals Capture the Farms of California?" Speech Before the Commonwealth Club, Mar. 23, 1934. University of California, Berkeley, Bancroft Library Files.

Martínez, Emilio. *Corridos,* 1936–50.

Rospow, Cecil—Letter to Author Dated Aug. 11, 1988.

Tarango, Hector. "Vote 'Yes' on Proposition No. 11 and Smash Discrimination," 1946.

Taylor, Paul S. "Citrus Strikes." Manuscript File Carton 15. University of California, Berkeley, Bancroft Library.

Orange County Department of Agriculture "Valencia Acreage—Orange County and State, 1919–1975." Statistical Report. Mimeo. Santa Ana, Calif.: Bowers Museum Archives.

Index

GILBERT G. GONZÁLEZ is professor in the Program in Comparative Culture and Chicano Latino studies at the University of California, Irvine.

Books in the Statue of Liberty–Ellis Island Centennial Series

The Immigrant World of Ybor City:
Italians and Their Latin Neighbors in Tampa, 1885–1985
Gary R. Mormino and George E. Pozzetta

The Butte Irish: Class and Ethnicity
in an American Mining Town, 1875–1925
David M. Emmons

The Making of an American Pluralism:
Buffalo, New York, 1825–60
David A. Gerber

Germans in the New World:
Essays in the History of Immigration
Frederick C. Luebke

A Century of European Migrations, 1830–1930
Edited by Rudolph J. Vecoli and Suzanne M. Sinke

The Persistence of Ethnicity: Dutch Calvinist Pioneers
in Amsterdam, Montana
Rob Kroes

Family, Church, and Market: A Mennonite Community
in the Old and the New Worlds, 1850–1930
Royden Loewen

Between Race and Ethnicity:
Cape Verdean American Immigrants, 1860–1965
Marilyn Halter

Les Icariens: The Utopian Dream
in Europe and America
Robert P. Sutton

Labor and Community: Mexican Citrus Worker Villages
in a Southern California County, 1900–1950
Gilbert G. González